LEADING CONGRESS
NEW STYLES, NEW STRATEGIES

When Everett McKinley Dirksen first envisioned the Dirksen Center, he pictured an institution where citizens could learn more about American government and politics, especially the role of congressional leadership. His interest grew naturally from a career of national public service that began in 1933 in the House of Representatives. Sixteen years in the House and eighteen more in the Senate, including ten as minority leader, convinced Dirksen that neither the public nor members of Congress fully understood the significance of legislative leadership.

Established in 1965 and located in Dirksen's hometown of Pekin, Illinois, the Everett McKinley Dirksen Congressional Leadership Research Center conducts many programs to foster an interest in congressional leadership. A not-for-profit, nonpartisan organization, the Center sponsors conferences and seminars, awards research grants, administers an archives and exhibit hall, and prepares educational materials about Congress for schools. It is the nation's only research center devoted to the study of congressional leadership in the United States.

LEADING CONGRESS
NEW STYLES, NEW STRATEGIES

John J. Kornacki, Editor

The Everett McKinley Dirksen
Congressional Leadership Research Center

Washington, D.C.

Library of Congress Cataloging-in-Publication Data

Leading Congress: new styles, new strategies/John J. Kornacki, [editor].
    p. cm.
  Includes bibliographical references.
  ISBN 0-87187-569-1
  1. United States. Congress—Leadership. I. Kornacki, John J.
JK1067.L43 1990
328.73' 0762—dc20   90-1669
                                            CIP

CONTENTS

Preface   vii

Introduction   1
   John J. Kornacki

1 Can Congress Be Led?   13
   Norman J. Ornstein

2 Fostering the Entrepreneurial Activities of Members
of the House   27
   Ross K. Baker

3 Party Leadership in the U.S. Senate   35
   Samuel C. Patterson

4 Committee and Informal Leaders in the U.S. House
of Representatives   57
   Susan Webb Hammond

5 Informal Leadership in the Senate: Opportunities,
Resources, and Motivations   71
   Steven S. Smith

6 Leadership and the Media in the 101st Congress   85
   Cokie Roberts

7 Congressional Leadership: A Review Essay
and a Research Agenda   97
   Barbara Sinclair

Appendix   163

Bibliography   167
Contributors   179
Index   181

PREFACE

In 1986 the Everett McKinley Dirksen Congressional Leadership Research Center began a four-year project to study the origin, nature, and operation of leadership in the U.S. House of Representatives and the U.S. Senate. In many ways this project was inspired by former Senate majority leader Howard H. Baker, Jr., R-Tenn., who, as senior adviser to the Dirksen Center, strongly recommended an extended investigation of the elusive and sometimes underappreciated leadership in the U.S. Congress.

The Center assembled a steering committee of congressional experts to assist in developing a plan for this project. Members of this steering committee included Richard Cohen of the *National Journal,* Roger Davidson of the University of Maryland, Alan Ehrenhalt of Congressional Quarterly, Susan Webb Hammond of American University, Thomas Mann of the Brookings Institution, Charles O. Jones of the University of Wisconsin, Norman Ornstein of the American Enterprise Institute, Richard Sachs of the Congressional Research Service of the Library of Congress, and Barbara Sinclair of the University of California at Riverside. Frank Mackaman, formerly executive director of the Dirksen Center and now director of the Gerald R. Ford Library, and Merle Glick, then president of the Dirksen Center's board of directors, served as project coordinators during the early stages of the study.

In early 1987 the Ford Foundation provided a $150,000 grant to support the Congressional Leadership Research Project.

A proposed plan called for the project to be conducted in three phases. The first phase would investigate contemporary information about congressional leadership from both scholars and practitioners. The second phase was designed to fill any gaps in information and would focus on research needs in particular. The final phase would disseminate the findings from earlier phases. Initially, a three- or four-year effort was contemplated.

For phase one, the Center commissioned six papers by distinguished authorities on Congress. These papers became the focus of discussion at six dinner meetings arranged in Washington, D.C., by the Center and the Congressional Research Service of the Library of Congress. Members of Congress, Capitol Hill reporters, and congressional staff and scholars were invited to attend these meetings. A list of the participants is included in the appendix of this volume. The six papers and transcripts of the discussions that occurred at the dinner meetings were then used to commission another paper that reviewed the overall status of research on congressional leadership. This latter paper also suggested an agenda for further research.

The six original essays were revised and updated to form the first part of this book; the major research paper forms the second part.

New components of the Congressional Leadership Research Project have been generated from these initial efforts. In 1988 the project supported a conference on Senate research held at the University of Nebraska. In 1989 the project also supported a conference on understanding Congress, organized by the Library of Congress in conjunction with the celebration of the congressional bicentennial. A study of leadership in the U.S. Senate is now under way. It is based largely on issues and findings addressed in this volume and will be the first effort at profiling individual leaders of the Senate. Congressional Quarterly will publish that study in 1991.

The Dirksen Center's board of directors has been steadfast in its support and encouragement of the work of the Congressional Leadership Research Project. On the staff at the Dirksen Center Anne Radic and Linda Sams have provided me with what has become an unusually consistent blend of professional talents and skills that turn ideas into substance.

The Congressional Research Service of the Library of Congress provided administrative and logistical support for the dinner meetings. Special thanks also go to Richard Sachs of the Congressional Research Service, who transcribed and summarized important information collected from the dinner meetings. His sensitivity to subtlety and nuance—so important in political discourse—is well appreciated.

David Tarr, Nancy Lammers, and Jerry Orvedahl of Congressional Quarterly Books provided the precise amounts of enthusiasm, patience, and guidance; I wish that their formula could be bottled for future projects. They are a vintage team, and I am thankful for their assistance.

John J. Kornacki

Introduction

John J. Kornacki

When the 101st Congress assembled in January 1989, changes in the way this nation would be governed were already apparent. A new president had taken office whose manner and experiences differed markedly from those of his predecessors. A new majority leader had been chosen in the Senate. Within a few months there would be a new Speaker, majority leader, majority whip, and minority whip in the House of Representatives.

Any of these changes alone would have influenced congressional operations and added a new element to congressional and presidential relations. Taken together, these changes have created a dramatically new environment for the development of public policies and political strategies in the 1990s.

One of the more remarkable patterns in the history of congressional leadership has been its stability and consistency.[1] But change seems to be the order of the day. What accounts for this?

Congress has always faced criticism of one kind or another. As an institution, it appears fragmented, confusing, and, at times, chaotic.[2] Despite appearances, however, the business of legislating and governing goes on. Leadership is at the center of this seemingly dysfunctional system, making the system work. In the past, tracking and describing congressional leadership may have been easier. For example, the Senate of the late 1950s was dominated by an "inner club" and personified by the consummate power broker, Majority Leader Lyndon Baines Johnson, D-Texas.[3] Understanding leadership meant understanding Johnson.

Understanding congressional leadership today requires more than understanding a dominant personality. For one thing, Congress itself has changed. Reforms of the mid-1970s altered power relationships. Ethical lapses and violations of the 1980s created institutional earthquakes that toppled the leadership. The aftershocks continue to reverberate.[4]

The political environment surrounding Congress also changed. Perhaps the most enduring of these changes stems from the growth, development, and pervasiveness of the media. Led by the availability of video transmissions of congressional proceedings through the C-SPAN public affairs cable system and increased network and local television coverage, Congress and its members are under constant scrutiny. As spokespersons for their parties, congressional leaders have become prime recipients of this increased attention. Other members, without formal positions of leadership but with facility in handling the "soundbite" format of television, have gained recognition for their ideas.

The changes in congressional leadership in 1989 may have resulted from all these factors. It is certain, however, that the productivity of the 101st Congress thus far is a function of its leadership.[5]

The pace and dimensions of recent changes in Congress provide a fitting backdrop for the ideas about leadership discussed in the following essays.

The Institutional Environment— Looking For Clues

Is Leadership Possible?

In the first essay in this book, Norman Ornstein notes that the increased challenge for congressional leaders today has "not precluded strong and assertive leadership." He traces some of these challenges to developments within the institution—particularly the reforms of the 1970s. As the committee system in Congress opened up, dispersing power to more junior members, party leadership also attained power.

Yet other developments such as the growing influence of the electronic media and special interest groups tended to create more independence among the rank-and-file members. This new external environment called for a different type of leader.

In focusing on the Senate, Ornstein compares and contrasts personal leadership styles with the changing institutional and political environments. For example, Majority Leader Lyndon Johnson could count on a contingent of "reflexive and reliable supporters." His gregarious and sometimes overbearing manner was well suited to the political climate of the 1950s. But by the 1960s, individual senators had grown more independent. The Johnson style was no longer sufficient. Sen. Mike Mansfield, D-Mont., who succeeded Johnson as majority leader, offered a fresh approach to leadership that reflected new institutional realities. The Senate was more decentralized and more democratic.

Ornstein next explains how the 1970s and 1980s demonstrated a further evolution in the Senate that both affected and was affected by its leaders. Senators Robert C. Byrd, D-W.Va., Howard Baker, R-Tenn., and Bob Dole, R-Kan., each brought unique personal skills, networks of support, and approaches to rules that influenced changes in the Senate. In fact, finding better controls for the inevitable changes that occur in Congress might best characterize the challenge for leadership in the 1990s.

Leaders as Entrepreneurs

At the outset of the second essay, Ross Baker concludes that the national party organizations will remain relatively weak and that publicly financed congressional elections will not be implemented soon, if at all. These conclusions allow him to describe how individual members of Congress who lack strict party controls have become like free agents in baseball: they owe some allegiance to their team or party but are more likely to pursue individual policy interests rather than party interests. This has contributed to a new strategy for congressional leaders as "patrons of policy leadership."

Baker contends that four techniques are available to party leaders to advance the policy interests of individual members. The first he terms "policy magnetism," or the ability of attracting outside experts. Policy expertise, although not a rare commodity in Congress, is not evenly spread, particularly in the House. A subcommittee is usually needed to pull in prominent policy experts to address an issue. "Such magnetism," notes Baker, "is well within the grasp of the instrumentalities of leadership."

The Committee on Party Effectiveness of the House Democratic Caucus serves as a useful example of the use of "policy magnetism" by the leadership. During 1982 and 1983 many of the academic advocates of industrial policy briefed this committee. Caucus chairman Gillis Long, D-La., was instrumental in mustering the expertise and making it available to the membership.

A second technique available to leadership is "policy action," or the redirecting of members' energies. Sometimes members' interests in policy are stifled by particular committees or, more likely, committee chairmen. Leadership can assist these members by providing nonlegislative committee assignments. Again using the example of Caucus chairman Long, Baker points out how Long was able to head off the possible defection of conservative Sun Belt Democrats by soliciting their active participation in the work of the caucus. Another example of this alternate forum for policy participation, notes Baker, was the Joint Economic Committee under Rep. David R. Obey, D-Wis., during the Ninety-ninth Congress.

Providing "policy cover" is a third technique available to leadership. This involves choosing party policies that will protect members from criticism back home. The Democratic leadership was able to respond to the budget challenges of the Gramm-Rudman-Hollings deficit reduction bill by insisting that some important social programs—critical to liberal members—were shielded in the legislation.

A final technique, what Baker terms "policy exposure," employs the use of the media. Journalists have a tendency to cover congressional leaders as authoritative sources for stories. Leaders can choose to share this attention with junior members. Such exposure assists not only in raising the visibility of the younger members but also in building networks of support for future policy initiatives and thus enhancing the power bases of leaders.

If these new policy techniques can be effectively translated into an overall legislative strategy by congressional leaders, the clearer definition of party values that results will strengthen party identity. Stronger party identity will, in turn, reinforce the positions of party leaders.

Peculiarities of Senate Leadership

Samuel C. Patterson relates recent developments in the Senate to a historical stream of change that can be traced to the early part of this century and the direct election of senators. A "tangled interaction" of six issues evolved, and they continue to shape and influence the modern Senate leadership. Patterson terms these six issues: context, management, party, succession, leader's role, and external relations.

The Senate leaders must work within the context of the Senate and its traditions, rules, and procedures. This environment continues to change however. What used to be a "club" in the days of Majority Leader Lyndon Johnson—with a few senior members calling the shots—is now an open-seat theater. Junior members are no longer willing to sit back. The ubiquitous television camera has given center stage to each senator. The challenge of Senate leadership has indeed become more complex.

Managing the Senate's work has also become more difficult. As senators spend more time in their home states, scheduling the legislative workload becomes "critical to the task of leadership." Patterson illustrates how in 1983 Majority Leader Howard Baker limited "holds" and "vote-stacking" to regain some control of the Senate's calendar and workload.

The Senate is organized along party lines, yet the degree of partisanship often depends on the styles of individual party leaders and their networks for gathering information and support. The whip system, policy committees, and Senate staff all play important roles in leadership, although the emphasis on these actors may change depending on who is directing them.

Leadership succession provides another challenge in the Senate. Democratic leaders generally have moved up from the post of whip to enjoy greater leadership responsibilities. Yet this did not happen with the selection of Sen. George J. Mitchell, D-Maine, in 1988. Republican leaders have a less apparent system of succession and a greater frequency of heated contests. Certainly this was true with the selection of Bob Dole in 1984.

Despite the importance of these contests and the renewed contentiousness, Patterson notes that leadership succession has not been the subject of much scholarly attention or discussion.

What is the appropriate role of the Senate leader? A considerable degree of leeway may be used to define how the leader leads. One way to describe leadership roles is to look at relationships between the president and the party leader, between the majority and minority leaders, and between the Senate and House leaders. Each of these relationships varies and is affected by which party controls the White House, Senate, and House of Representatives. Interestingly, only in the Senate has party control changed in the last decade, making Senate leadership an increasingly strategic position for both parties.

Related to this is the more general issue of the external environment. Just as Senate leaders are affected by the Senate as a formal institution, so are they affected by what lies outside the Capitol. Leaders are thrust into the limelight of celebrity status by the television networks. Presidents court them for their influential support. Colleagues and petitioners pressure them for the same. Certainly the leadership has become more visible. This increased visibility, and the ability to deal with it deftly, has contributed to the selection of George Mitchell as majority leader.

Patterson concludes with a reminder about the paucity of material that systematically examines any of these six issues that critically influence the Senate leadership of today.

Informal Leadership in the House

"The contemporary House of Representatives," Susan Webb Hammond states in Chapter 4, "is characterized by structural decentralization and member individualism." This, in turn, presents new opportunities for informal leadership in the House.

Hammond identifies two types of informal leaders in the House: "leaders with portfolio," such as committee and subcommittee chairs; and "leaders without portfolio," such as issue-oriented leaders or coalition builders. Informal leaders with portfolio are comparable to midlevel managers with responsibilities to both party leaders and their own constituencies of junior committee or subcommittee members. Informal leaders without portfolio rarely have a stable constituency and may work in opposition to the party leadership; their prominence may increase because of expertise in a policy area.

These informal leaders—with or without portfolio—are part of a leadership network quite apart from that of the party leadership. "Our understanding of House leadership," states Hammond, "is incomplete without consideration of . . . the role of informal leaders." She then suggests a framework for analyzing individual types of informal leadership and poses specific concerns for each that require further examination.

Committee leaders, for example, are influenced by both the structure of their committees and party hierarchy. Committee chairs may be issue experts and rise in rank because of it. Sometimes the holding of a formal leadership position may cause a member to become an issue leader. Do these positions now overlap? And if so, poses Hammond, why do there appear to be more rather than fewer leaders in the House?

Similar concerns are raised for other types of informal leaders, such as discussion group leaders. Discussion groups are very informal gatherings of party members who share common concerns about issues. A recent example is the arms control group led by Rep. Thomas J. Downey, D-N.Y. Arms control has become a higher priority with the House Democratic leadership due to this group's involvement. Yet why are these discussion group members so effective? What strategies are employed?

The congressional caucus system, individual issue leaders, coalition builders, and congressional staff all function at various times as part of an informal leadership structure. Each has its singular mechanisms. Each poses a challenge to the formal leaders and enhances the further decentralization of power.

Informal leaders may also be described functionally, what Hammond characterizes as "heralds, honchos, and henchmen." "Heralds," like voices from the desert, are informal leaders who identify issues or help set policy agendas. "Honchos" are informal leaders responsible for monitoring the policy process. "Henchmen" are the strategists, the informal leaders who cut deals, influence their colleagues, and shape debates.

Whatever the functional manifestations of informal leaders, much work remains if we are to better understand this growing element of congressional leadership. Hammond advances our grasp of this elusive subject while suggesting several important issues for scholars to pursue.

Informal Leadership in the Senate

In Chapter 5, Steven Smith asserts that unlike the more anonymous House, the Senate is filled with personalities. That the Senate is more individually distinct, he notes, is largely the result of senators gaining political identity through activities "not directly related to formal positions of party or committee leadership." Senators gain informal leadership through their recognition as authorities on specific issues. Sen. Bill Bradley, D-N.J., demonstrated this on the issue of tax reform.

Smith notes that a senator's decision to pursue an issue is influenced by three factors: opportunities, resources, and goals.

Opportunities abound. Issues are raised in constituent mail and by growing numbers of interest groups. Also, the issues themselves have become more complex, creating subsets of issues and interests. Another opportunity for informal leadership exists in the growing number of committees and subcommittees, which provide areas where individual senators can "stake a jurisdictional claim."

Resources control the ability to delve into issues. Like spare staff time, discretionary resources available for policy or issue leadership are usually very limited. Senators benefit, however, from a slightly larger staff and the capability to continually attract high-quality personnel. Coverage by the media is another key resource for informal leaders in the Senate. An individual senator's time is perhaps the most precious of these resources and, asserts Smith, "it's becoming ever more scarce."

The precise motivations that guide individual interests in policies or issues are not easily discerned. Senators make choices about issues based on personal and public convictions and commitments. In citing a recent survey of key legislative aides, Smith notes that presidential ambition, however, does not seem to be one of these motivations.

Smith identifies several conditions that enhance informal leadership. New issues, for example, are more likely to involve informal leaders. Issues that do not fall neatly under a single committee jurisdiction also encourage the participation of informal leaders.

In essence, the informal leaders in the Senate are a "floating pool" of interested and talented members who exert influence on issues and shape debate. This occurs despite the extraordinary amount of time now devoted to raising money for future campaigns.

New developments in the Senate, such as more committees, have enhanced the opportunity for policy participation and leadership. Yet these new committees also make large claims on members' diminishing available time. This essay suggests that if informal policy leadership is to be fostered, then the problems of time and its alternative uses must be addressed.

A Matter of Media

In Chapter 6 Cokie Roberts discusses how the media influences and, in turn, is influenced by leaders in Congress. Some junior members, such as Sen. Phil Gramm, R-Texas, have gained power and stature through the deft courting of media attention. Yet formal party leadership still commands most press coverage, particularly on television. Roberts asserts that network producers make decisions on whom to cover with a "round-up-the-usual-suspects" frame of mind that often works against all but a handful of party leaders and committee chairmen. Leadership encourages this centralized focus of attention. The Speaker of the House may hold formal press conferences. The same is true for other leaders. House Minority Leader Robert H. Michel, R-Ill., notes Roberts, "is regularly available for conversations [with reporters] in the Speaker's lobby."

Other members, however, have ways to break into the media limelight. Individuals who are able to answer questions quickly and understandably have an advantage in the soundbite format of network news. The televising of the Senate and House floor debates also offers the opportunity for increased visibility.

One person who combines the advantage of having a leadership role with a comfortable and direct communication style is Senate Minority Leader Bob Dole. Roberts cites a study that showed that Senator Dole appeared on the evening news twice as often as any other senator in the Ninety-ninth Congress when he was majority leader.

Televised hearings, the employment of the special orders segment at the conclusion of the legislative workday, and the deft use of media contacts all assist in increasing visibility and sometimes prestige for members of Congress who may not be in the leadership chain of command. Sometimes effective cultivation and handling of these media opportunities lead to positions of leadership. The elevation of Senator Mitchell to majority leader was certainly aided by his strong performance during the widely covered Iran-Contra hearings. The election of Rep. Newt Gingrich, R-Ga. as house minority whip and his active participation during special orders and other televised events are similarly linked.

Yet Roberts warns that media exposure can cut both ways. Some members resent those who appear too frequently on television: "the old distinctions between workhorses and showhorses still carry some weight inside the caucuses."

The differences between those who come across well on television and those who do not may be fading. Roberts concludes that soon all members of Congress—not only its leadership—will need to perform well for the media, particularly on television.

The Research Environment— Looking for Clues

A Synthesis and a Search

In the final portion of this book, Barbara Sinclair addresses many of the issues suggested by the previous chapters. She also undertakes an in-depth review of the current status of congressional leadership research.

Finally, she provides a map of largely under- or unexplored areas of research that require further study.

Sinclair begins by looking at a few fundamental concerns: What are congressional leaders expected to do? Have these expectations changed? Do others now fulfill them? Addressing these central questions becomes the basis for the literature review and the suggestions that follow.

The External Context

Determining the strength of the party system is a key element in understanding the roles of party leaders. Sinclair points out that several previous studies confirm that the number of fellow partisans and their ideological cohesiveness are strong determinants of legislative success—an important measure of accomplishment for the congressional leader. The social, economic, and ideological characteristics of the political parties also influence the effectiveness of party leadership. A relatively homogeneous party provides for fewer conflicts for the leadership to resolve. The party system itself is buffeted by continuous change. Recession and scandal may have a short-term effect on party cohesion and strength and thus constrain leadership. Sinclair suggests that a long-term constraint for leadership is the increased congressional workload.

Sinclair acknowledges that the media, largely through increased availability of television, has further weakened political parties. She notes, however, that some disagreement exists about whether this has enhanced or detracted from the power of congressional leaders. She questions whether or not the increased television coverage has changed members' expectations of the leaders.

The proliferation of interest groups also has had an effect on congressional leadership. Do these issue-oriented groups compete with party leaders for allegiance? Is coalition building enhanced or made more complicated?

Institutional Environment

Many of the tools available to congressional leaders are a function of how Congress is organized to perform tasks and distribute influence. The congressional workload and the strength of the party are important determinants in task performance and in distributing influence.

Sinclair reviews the development of important leadership offices. She notes the significant distinctions between leaders of the House and leaders of the Senate. For example, House leaders function by rounding up majority votes, while their Senate counterparts seek unanimous consent. The mechanisms of Senate leadership are not well understood.

Reforms have also altered the organizational setting. During the 1970s power was redistributed from a few powerful committees to numerous subcommittees—what Sinclair refers to as a decentralizing force. Other changes have had centralizing effects. For example, the requirement that committee chairmen and appropriations subcommittee chairmen win majority approval in the Democratic caucus has made these leaders more responsive to the party and, hence, the party leadership.

Leaders and Leadership

One of the constants in the study of congressional leadership has been its stability. With the possible exception of minority leaders in the House, changes in congressional leadership have been free of visible struggle and rancor. Yet new leaders are emerging, and their rise to power may provide important clues to determining the expectations of congressional leaders in the 1990s.

Congressional leaders occasionally attain their positions by ascending a ladder of increasing responsibility. This was the case with current Speaker Thomas S. Foley, D-Wash., who moved up from majority leader and majority whip, although this type of succession system has not developed for Republicans in the Senate. In citing the earlier work of Peabody, Sinclair confirms that leadership selection is affected by a broad range of variables that include both early traditions and emergent technologies.[6] The relative importance of these variables in selecting leaders calls for further examination.

Determining the characteristics of leaders has proved a difficult task for the social sciences. Legislative leaders, however, do have certain responsibilities that offer a perspective on this type of leadership. The ability to develop consensus or broker various interests—"the middle-man hypothesis"—is one such characteristic.

Party organizations provide yet another view of leadership. These structures may be valuable tools for the leadership. Knowledge about party structures, however, is uneven. Sinclair identifies the fairly rich source material about the House Democratic party and the dearth of similar information about the other three congressional parties. A need for further examination of the party structures of the Senate in particular seems to beckon scholars interested in Senate leadership.

Interactions among congressional leaders, between these leaders and committee chairs, and also the rank-and-file members provide additional sources for study. Data on the frequency and content of these interactions would help define the precise role of leadership in the legislative process.

An area of leadership that illuminates how the nation is governed involves the relationships and interactions between congressional leaders and the president. The working relationship between the president and the congressional leadership has waxed and waned over time. Is the party leader an advocate (or opponent, if of the other party) of the president's program? In Congress, notes Sinclair, the leaders' obligation to the membership rather than the president is considered paramount.

The purpose of Congress is to make laws. Perhaps, then, the most elemental aspect of congressional leadership is legislative success. Sinclair reviews this aspect of leadership and suggests that "skillful congressional leadership is neither a necessary nor a sufficient condition for legislative success." She also notes that institutional maintenance factors—the rules, norms, and resources available to the leadership—are largely unexplored by researchers.

A Research Agenda

Sinclair's approach closes some of the gaps in an often-fragmented understanding of congressional leadership. First, she suggests that a systematic study be undertaken of the members' expectations of leadership. As yet, direct evidence of these expectations is sparse.

Second, she recommends looking at leadership by studying public policy development. At each significant point in the process, researchers could compile information on the role of the leadership. Policy development in different areas could be compared and contrasted by examining the roles played by the leadership.

A final recommendation calls for better descriptive work on congressional leadership, including a full examination of party offices and the people who operate them. This is particularly important for Senate leadership, which has not received the same amount of scholarly attention as House leadership.

Conclusion

The study of congressional leadership tends to linger on the academic sidelines while researchers tackle the more glamorous trappings of presidential leadership. Until the Constitution is rewritten, however, the nation will continue to be governed by a shared arrangement of power. The leaders of Congress are often at the crossroads of the competing branches of U.S. government. An incomplete understanding of congressional leadership means an incomplete understanding of government in the United States.

Now is a propitious time to promote a new look at congressional leadership, not only because of the magnitude of changes in Congress but also because the entire world has changed dramatically. Eastern Europe has begun again to develop and sustain a truly representative government. The model in this effort at democratic nation building will undoubtedly have familiar American attributes. The roles and functions of the U.S. Congress and its leadership will likely receive plenty of attention from the founders of these new democracies.

Notes

1. Lynne P. Browne and Robert L. Peabody, "Patterns of Succession in the House Democratic Leadership: The Choice of Wright, Foley, and Coelho, 1986" (Paper prepared for the 1987 annual meeting of the American Political Science Association).
2. Frank H. Mackaman, "Introduction," in *Understanding Congressional Leadership*, ed. Frank H. Mackaman (Washington, D.C.: CQ Press, 1981), 1.
3. See Rowland Evans and Robert Novak, *Lyndon B. Johnson: The Exercise of Power* (New York: New American Library, 1966); and Howard Shuman, "Lyndon Baines Johnson," in *Profiles in Senate Leadership*, ed. Richard A. Baker and Roger H. Davidson (Washington, D.C.: CQ Press, forthcoming).
4. For a particularly insightful look at the resignation of Jim Wright, see John M. Barry, *The Ambition and the Power: The Fall of Jim Wright: A True Story of Washington* (New York: Viking Press, 1989).
5. Janet Hook, "New Leaders Felt Their Way Gingerly Through the Session," *Congressional Quarterly*, December 2, 1989, 3284; and Richard E. Cohen, "It Was a Transition Year in the House," *National Journal*, December 2, 1989, 2948.
6. Robert L. Peabody, "Senate Party Leadership: From the 1950s to the 1980s," in *Understanding Congressional Leadership*, ed. Frank H. Mackaman, 104-105.

Can Congress Be Led?

Norman J. Ornstein

Can Congress be led? The question itself suggests that today strong leadership in Congress is unlikely, if not impossible. Assertive and centralized leadership has waxed and waned in Congress over the years, as personalities, rules, presidents, majorities, internal and external norms, parties, and other conditions inside the legislature and outside in the broader political system have changed. But to suggest that weak leadership has been made inevitable in the contemporary political world means that something far more fundamental has occurred.

In this essay, I will look at what makes leadership in Congress work. At the same time, I will examine the notion that the changes in the contemporary Congress have weakened fundamentally the institution and its leaders. I will argue that while the challenges to leadership have increased dramatically in recent years, they have not precluded strong and assertive leadership. Using the Senate as an example, I will compare the leadership opportunities and styles of Lyndon Johnson with two of his contemporary counterparts, Howard Baker and Bob Dole, to shed light on the limits and possibilities of leadership in the new Congress.

Congressional Change and Leadership Challenge

Why do so many assume, or at least accept, the notion that real leadership in Congress today is close to impossible? Clearly, this attitude has been shaped by the tremendous changes that have taken place in the past fifteen years in American politics and in Congress. Given that changes in internal congressional rules, norms, and resources, external institutions like the media and interest groups, and the attitudes of rank-and-file members were accompanied in the 1960s and 1970s by a shift from strong to unassertive leaders, the stereotype of inevitably hopeless leadership took hold. It has been reinforced by an exaggeratedly rosy remembrance of the strong leaders of the 1950s, Lyndon Johnson and Sam Rayburn.

What changed in the reform era to weaken leaders and leadership? We can start with rules changes. It is a commonplace that rules matter to leaders and help shape their influence; formal rules are perhaps the most important weapon in a leader's arsenal. Conventional wisdom would suggest that the reforms of the 1970s that gave power to rank-and-file members and to subcommittee chairmen came at the expense of committee chairmen and other senior leaders. In addition, the series of changes that opened up congressional deliberations, through more roll-call votes on significant floor and committee decisions, and through open committee meetings and markups, took away leaders' ability to influence their colleagues behind the scenes, with other potential influences—public opinion, interest groups—absent, and with individual decisions hidden from their view, but not from the leaders. It is often overlooked, however, that the rules changes, especially in the House, also explicitly added substantial formal powers to party leaders—power of committee assignments, the makeup and role of the key House Rules Committee, and bill referral, in particular. On balance, rules changes perhaps weakened the climate for assertive leadership—but only on balance.

Second, we saw norms change. The informal do's and don'ts of the legislature relaxed in general in the 1960s and 1970s, starting with the folkway of freshman subservience. Indeed, the notion that junior members should be seen and not heard began to fade after the 1958 election. The norm continued to apply in principle for a few years, but by the mid-1960s it was no longer in existence. By the late 1960s, as tensions grew over Vietnam, norms of courtesy and institutional patriotism were honored more in the breach; by the early 1970s, the idea that antisocial or anti-institutional behavior should be ostracized or punished in any significant way was dismissed. And with the Vietnam era, the norm of deference to elders and authority figures declined generally in society and followed suit in Congress.

During and after the major reform era, norms and rules changed to make a wide variety of rewards—staff, committee assignments, office resources, junkets—virtually automatic to all members, thereby making the selective use of reward and sanction virtually unemployable for the leadership. The expansion of rewards came as reforms greatly multiplied the resources available to Congress and its members. An explosion of staff occurred in the 1970s, along with a tremendous expansion of computer and other electronic resources, from data processing to communications innovations. As subcommittees and subcommittee chairmen multiplied, the opportunities for committee-oriented travel, slots on conference committees, and positions as floor managers of bills multiplied accordingly. What had been precious commodities to be doled out by leaders and their allies became greatly expanded and diluted currency.

As these changes occurred internally, enormous changes were occurring in the political world outside Congress. During the 1960s, as television increased its penetration among citizens, becoming the overwhelming primary medium for news, it increased its coverage of Washington, and of Congress. During the 1970s, there was a tremendous expansion of interest-group activity in Washington, which began with a spurt of new "public interest" groups forming and advanced as business interests counterlobbied and as other groups formed or expanded to take advantage of the new openness and points of access in the reformed Congress.

Enhanced television coverage of Congress had many effects. First, it contributed to the outside attention placed on the previously insular institution. Congressional leaders accustomed to working strictly inside, mostly behind closed doors, but more generally with little attention paid by the broader community, suddenly found that more of their activities and those of their colleagues came under scrutiny. At the very least, this development crimped the styles of traditional, inside-oriented leaders. It was not surprising, then, that Speaker Sam Rayburn resisted any television presence in the House, leaving even occasional coverage of hearings to his successors, and that the Senate resisted any media presence more extensive than hearing coverage into the 1980s.

Television coverage also altered the career incentives of lawmakers. More media attention left open more possibilities for members to become celebrities of sorts—profiled in newspapers, gaining notoriety in the broader Washington community to become a social presence in the capital city, or having a springboard to a higher office or a lucrative outside career. More outside incentives meant less inside leverage for leaders. It was no longer necessary, using Rayburn's dictum, to go along to get along; a member could get along, in another fashion, by going his or her own way, or even by deliberately challenging the leadership.

The expanding presence of interest groups, and their new reach to subcommittees, rank-and-file members, and staff, also added to the complications for leaders. The fewer such outside pressures, the greater the ability of the leaders to have their own impact; as the outside pressures increased, the leaders faced more competition for the time and attention of their followers and also had to cope with increased cross-pressures on followers.

The combination of changes throughout the 1960s and 1970s clearly made the task of party leaders far more formidable. With the open, fluid, unpredictable, decentralized Congress, it was no longer possible for a leader to bury a losing bill quietly in committee or to kill an amendment by a nonrecorded vote on the floor. So, even if leaders were no less able than predecessors like Rayburn or Johnson, they *looked* less powerful because their failures were more public.

In the 1960s and early 1970s, the hurdles facing leaders thus required individuals with great leaping ability to surmount them. In keeping perhaps with the institutions, the leaders of the times either did not try or tried but did not quite measure up—some, like Sen. Mike Mansfield, D-Mont., and Carl Albert, D-Okla., because of their mild personalities; others, like John W. McCormack, D-Mass., because they were generationally and temperamentally unsuited for the sweeping changes they confronted. But by the late 1970s, as one generation of congressional leaders retired, lawmakers had an opportunity to pick new leaders more attuned to the new Congress. Given the traditions of leadership selection, their choices were not "new wave" junior members, but senior figures like Rep. "Tip" O'Neill, D-Mass., Rep. John J. Rhodes, III, R-Ariz., Sen. Robert C. Byrd, D-W.Va., and Sen. Howard Baker, R-Tenn. Still, all tended to be more assertive than their predecessors (with the possible exception of Rhodes for Ford as House Republican leader), fitting the mood of the era for less decentralization and somewhat more consolidation.

These leaders were all selected for their posts between 1974 and 1977; only Byrd has remained, however, as we have progressed through another generation of leaders. Yet replacements Rep. Jim Wright, D-Texas, Rep. Robert H. Michel, R-Ill., and Sen. Bob Dole, R-Kan., also fit within the longstanding traditions of leadership selection. But as Congress has changed, and begun to change again, and as several new leaders have passed through the House and Senate, we can make some fresh generalizations about leadership in Congress. Most significantly, the leaders of the late 1970s and early 1980s show that strong and assertive leadership is not a thing of the past. Granted, in many key respects, leadership is different in a different era—but Congress, throughout its history, has constantly changed. Party majorities swell and recede; partisan dominance comes and goes; crises emerge and fade; presidents change. And periodically, leaders have emerged who understand enough about the verities of politics and human beings, and enough about the constants and the changes in the legislative process, to make the institution work—even if, on the surface, it does not appear to do so. Just as often, leaders are selected who do not measure up or who are unable to respond adequately to the changes around them.

Component of Individualism in Leadership

There are many reasons why strong leadership emerges and disappears in Congress that correspond to the many and interrelated variables that shape a legislature. What makes leadership work? Apparently, there are institutional factors that create greater, or lesser, opportunities for leadership at different times. But equally evident is that individual talent and adaptability matter. Certain eras may call out for strong leaders, but for various reasons the individuals who find themselves elected or appointed to leadership posts do not measure up. At other times, clever, assertive, and adaptable leaders may be able to overcome considerable institutional impediments to provide surprisingly strong leadership. Some individuals are strong leaders under certain circumstances, but find their ability to lead faltering when conditions change; others can vary their styles and approaches as the times change. Sorting out circumstances, personalities, and tactics is complicated. Let us begin by looking at the Senate and comparing leadership in Lyndon Johnson's era with that in more recent Senates.

Senate Leadership in Institutional Context

Like most legislative bodies, the United States Senate has several core characteristics that do not change much from year to year or decade to decade. Its small size, informal atmosphere, and emphasis on the prerogatives of individual members and minority rights all have been a part of the Senate virtually since its beginnings. All shape and constrain what any individual Senate leader can do or not do to influence the actions of fellow senators or the Senate itself.

But there are also many characteristics of the Senate, and its political and social environment, which can and do change considerably from year to year and era to era. The size of party majority and the homogeneity of party members are two issues that can affect and constrain Senate leaders. So, too, can the general political context, Senate rules, majority or minority status, the openness of the political system within the Senate, the party and personality of the president, and many other more temporal concerns.

In almost all these aspects the Senate and its world have changed, sometimes several times, in the past decade or two, thus altering what a leader can or cannot do to shape the institution and influence its members. In the 1950s, Lyndon Johnson saw many changes in his political world, moving as his party's leader from minority to majority status, facing both a razor-thin party edge and a swollen party majority. Johnson also saw the overall political environment shift, especially after the landmark election of 1958. During most of his tenure as party leader, up to 1958, Johnson had more control over the Senate's internal operations and incentive structure than either his predecessors or his successors. But Johnson's own clout as leader diminished when the political environment changed in 1959.

Although Johnson's clout in the Senate lessened over time, he was acknowledged universally to be a powerful leader. How did Johnson shape the Senate's agenda and outcomes? Clearly, his ability to lead was determined by a combination of the institutional norms, members, and rules; the nature of the Eisenhower presidency; and Johnson's own extraordinary personal and political abilities. His individual style and techniques were outlined effectively by Rowland Evans and Robert Novak in their book *Lyndon B. Johnson: The Exercise of Power*.[1] As they describe it, Johnson's ability to lead the Senate depended on two major elements: the Johnson Network and the Johnson Procedure. The Johnson Network, in essence, was Johnson's coterie of reflexive and reliable supporters—those senators he could count on for any vote at any time, and those who were there in a pinch if he absolutely needed them. As Evans and Novak detail, the Johnson Network did not spring up full blown; Johnson worked at it constantly, stroking and cultivating senators and influential outsiders, and maintaining through his staff constant contact and communications with these leaders to be certain at all times of how votes or potential votes would break down.

The Johnson Procedure, in essence, was Johnson's set of tactics to bend the Senate's rules to his own will and to make such arcane procedures as unanimous consent and the quorum call work to his substantive advantage. The majority leader's ability to shape the Senate's schedule—to use filibusters and stop-and-go timing to influence the agenda, and to maximize leadership support present and voting when a crucial test occurred—was the key to the Johnson Procedure.

The Johnson Network was undeniably successful but not only because of the times. Leaders before Lyndon Johnson who lacked his energy, political savvy, skill, and drive were not able to mold a consistently winning coalition. It took Johnson's unique political skills, which were in sync with a set of rules, informal norms, and an overall political context, that made it possible to predict the inclinations of most senators and to use leverage over a large number of them.

By 1959, however, and throughout the final two years of Johnson's majority leadership, the political context had shifted enough that the Johnson Network was in decline. The 1958 election brought in fifteen new Democratic senators, most of whom were independent, aggressive, urban, northern liberals not inclined to bow to Lyndon Johnson's dictates without question. They wanted to play an active role as freshmen, fulfill their campaign pledges, and influence the course of the policy debate as the open presidential election of 1960 approached. Thus, they were not eager to listen to the majority leader plead for bipartisan compromises with a lame-duck Republican president.

After the 1958 election, the Senate began to change a great deal. The large number of aggressive freshmen weakened the internal norms of the Senate, making it harder for leaders to use the Senate's social system to shape the agenda and outcomes. Fewer of these freshmen, too, were products of party organizations, making the party tie—never overwhelming—even less of a lever for leaders. The increasing dominance of television as the national medium, and its focus on the Senate as a national policy-making institution, served as well to remove more of the leadership's leverage. The careers of senators were no longer controlled simply by internal considerations—committee assignments, opportunities for foreign junkets, positions on conference committees, or pats on the back. It was increasingly possible to build a major career based on *external* acknowledgements—becoming a national celebrity or spokesperson for outside groups, without being terribly damaged or ostracized inside the Senate.

In addition, the political and policy worlds became more complicated, making the votes or inclinations of most senators increasingly difficult to predict. As one veteran senator commented in the 1970s, looking back on the Johnson era:

> Back then, you pretty much knew how 90 percent of the senators were going to vote on any given issue; maybe 10 percent were unpredictable. These days, it isn't quite reversed, but, on many votes, you just can't tell in advance how most of the members will come down.

These changes did not make it either impossible or undesirable to form a network like the Johnson one, but they did make it more difficult. Some of the interpersonal skills that Johnson displayed—making people indebted to him, finding the right way to stroke and the right time to threaten or pressure individual senators, building up a bank of IOUs, remembering each one and calling it at the appropriate time—all have proven useful or indispensable since, for party leaders who are fortunate enough to possess them and savvy enough to use them. But with fewer chits to use, with more unpredictability among individual senators, and with more and more lawmakers possessing or building outside networks and power bases, these interpersonal skills are a necessary but not sufficient condition to construct a reliable and enduring Johnson-type network.

As the Johnson era progressed to the Mansfield era, the role of the majority leader changed. Mansfield's personality and approach to leadership differed dramatically from his predecessor's; he saw the Senate as a body of one hundred equals, with the leader serving more as a coordinator than a field general. Mansfield's style meshed well with the 1960s and early 1970s, an era of continuing decentralization and democratization in Congress, and continuing movement from a closed system—with rewards and incentives largely internal to the institution—to an open system. Unquestionably, Mansfield encouraged and accelerated such trends, as he did a full and immediate role in the Senate for freshmen.

By the end of the Mansfield era, after Vietnam, Watergate, and the other tumultuous events of his congressional period, there was a desire in the Senate to consolidate a bit. This was partly reflected in the 1976 creation of the Stevenson Committee and the Commission on the Operation of the Senate and further suggested by the choice of Robert Byrd as Mansfield's replacement. The trend to consolidation increased four years later, with the first Republican Senate in a quarter-century working with a new Republican president.

After observing Senate majority leadership under Howard Baker and Bob Dole, we have an opportunity to compare their styles and approaches to leadership with Lyndon Johnson's. Do conditions in the contemporary Senate make it impossible for a leader to lead the way Johnson did in his heyday? Are followers so different that they cannot be molded into a majority coalition? Are processes so open that Johnson-style wheeling and behind-the-scenes dealing are impossible? A brief examination of Baker and Dole as leaders can help us to answer such questions and shed light on the limits and possibilities of contemporary leadership in Congress.

By almost any set of standards, both Howard Baker and Bob Dole, despite different personalities, approaches, and circumstances, have been strong leaders. Like all successful leaders, Baker and Dole have used their personal assets to mold individual senators, although in the individualized Senate of recent years, molding anyone is quite difficult. Baker's approach was to meet endlessly with his Republican colleagues, singly and in groups, letting them talk and argue until they would finally go along with him, if only because they felt sorry for their leader as his shoulders slumped from their burden. Realizing over time the difficulty of maintaining a wholly cohesive party, Baker was also flexible and generous with his Democratic counterparts in the hope that his decency would attract some opposition votes or at least prevent implacable obstructionism. Under some conditions—when his minority party was naturally united in purpose (1979-1980) or when, as a new majority, it faced the need to advance and protect the new Republican president's program (1981-1982)—the "Baker Network" coalesced nicely. But when conditions changed from 1983 to 1984 with the approaching presidential election, and Republican senators began to lose their sense of united purpose and scrambled for individual positions, the opportunity to build a consistent network faded.

Dole's approach has been more hard nosed, aggressive, and partisan than Baker's but has also succeeded under conditions where Baker had begun to falter. Faced with a bare majority, Dole as majority leader in the Ninety-ninth Congress attempted to mold a partisan majority on a number of issues, gathering groups of GOP senators in his office and pushing them to agree on strategy and substance. Using time pressure as a lever (these meetings often took place during quorum calls, with the Senate put on hold until the difficulties were resolved), and working tirelessly to touch all bases, Dole had surprising success. Ironically, his success came in part because of the narrowness of the GOP majority. Each vote counted and individual senators thus faced more attention and internal pressure when the votes were cast. Moreover, with the Republican majority so directly on the line in the coming election of 1986, the common interest in party unity was clear to everybody.

But this strategy has not always worked. In the contemporary Senate, individual senators have enormous leverage. Perquisites and prerogatives have multiplied and are given almost automatically to all senators—whether leaders like it or not. There have been many times when the personal skills of Howard Baker or Bob Dole were unable to stop a strong-minded colleague like Lowell Weicker, R-Conn., or Jesse Helms, R-N.C., from wreaking havoc with their agendas or voting against the leadership position. Lyndon Johnson, too, was not invariably successful at persuasion and frequently found colleagues like Paul Douglas, D-Ill., William Proxmire, D-Wis., Wayne Morse, D-Ore., and Joseph Clark, D-Pa., voting against him. But Johnson was better able to manipulate the Senate's agenda, in the era before open committee meetings; moreover, the committee chairmen—Johnson's natural allies for the most part—had greater ability to mold their own coalitions during a time when the seniority system reigned supreme. While Baker and Dole developed their own strong alliances with key committee chairmen, they found it more difficult to line up votes; to kill quietly embarrassing or losing bills and amendments; and to use subcommittee chairmanships, committee assignments, or staff slots as rewards or incentives for individual members.

The changes in the Senate's environment have affected more than the ability of leaders to form networks or convince colleagues. They have also altered the ability of leaders to use procedures to shape issues and outcomes. Some of the changes have occurred in the Senate rules themselves. True, in the years since Johnson's leadership, the Senate's rules have not changed dramatically. But the changes that have occurred have also altered the context in which leaders can apply them. One of the primary areas of change has been in the rules regarding the filibuster. On the one hand, filibusters have become harder to sustain, with fewer votes required to invoke cloture. But more significantly, they have become easier to initiate since Mike Mansfield began "two-track" scheduling in the 1960s, allowing other business to proceed while the filibuster blocks action on only one bill.

Thus, both the number and unpredictability of filibusters have increased dramatically, thereby complicating the lives of the Senate's leaders. But the ability of a leader to use the filibuster to schedule round-the-clock sessions, and manipulate them to his own ends, has declined. In Johnson's era, nearly all filibusters were civil rights related and initiated by southern Democrats to prevent civil rights bills. These southern Democrats, like Richard Russell, D-Ga., for example, were regular Johnson allies who were loath to blindside their leader. Today, filibusters come from all quarters, ranging from liberal Democrats like Howard M. Metzenbaum of Ohio to conservative Republicans like Jesse Helms, and are rarely planned or announced in advance.

Another major set of rules changes opened up Senate business to the public, press, and others. Committee meetings and hearings, not to mention markup sessions, were nearly all opened in the 1970s, while in the Johnson era virtually any important session was closed to all but lawmakers and selected staff. In this closed environment, the ability of leaders and their allies to wheel and cut deals was greater than in the public sessions that became the norm in the 1970s.

Even with these and other rules changes, Senate leaders have found that control over scheduling and setting agendas is their greatest lever to influence the Senate and senators. In some respects, the more open, freewheeling, and unpredictable Senate of the past decade has been advantageous to leaders. The same senators who abuse their privileges and take advantage of the rules also insist on having votes rescheduled so that they can travel abroad or give speeches, and want themselves to avoid being surprised or blindsided by the Senate's schedule. Thus, leaders do favors for their colleagues and generate due bills. And leaders can still use unanimous consent agreements, the power of recognition, and "stop-and-go" scheduling, especially near the end of a session, to time bills and amendments to maximize support and minimize opposition.

In the past few years, the rules and their applications have changed again, moving slightly away from the reforms of the 1970s. For example, closed meetings and markup sessions are no longer impossible; while still rare, they have been used to build the necessary support for several crucial pieces of legislation. The major tax bill of 1982 initiated in the Senate was put together by Finance Committee Chairman Bob Dole in several closed sessions with key committee colleagues; so, too, was the landmark tax reform bill of 1986. In both cases, Senate leaders took advantage of the relaxation of the rules to build coalitions that would have been otherwise impossible.

As majority leader, Bob Dole used the drive to televise Senate sessions, long promoted by his predecessor, Howard Baker, to insist on several rules changes as prerequisites. All the changes were aimed at giving the majority leader greater control over the Senate's schedule to prevent the institution from embarrassing itself on national television by appearing unable to control its own agenda. In the process, the tough-minded leader in the Johnson mold seized the opportunity to gain more personal leverage and used it to advantage in the second session of the Ninety-ninth Congress. In his run for president, Dole faced very different circumstances as minority leader; in the 100th Congress, he was down a full five votes and put on the defensive at the outset because of the Iran-Contra affair.

It was also interesting to watch Robert Byrd in his second tour as majority leader, beginning in 1987. Byrd beat back a challenge from within and then faced pressure to perform not only as a strong parliamentary strategist on the floor but as a telegenic spokesperson for his party. In the House, Byrd's counterpart, Jim Wright, started off on strong and assertive footing but with a good deal of internal and external criticism for his independent, unpredictable statements and his penchant for carrying out matters himself, without delegating appropriately to his colleagues or staff. In each of these cases, though, it is clear that the institutional impediments to leaders who assert themselves and make things happen are not insurmountable.

Congressional Leadership Under Challenge

Robert Byrd stepped down as Senate majority leader at the end of the 100th Congress, assuming the dual posts of president pro tempore of the Senate and chairman of the Appropriations Committee. He was replaced, after a vigorous contest, by George Mitchell of Maine. After a controversial but highly productive term as Speaker of the House, Jim Wright found himself embattled from the first days of the 101st Congress by an ethics controversy and by the congressional pay raise. Halfway through the first session, he resigned, as did House Majority Whip Tony Coelho, D-Calif. A new Democratic leadership team took over, led by Speaker Tom Foley, Majority Leader Richard A. Gephardt, D-Mo., and Majority Whip William H. Gray, III, D-Pa. Early in the 101st Congress, House Minority Whip Dick Cheney, R-Wyo., was appointed secretary of defense; he, in turn, was replaced by Wright's nemesis, Newt Gingrich, R-Ga. In each instance, the leadership changes produced sharp contrasts in personal style and outlook between predecessors and successors. It appears, however, that the potential for strong and assertive leadership remains for all the new leaders.

George Mitchell was chosen Senate majority leader over his rivals for the post, J. Bennett Johnston of Louisiana and Daniel Inouye of Hawaii, in significant part because Democratic senators saw Mitchell as possessing the combination of resources that fit their own conception of what was required for the post in 1989 and beyond. Their contextual analysis was no doubt driven by the reality of a continuing Republican presidency facing a continuing Democratic Congress, a situation that put a premium on the ability of their leader, as a prime national spokesman for the Democratic party, to communicate well, especially on television. No senator could begin to contend for this top leadership post without having shown a command of the rules or other legislative skills. But in the absence of a president who would aggressively push a massive legislative agenda or hostilely attack congressional prerogatives, there was less need for a leader whose major strength was command of the rules on the floor or who could knock heads together to build a majority better than he could communicate to the Washington community and the outside world.

With the battle over cutting capital gains taxes, however, Mitchell showed that he could be a tough partisan infighter, using the rules of the Senate and hard-nosed coalition-building techniques to deny a popular president his top legislative priority. By strongly and effectively criticizing the Bush administration for its passivity toward the revolutionary changes in Eastern Europe and its secret diplomatic mission to China shortly after Tienanmen Square, both inside Congress and on national public affairs television Mitchell showed the growing importance that communication can play for a congressional leader and its effectiveness as an institutional and partisan resource. With a personal style vastly different from that of Lyndon Johnson, Mike Mansfield, Robert Byrd, or Bob Dole, Mitchell managed his first year to maximize his own skills and resources to fit the political and institutional context and to emerge as a strong leader. In his second year, as the context moved toward passing major pieces of legislation, Mitchell faced another set of challenges that required somewhat different skills and resources.

In the House, the bitter and difficult departure of Jim Wright, and the early experience of his successor, Tom Foley, provide a different set of lessons. In terms of the successful passage of major pieces of legislation, the 100th Congress was the most productive in modern memory—in no small part because of Jim Wright. Wright effectively used House rules and his own partisan majority to set and pursue an aggressive legislative agenda, often ignoring and sometimes exploiting the outrage voiced by House minority Republicans. While legislation passed, one side effect of Wright's strong and assertive leadership was sharply heightened partisan conflict, exacerbated by frayed tempers and personal clashes. Partisan tension in the House was a major factor in Wright's eventual resignation.

With a personality in dramatic contrast to his predecessor's, Tom Foley moved quickly and effectively as Speaker to heal the partisan wounds. While Foley did not have any stunning legislative victories in his first months as Speaker, his personal qualities—a mastery of the House, including its rules, history, and policies, the universal respect he commanded from the Washington community, and his breadth—raised the intriguing possibility that he could be as productive and powerful a Speaker as Wright but with a radically different style of leadership.

Conclusion

Indeed, no matter who leads the House and Senate, or how it changes, chances are that leaders will strive to build a network of support and working relationships with individual lawmakers and will find ways to mold the rules to advantage. As the context of leadership changes—and it most assuredly will—both inside the legislature and in the outer political environment, the ability of leaders to manipulate these key elements will change as well. Some leaders will be able to adapt easily, depending on their personal abilities and flexibility, and will still find ways to build coalitions, construct networks, and apply procedures to advantage, even if the context has made strong leadership tougher to implement. Other leaders have personal styles or bents that make assertive leadership impossible no matter what the conditions. Yet other leaders can be dominant under some conditions but not others. Ability, personality, and context all must be taken into account to appreciate how leaders can operate in the legislative setting.

All these changes, however, provide the same answer to the title of this essay. Can Congress be led? The answer is yes, in a myriad of ways and by a myriad of people, in very different contexts and times.

Notes

1. Rowland Evans and Robert Novak, *Lyndon B. Johnson: The Exercise of Power* (New York: New American Library, 1966).

2

Fostering the Entrepreneurial Activities of Members of the House

Ross K. Baker

It may strike the reader that the title of this paper might be likened to one reading, "Encouraging Your Dog to Eat Red Meat," or "Persuading Malpractice Attorneys to Pursue Negligence Claims." The purpose of the essay is not to advocate self-evident courses of action; rather, it is to ask the question, "What is a realistic expectation of party leaders in Congress given the nature of today's members?"

It is important to put aside the notions of responsible party government learned in introductory comparative government courses that taught us to envy the consistency and unity of the parliamentary form of government. Nor should we berate ourselves for the illogic and messiness of having a head of government who is not drawn from the national legislature or congressional members remarkably autonomous of the party on whose benches they sit. Let us banish from our minds the prospect that anytime soon national party organizations will be sitting atop huge mounds of money meted out only to the loyal. Let us also put aside any immediate hope that national party organizations will regain control of congressional nominations, or even that public funding is around the corner. These eventualities, it seems to me, are only slightly more likely than the chance that strong party identifiers will come to dominate the electorate.

Instead let us think about the challenges of generalship in an army composed of colonels or of heading an academic department in which everyone is tenured. Such is the environment in which representatives Tom Foley, D-Wash., and Bob Michel, R-Ill., must work. To be sure, there are days in December when the Steering and Policy Committee and the Committee on Committees have an opportunity to weigh the souls of some members on the scales of party regularity. But for those so senior or well ensconced in their chairmanships or committee assignments, the most serious threat comes not from a party leadership scorned but from a volatile and unpredictable caucus.

That authoritarian and directive leadership has been interred with the bones of Thomas Brackett Reed and Joe Cannon is, I would hope, a truism by now. We accept the concept of the candidate-centered campaign, the member-centered perspective reflected in Richard Fenno's work,[1] and the concept of service-centered leadership that Barbara Sinclair called to our attention.[2] I think we need to go one step further and come to appreciate what people like Burdett Loomis have been telling us—that is, the quality of the House has never been better, but it might be realistically viewed as a mail drop for a group of 435 venture capitalists.[3]

Why would we expect legislators who have won such signal victories by and for individualism to submit to the yoke of party regularity or, indeed, even pay much attention to the public face of the party if such deference yields them little and might even get them into trouble with their constituents? Why would we expect bright and able young members with a desire to shape national policy to refrain from doing so in any way they could—with or without the blessings of their party's leaders? We would probably not be realistic to expect any of these, except momentarily or intermittently, without some persuasive evidence that the policy-shaping activities that the best members pursued would be underwritten by their party's leadership—not simply tolerated but fostered and cultivated.[4]

How does this suggestion that party leaders serve as patrons of policy entrepreneurship square with the obligations that they have to present a more or less consistent array of policies that give form and identity to a party nationally?

It is a reasonable assertion that the policy activism of modern House members and the obligations of leadership to mediate, integrate, and fashion broadly acceptable winning policies are not zero-sum games. And while the freewheeling independence of many modern members is a challenge to the resourcefulness and ingenuity of leaders, it does not make leadership impossible. Such leadership becomes impossible only if leaders harbor unrealistic or outmoded ideas of what can be accomplished in a member-centered House.

In prefacing a set of suggestions on what techniques and resources might be used by leaders, I would like to highlight an assumption that underlies this paper: while many members have the desire to be shapers of policy, only a few have the wherewithal to do so. Those members with important or favored committee assignments may pursue policy innovation with considerably greater ease than those less strategically situated. It is this latter group, in particular, for which leadership can actually improve the terrain for policy entrepreneurship. Leaders can then integrate this activity into the framework of the congressional party and make it part of the party's public face.

Based on my own observations of a party instrumentality, the House Democratic Caucus in the years 1982 and 1983, I would like to discuss four techniques available to party leaders in the House. These activities assist the policy-inclined member while at the same time render entrepreneurship more compatible with the broader policy concerns of party leaders. While these activities have been undertaken by various party leaders and instrumentalities in the past, they might benefit from codification; I call them magnetism, action, cover, and exposure.

Policy Magnetism: Attracting the Experts

There is now broad acceptance of the "percolation" model as a plausible view of how congressional policy making originates. There is, at the very least, an array of sources of policy inspiration outside Congress that pass through its permeable walls and eventuate in legislation. But the ability to summon up policy expertise from outside the House is not distributed uniformly across its membership. While an individual senator might be able to command a briefing from a prominent expert, it generally takes at the least a House subcommittee to exert that kind of pull. Such magnetism, however, is well within the normal grasp of enterprises headed by members of the party leadership.[5]

In the 1982-1983 period, the Committee on Party Effectiveness of the House Democratic Caucus developed a major economic policy initiative, the centerpiece of which was industrial policy. During that period, most of the academic advocates of industrial policy and experts in the private sector briefed the committee. While it is true that some influential members of the committee such as Rep. Tim Wirth, D-Colo., and Rep. Richard A. Gephardt, D-Mo., were able to arrange private meetings with policy experts, most of the other members received their only direct exposure to the outsiders from the seminars arranged by Caucus Chairman Gillis Long, D-La.

There was nothing magical about the caucus committee as the forum for these briefings. It might just as easily have been undertaken by the Democratic Steering and Policy Committee or the Republican Conference. But the point is that a summons from the leadership was much more likely to attract the outsider with ideas. There was, accordingly, a real incentive for junior members to be associated with the work of the Committee on Party Effectiveness if for no other reason than to improve their own entrepreneurship. Reliance on a party group for policy inspiration led, almost necessarily, to a firmer bond between leadership and members.

Policy Action: Directing the Energies of Members

If the average member finds it difficult to acquire individually much in the way of personalized policy expertise from the outside, he or she may also be frustrated by the inactivity of his or her own committee. It seems especially the case in this period when the chance for real legislative accomplishment is within the reach of so few. Leaders ought to be able to profit from the distress of their long-term antagonists, the committee chairmen.[6]

While the attraction of a nonlegislative committee may not be as alluring as that of a major committee that processes "must-pass" legislation—such as appropriations or budget bills—party policy making can be challenging and engrossing. Indeed, in a paradoxical way, some members may feel even *more* comfortable developing policies that have no immediate chance of enactment or have doctrinal or symbolic, rather than statutory, importance. Such activities present an opportunity to be freewheeling and imaginative without having to worry too much about what follows the enacting clause.[7]

The Committee on Party Effectiveness absorbed the energies of about two dozen relatively new members while it prepared two major reports on industrial policy and competitiveness between 1981 and 1984. Chairman Long sought to reduce the alienation of them with a program of "participatory democracy" in the activities of the caucus. He reached out specifically to a group of Sun Belt Democrats who, he feared, might drift irretrievably into the Boll Weevil camp or even join the handful of outright defectors to the Republican party. By engaging this group of right-of-center Democrats in party policy activities while attempting also to provide policy action for a larger number of moderate-to-liberal members, Long additionally contributed to coalition maintenance during a perilous period for the party.

Another remarkable example of a nonlegislative committee providing policy action was the success of the Joint Economic Committee (JEC) under Rep. David R. Obey, D-Wis., during the Ninety-ninth Congress. More than any other source, the JEC placed the issue of the "bicoastal economy" on the national agenda and probably influenced the outcome of the 1986 congressional elections more profoundly than the Ways and Means Committee with its tax reform.

Political Cover: Inoculating the Members

The third leadership activity is directed, perhaps, less to policy entrepreneurship than to policy as a tool for political survival. As a component of a party that was both out of power and out of favor, the protection of its incumbents was a major task for the Committee on Party Effectiveness.

The choice of party policies that Long's committee chose to emphasize—industrial policy, competitiveness, and military reform—served to inoculate many Democrats with the antibodies of political centrism at a time when many viewed the party as committed only to redistributive social programs. For some Sun Belt moderates, the much-publicized work of the Committee on Party Effectiveness flashed an important message that being a Democrat was not politically incapacitating in a period when being tagged a liberal was a heavy political liability. This image doctoring by an element of the party-in-Congress was an astute undertaking that gave political cover to a number of moderate southerners and westerners who probably would have survived anyway but felt reassured that they were not saddled with a party whose mythology was damaging to them.

Democratic leadership in the Ninety-ninth Congress was successful in providing political cover for members when Jim Wright, D-Texas, helped to fashion a drug bill to respond to public indignation over narcotics abuses but failed in the 101st Congress to structure a pay-raise bill that would enable members to receive raises without incurring political heat. Majority Whip Tom Foley acted with great skill in the House's response to Gramm-Rudman-Hollings offering a compromise that was seen as responsive to the political exigencies of budget cutting and to the need on the part of liberals to shield important social programs from cuts.

The success of the Committee on Party Effectiveness in spreading the message that Democrats could be thoughtful, measured, and judicious people underscores another activity of user-friendly leadership: exposure.

Media Exposure: Edging Close to the Celebrities

Long was very successful in getting the media to pay attention to the reports of the Committee on Party Effectiveness, particularly the first one, which was entitled "Rebuilding the Road to Opportunity" but quickly dubbed "The Yellow-Brick Road" because of the color of the report's cover.

Recent research that explores the relationship of members to the media suggests that journalists seek out appropriate leaders for comment and turn to authoritative sources for their stories.[8] If that is indeed the case, there would be an incentive for members to be associated with leadership activities if they sought media attention but feared they could not attract it on their own. This presupposes, though, a disposition on the part of leaders to share the limelight with members.

For their part, members seemed eager to participate in broad-gauged party policy-making activities as much for the considerable media attention generated from the proposals as for the merits of the proposals themselves. Indeed, the members could ascribe whatever meanings they chose to such concepts as "industrial policy" or "competitiveness."

There was at the time a very attractive mythology that attached to such terms as "high-tech" and "industrial policy" that the press found irresistible. The promotional activities by the committee itself helped to heighten the media's eagerness to see what the Democrats were up to. Long, for his part, was willing to push newer members in front of the cameras—not a practice we have come to expect in leaders but one that set up a bond of personal loyalty to and affection for the caucus chairman. For their part, certain members emerged from the party policy-making process with increased visibility—a visibility they might not have achieved so efficiently or quickly by working strictly on their own or through their assigned committees.

Policy Entrepreneurship and the Public Face of the Party

The aggressive pursuit by its members of policy-making opportunities is, for a national party, more of a blessing than a curse. Party leaders in Congress have always been good at making virtues out of necessities, and this situation does not constitute an exception. Indeed, given the process by which members arrive in the House and the means they employ to stay there, the consistency and distinctiveness that leaders are able to imprint on their overall policies are quite remarkable. House Republicans, for example, seem to have developed policies quite distinct from both the White House and Senate Republicans but at the same time not discordant with these others.

While leaders in the House seem willing, or perhaps resigned, to let a hundred flowers bloom, they may profitably go one step further and cultivate them. Their powers to command expertise, provide useful party-related activities, and confer political cover (and damage control), as well as their superior ability to attract the media, are resources of incalculable value to the entrepreneurial member. The process by which these many ideas are translated into the party's overall program is the activity that allows a political party to define itself.

The more open and receptive leaders are to the ideas and proposals of members, the more likely the party is to go forth with a public face that all have had a share in composing. Themes that all have shared in composing are those that all will be more likely to defend.

Notes

1. Among the most influential of the congressional scholars of the last two decades, Richard F. Fenno has produced a body of literature that focuses increasingly on the individual member. In *Congressmen in Committees* (Boston: Little, Brown, 1973), Fenno examines the components of members' individual calculations in deciding on which committee to serve. *Homestyle* (Boston: Little, Brown, 1978) highlighted the importance of the perceptions

members had of their districts and the distinctive and highly individualized manner in which these perceptions were shaped.

2. Barbara Sinclair's exploration of House leadership at a critical time in the late
1970s and early 1980s shows dramatic evidence of the resort to the provision
of politically useful services by ranking party officials to build coalitions. This
emphasis on members and their needs demonstrates that in a postreform
House, individual members are being cultivated by leaders to an unprece-
dented degree. See Barbara D. Sinclair, "Majority Party Leadership Strategies for Coping with the New House," *Legislative Studies Quarterly* 6
(August 1981): 391-414; and *Majority Leadership in the U.S. House*
(Baltimore: Johns Hopkins University Press, 1983).

3. Burdett Loomis isolates one particularly influential group of House members,
the Watergate class of 1974, and holds them out as emblematic of a new and
more individualistic Congress. He writes, "By the mid-1970s, freshmen
legislators were encouraged, even expected, to participate actively within
both Senate and House. With such expectations for activism and a loosening
of the straitjacket of apprenticeship came increasingly diverse individual
styles. Such stylistic variety has complemented the structural fragmentation
of Congress. . . ." Burdett Loomis, *The New American Politician* (New York:
Basic Books, 1988), 24.

4. Ibid., 42.

5. Salisbury and Shepsle have made the point that "in seeking power within the
institution, the modern member utilizes not only his or her personal skills and
opportunities but those afforded by the whole enterprise a member heads. It
follows that, by and large, the bigger and more well-placed that enterprise in
its various elements may be, the better the chances for additional power to be
secured. Hence, a committee chair confers power, not simply any more by
the sheer authority of the position, but through the increment of staff to the
member-centered enterprise." This description applies with greatest force to
leaders who are able to marshal even more imposing resources. See Robert H.
Salisbury and Kenneth A. Shepsle, "Congressman as Enterprise," *Legislative
Studies Quarterly* 6 (November 1981): 566.

6. In interviews with Democratic House members who had been associated with
the caucus's Committee on Party Effectiveness, I found that the breadth of
the panel's concern served to broaden the horizons of those who felt too
closely tied to the jurisdictional concerns of their own committees. Typical
was the comment: "[The Committee on Party Effectiveness] was party-wide
and avoided the kind of narrow policy focus of the single committee. You
usually stick with your committee and caucus with the Democrats and you
talk about what's going on in Energy and Commerce or Foreign Affairs. But
this was party-wide and not in a single policy area." Ross K. Baker, "What's
in It for Me: Benefits to House Members for Association with Industrial
Policy" (Paper presented at the annual meeting of the American Political
Science Association, New Orleans, August 30-September 2, 1985).

7. A member of Congress may gain political advantages by being identified
with an issue even when there is no serious possibility that any enactments
will take place. This is the technique known as "position taking" described in
David R. Mayhew, *Congress, The Electoral Connection* (New Haven,

Conn.: Yale University Press, 1974). Members may also see political advantage in policy fads and fashions that attract early intensive media attention but on closer examination may raise problems that are insoluble or can be addressed only at unacceptable cost. Nonetheless, the well-publicized exploration of the issues often yields political dividends. See John W. Kingdon, *Agendas, Alternatives, and Public Policies* (Boston: Little, Brown, 1984).

8. Stephen Hess, *The Ultimate Insiders* (Washington: Brookings Institution, 1986), 30-43.

3 ■■■

Party Leadership in the U.S. Senate

Samuel C. Patterson

The first steps in understanding party leadership in the U.S. Senate are mapping and analyzing its properties and problems. Here, leadership is situational, personalized, partisan, collegial, and mediating. Senate leaders face perplexing institutional problems—problems of context, management, party, succession, formalized power, and external relations. Investigating the salient features of Senate leadership and the institutional problems leaders confront will help in understanding the behavior of Senate leaders.

The United States Senate remains a remarkable political body. Surely it has changed in various ways in the years since World War II, and these changes rightfully excite the interest of journalists and scholars. But the import of recent changes in the Senate is easy to exaggerate. The most important and indelible change in the Senate occurred around the turn of the century, when the development of an active party organization and leadership made the institution what it is today. One historian has said, "By 1900 the United States Senate had become more modern, enjoying a life of its own." [1] And it had become an institution markedly different from what had been intended.

In 1926 historian Lindsay Rogers said of the Senate, which was now directly elected by the people:

It is a body whose development has completely falsified the confident anticipations of the framers of the American Constitution: few if any issues have arisen to make the small states require protection against the

---

* This research is part of a larger analysis of the congressional parties for which I acknowledge the support of a John Simon Guggenheim Memorial Fellowship, a visiting fellowship at the Brookings Institution, and a research grant from the Everett McKinley Dirksen Congressional Leadership Research Center. An earlier version of this study appears in *Legislative Studies Quarterly* 14 (August 1989): 393-413.

more populous states, and, instead of being only a check in the congressional system, the Senate is now a senior partner.[2]

In his doctoral dissertation, written in 1884, Woodrow Wilson chided the Senate for weak leadership, characterizing it as merely a small House of Representatives—equally "a disintegrate mass of jarring elements."[3] But closer, more thorough observation belies this. In the 1880s party leadership was unmistakable, and by the end of the century Senate party organization was well developed.[4] In the Fifty-fifth Congress (1897-1899), William Allison, a Republican from Iowa, and Arthur Gorman, a Democrat from Maryland, served as their parties' leaders in every modern sense.

As in the late nineteenth century, we refer to those who hold particular party offices and party committee memberships when we speak of the Senate leadership today. Preeminent among these is the party floor leader, although the designation "leader" was not formalized in the Senate until the 1920s. Today, the party leaderships include the floor leaders, caucus chairs and secretaries, whips, and members of committees on committees, policy committees, and campaign committees. All or most chairs of full committees are likely to be included in the party leaderships. For instance, in the Ninety-ninth Congress, all standing committee chairmen were also members of the Republican Policy Committee. Until the 101st Congress (1989-1991), Democratic floor leaders also served as the chairs of the caucus, the policy committee, and the steering committee, whereas the Republicans traditionally filled these offices with different senators.

Leadership in the Senate

"Congressional leadership," wrote Charles O. Jones, "is an uncommonly difficult phenomenon to analyze."[5] In a highly institutionalized group like the Senate, leadership is a subtle and complex matter. Senate leadership develops from a tangled interaction of individual personalities, institutional constraints, and external forces. It is not easy to understand how leadership works.[6] What are the salient features of party leadership in the Senate?

Leadership Is Situational

Observers note first and foremost that leadership in the Senate is highly situational. A British scholar who came to Washington in 1983 to study Senate Republicans was notably impressed with the constraints that the institutional context placed on leaders' behavior. "The problem faced by all majority leaders," he wrote, "has been to organise the Senate within the limitations imposed by the Senate's structure." [7]

It is often said that Senate leaders have few formal institutional powers.[8] The party system and its reflection in the Senate shape the possibilities of leadership in that body.[9] The shaping effect of party structure may incline Senate leaders to serve as "middlemen," consistent with "the mediate function of the legislative party." [10] Again, the majority or minority status of the legislative parties surely helps to fashion the extent and reach of centralized leadership.[11] And because the organizational hierarchy of the Senate is, as Robert L. Peabody has said, "flatter" than that of the House, Senate leadership tends to be more personalized.[12]

Leadership Is Personalized

Indeed, Senate party leadership is highly personalized. Characterizations of the performance of Senate leaders commonly underscore their personal styles, preeminently in exercising the power of persuasion. The significance of personal style is epitomized in the leadership of Texas Democrat Lyndon B. Johnson.[13] But personalized leadership is also exemplified by the manner in which Senators Mike Mansfield, D-Mont., Robert C. Byrd, D-W.Va., Howard Baker, R-Tenn., and Robert Dole, R-Kan., exerted personal influence. Senate leadership in general is personalized, and "party leaders exist to serve the needs of other Senators." [14] The activities and influence of the Senate party apparatus—the conference, or the policy committee—depend heavily upon the personal style of the leader.[15]

In countless studies of the emergence and performance of leadership in small groups, it has been demonstrated that two crucial leadership roles tend to develop: the socioemotional specialist and the task specialist.[16] Affective leadership—that of the socioemotional specialist—is plainly exhibited in congressional leadership behavior. Barbara Sinclair wrote of the importance House leaders attach to "keeping peace in the family." [17] At the same time, a considerable proportion of congressional leadership effort is invested in performing the myriad tasks essential to the smooth running of the legislative process. Examples of affective behavior abound in accounts of Senate party leadership. Lyndon Johnson's interpersonal style is often celebrated for its affective power, but Mike Mansfield was a master of affective politics as well. A contemporary Democratic senator said of Mansfield's leadership: "He will sometimes call a meeting of some eight or ten senators and have coffee and cookies in his office . . . as some sort of pep meeting. . . . He wants to get everybody together." [18] Sen. Everett M. Dirksen, R-Ill., who became Republican leader at the outset of the Eighty-sixth Congress (1959), succeeded in mollifying dissident factions after the failure of his predecessors, Sens. Robert A. Taft, R-Ohio, and William Knowland, R-Calif., to "keep peace in the family." [19]

Occasionally Senate leaders are called upon to keep peace in the Senate as a whole and not merely within their own party. On July 18, 1979, Sen. J. Bennett Johnston, D-La., was called upon to manage the bill continuing the construction work on the Hart Senate Office Building, which had been labeled a "Taj Mahal," a "palace of Versailles," and a "monument to government extravagance and waste." Sen. John C. Danforth, R-Mo., attacked the Hart building appropriation, implying that the conservative Johnston was a "profligate spender." Sen. William S. Cohen, R-Maine, reported what transpired next:

> The mood in the chamber turned into a sour malignity. The presiding officer called attention to the Senate Rules requiring Senators to speak to the Chair and to refer to other Senators in the third person.
> Majority leader Robert Byrd, who was listening to the debate on his "squawk box," rushed to the floor and came to Johnston's defense. He reminded everyone that the Senate Rules existed "in order that acerbities might be avoided and the debate might not get too personal."
> Tempers cooled somewhat. . . .[20]

Keeping peace in the family may also require the leader and his or her staff to work tirelessly to smooth relations between senators and the White House or executive agency leaders, as when Majority Leader Howard Baker sought to quell a feud between Sen. Dan Quayle, R-Ind., and the Reagan administration's labor department over the job training bill in 1982.[21]

Effective performance of socioemotional leadership in the Senate may require skill at accommodation and empathy but not necessarily close personal friendship. Both as majority and minority leader, Senator Byrd was lionized occasionally on and off the Senate floor for his skill at accommodation and finesse in resolving conflicts among Senate Democrats. But Byrd is often said to be a "loner"; one day on the Senate floor, he remarked, "I understand that I am not very well liked around here anyhow. I did not get elected to be liked here. I got elected because I thought I could do a job." [22]

A good many Senate party leaders over the years have been without close friends among senators. Personal friendships are not necessary to leaders' performances of the affective function:

> The leader or potential leader need not have a wide network of personal friends or even be capable or willing to forge such ties of intimacy; but he must be a good enough 'friend', in the senatorial context, to be able to appreciate the individual needs of his colleagues as politicians and people.[23]

It is difficult to overstate the importance of interpersonal skills that can be directed to effective socioemotional leadership in the Senate. Nevertheless, modern Senate leadership is heavily task oriented. Although socioemotional performance and task performance are analytically distinct leadership functions, in reality they are intertwined. The agenda places unmistakable burdens on leaders to conduct legislative business as expeditiously as possible. Notwithstanding the perceptiveness of David B. Truman's observation that "the legislative party in the Senate is not closely analogous to the problem-solving type of group," Senate leaders' function is actually defined largely in terms of legislative tasks.[24] The overriding job of the leaders, and especially the majority leader, is to get the job done, to manage the Senate's business. "Perhaps," commented Peabody, "the primary responsibility of majority leaders, working in generally close harmony with the minority leaders, is to oversee the scheduling of legislation for the floor." [25] Much of the effort of contemporary Senate leaders, and much of the agony of leadership in the Senate, concerns managing the enterprise.

Leadership Is Partisan

Party leadership in the Senate is partisan, a redundancy that is necessary only when speaking about legislative leadership in the United States; in other countries partisan leadership goes without saying. Partisanship gives Senate leadership a special character in relation to external constituencies, the president, and senatorial colleagues. Although "on Capitol Hill everyone is a partisan," the leadership bears special organizational and ideological responsibility.[26] Party voting is not as prevalent in the Senate as in the House, and Senate party voting levels respond over time to somewhat different variables.[27] And although senators may not be as concerned about the policy positions of their leaders as House members are, even in the Senate "bland moderation does not prevail against the spice of partisanship." [28]

Senate leaders since World War II have tended to show higher levels of party loyalty on roll-call votes than have rank-and-file members.[29] As Senate roll-call voting became increasingly more partisan beginning in the late 1960s, the differential in party unity between leaders and rank-and-file members slackened. Still, as Table 3-1 shows for the 1980s, the average unity of Senate party leaders is marginally higher than that for all party members and is higher than the unity of committee chairs. Interestingly, the high scores for the Republican leaders are, in fact, equalled or exceeded by southern Republicans in these four Congresses. The party unity of Democratic leaders is close to the average for rank-and-file Democrats from northern states. In the 1980s, Republican leaders' party unity ebbed somewhat; Democratic

Table 3-1 Party Unity of Senate Leaders (in percentages).

Party and position	97th Congress (1981-1983)	98th Congress (1983-1985)	99th Congress (1985-1987)	100th Congress (1987-1989)
Republicans				
Leaders	85	84	80	75
Committee chairs	76	73	73	—
All Republicans	79	76	76	72
Northern Republicans	77	74	74	70
Southern Republicans	87	84	83	83
Democrats				
Leaders	79	71	81	84
Committee chairs	—	—	—	79
All Democrats	72	70	74	80
Northern Democrats	77	74	79	83
Southern Democrats	60	60	61	74

Sources: Congressional Roll Call, annual volumes for 1981 to 1987 (Washington, D.C.: Congressional Quarterly); *Congressional Quarterly Weekly Report,* November 19, 1988, 3334-3342.

leaders' unity edged up after the Ninety-eighth Congress, in keeping with the generally growing party unity of Democratic senators.

These patterns in party unity only illustrate the partisanship of Senate leaders. Because successful leadership of the Senate entails "a constant balancing act between demanding partisan unity and loyalty and deferring constituency interests and the dictates of individual judgment," leaders face "a complicated process of interaction with the members." [30] The extent to which these interactions present urgent and profound partisan cues depends upon a number of variables, including the partisan role orientation and ideology of the leaders and the partisan predispositions of the rank-and-file senators. While the partisanship of Senate leadership is problematic, it is nonetheless real and important.

Leadership Is Collegial

Although the Senate parties differ in allocating leadership jobs—the Democratic leader chairs the caucus, the committee on committees, and the policy committee, while Republicans give these posts to members other than the leader—fundamentally Senate party leadership is collegial.[31] In the Senate, leadership is markedly less centralized than in the House of Representatives. This was certainly true in the nineteenth century. Daniel Webster said, "This is a Senate, a Senate of equals. . . . We know no masters. . . . This is a hall for mutual consultation and discussion, not an arena for the exhibition of champions." [32] By 1975, Sen.

Edmund S. Muskie, D-Maine, was calling this dictum the "Mansfield Principle." Referring to the majority leader, Muskie said, "He doesn't run the Senate . . . the Senate is a body of equals. . . ."[33] In reality, those who are "more equal"—the occupants of party leadership posts and committee chairs—run the Senate.

Over the years, patterns of collegiality or centrality in Senate leadership have changed.[34] But differences between Democrats and Republicans in these patterns appear to stem largely from the nature of the party majorities and the affinities of the Senate parties to the president,[35] rather than reflecting a particularity endemic to each party.[36]

Leadership Is Mediating

David B. Truman came to understand the congressional parties as "mediate and supplementary rather than immediate and inclusive in function." [37] This conception led him to think of congressional leaders as "middlemen," both in the structural and active senses.[38] Truman reasoned that:

> . . . this characteristic of the Senate floor leader's role—holding a position in the structural middle of the party—is a logical correlate of the mediate function of the legislative party. The party as a mediate group both reflects and fosters the self-conscious independence of the individual senator, records and in a degree perpetuates the deep cleavages that persist within it. And the mediate group imposes upon even a most talented leader the necessity to build his influence upon a combination of such fragments of power, and hence such groupings of men, as are available to him. He must, in other words, be a middleman in the sense of a broker.[39]

Based on his observations of voting blocs in the Eighty-first Congress (1949-1951), Truman also thought that Senate leaders were likely to be middlemen in the structural sense as well, located ideologically and behaviorally in the middle of their parties.

Evidence of whether or not Senate leaders occupy the structural middle—are ideologically moderate, or take mediate positions in Senate voting—is mixed. Some think the Senate's recruitment function works so that leaders tend to be moderate or are drawn from among those who are highly tolerant of conflicting policy positions or have only tepid programmatic interests and are willing to build coalitions for whatever can succeed. Senate leaders do not always occupy the "moderate" zone in voting; frequently they are to be found at the extremes.[40] Moreover, as Table 3-1 indicates, Senate leaders often show higher levels of party loyalty than rank-and-file members. The weight of the evidence suggests that Senate leaders are not necessarily middlemen insofar as their spatial location in voting goes.

At the same time, a mediating role—that of broker, compromiser, builder of coalitions, or negotiator—is undoubtedly central to successful Senate party leadership.[41] In this sense, Senate leaders certainly are middlemen. Lyndon Johnson's persuasive treatment provides an ideal for the mediating function of Senate leaders. But Everett Dirksen knew that the first requirement of the minority leader's job "was to find out what senators want and what they will settle for and then to work out a compromise," and his effectiveness evanesced when he faltered as a mediator and communicator.[42]

Problems of Senate Party Leadership

Where theoretical helmsmanship is difficult, we may derive a better understanding of Senate party leadership by focusing upon practical problems in Senate leadership today. We can view a problem not so much as a specific difficulty that calls for solution but rather as a perplexing situation to be dealt with accordingly. We are not talking about policy problems here—how the Senate can cut the budget deficit, or how the majority party's program can be approved. We are talking about institutional problems, involving the conditions or circumstances of leadership. What major problems do Senate party leaders face? A half-dozen are readily apparent; most have been discussed frequently by scholars and senators; and some are very long of tooth. Some may be amenable to particular solutions; some can only be attended to temporarily without being resolved forever; and perhaps some can safely be ignored, in the hope that they will go away. All are worthy of reflection and speculation. Six primary problems are: context, management, party, succession, the leader's role, and external relations. They each deserve comment in turn.

The Problem of Context

Every Senate leader operates in a particular time and place; the Senate itself is profoundly affected by the world around it. Woodrow Wilson grasped this well, observing that "in order to understand and appreciate the Senate, . . . one must know the conditions of public life in this country." [43] Accordingly, Senate leadership must adjust itself to the environment and circumstances of a particular time. How can Senate party leadership best adapt to today's Senate?

Senator Byrd has commented several times on how changes in the political world of the Senate have affected the capacity of the party leader to perform. In 1980 he told the Senate: "Lyndon Johnson was a great majority leader. His prowess as majority leader is legendary. But Lyndon Johnson could not lead this Senate today as he led the Senate in his day. I do not say that with any measure of disrespect for him, but it is a different Senate." [44] Today's Senate is indeed more difficult to lead.

The Senate presents to its leaders a different institutional situation from the one it presented in the halcyon days of Lyndon Johnson. It is a much more individualistic body, one in which all members demand opportunities to participate. What a contrast to the 1950s, when a small group of senators, the "Senate Club," called the shots, and the majority leader could use a "procedure" of persuasion to maintain control. Committees have become increasingly active, and senators face a dismaying array of conflicting committee responsibilities. Junior senators play a much more significant role in committees and subcommittees than they once did.

Senate floor activity has also accelerated, and the floor has become a much more important arena for decision making than it was. Nowadays individual senators make greater use of the rules of procedure to gain or assert leverage over policy making. Freshman senators no longer expect to serve an apprenticeship, and beginning in the 1970s, they "increasingly adopted the new style of unrestrained activism as soon as they entered the chamber." [45] In short, the Senate has become a more complex challenge for leadership.

The Problem of Management

It is one thing for Senate party leaders to adapt in a general way to a more activist and individualistic membership by taking on new, more appropriate leadership styles; it is something else for them to confront the explicit problems of managing Senate business on a day-to-day basis.[46] Today's Senate leaders have been struggling to cope with the increasingly difficult job of managing the institution's legislative work. The Senate's business has become much more pressing than it was even in the recent past. In numbers of bills engendering at least one roll-call vote, the Senate workload tripled between the mid-1950s and the mid-1970s. The sheer number of contested bills declined in the 1980s, but this decline represented no diminution in the Senate workload because bills became larger and more complex. The average length of bills very nearly doubled from the mid-1970s to the mid-1980s. Perhaps even more indicative of the growing burden of legislative work in the Senate has been the mushrooming of amendments: the average number of amendments forced to a vote more than doubled between the 1950s and the 1980s. Managing the escalation in workload has been a continuing problem for Senate leaders. Scheduling the expanding corpus of legislative work has become an especially salient problem for the majority leader.[47] As scheduling is critical to the leadership's effectiveness, Senator Byrd put his finger on the crux of the issue:

> Let it be said for all time that one of the cardinal principles of leadership is to have the right senators—the right senators meaning senators who are going to vote with us—the right senators at the right place, and at the right hour, when the clerk starts calling the roll.[48]

In the 1980s, majority leaders were especially frustrated by scheduling problems in the Senate. In 1983, Republican Majority Leader Howard Baker clamped down on "holds" and ceased "vote stacking" in an effort to gain control of the legislative schedule. He referred to the scheduling task as like "trying to push a wet noodle." Democratic Majority Leader Byrd commented often on his own scheduling frustrations:

> It is extremely difficult to deal with the wishes and needs of 99 other senators, attempting to schedule legislation because almost in every case at any time it is scheduled it inconveniences some senator and I cannot fire any of them. . . . I often say when I am to fill out a form and the form says "occupation", I should put "slave." [49]

In reflecting on his experience as Republican majority leader, Robert Dole expressed similar frustrations:

> I know one of the greatest frustrations I had . . . as a majority leader was trying to accommodate every senator and still get the work done because we were told, 'We cannot vote on Monday,' 'I have to leave early on Friday,' 'I don't want to be here on Tuesday.' . . . That is one day. And then you have that 100 times or maybe 98 times.[50]

At the end of the Ninety-ninth Congress, Dole lamented that a majority leader is "in some ways . . . the slave of all." [51]

In recent years, majority leaders have found delay in completing roll-call votes extremely frustrating. Majority Leader Byrd often complained of unwarranted delay in his comments on the Senate floor. For instance, he once said:

> The majority leader is under a great deal of pressure, because I have Members on my side who do not make it here by the time the 15 minutes are up and I try to check on them. I hear they are on the subway, they have left the office and they will be here, should be coming in the door any moment. So we wait. . . . It is very inconsiderate on the part of a Senator to hold up a vote. [52]

As the remarks of these majority leaders suggest, part of the scheduling problem lies in the great increase in senators' proclivity to spend time in their home states.[53] In the Eighty-ninth Congress (1963-

1964), senators spent an average of 9 days a year in their home states; by the Ninety-third Congress (1973-1974), this average had increased to more than 70 days per year.[54] More immediately, scheduling problems have been grossly compounded by the use of obstructionism as a standard operating procedure. Whereas filibustering used to be an extraordinary effort mounted only in the direst of circumstances, now it has become commonplace. And alteration of Rule XXII to make cloture easier has not resolved the problem.[55]

The Problem of Party

On important matters of national public policy, the Senate usually divides along political party lines. What is the extent and basis of partisanship in the Senate? To what degree do Senate leaders contribute to partisan cleavage? Can the Senate provide more party government than it presently does? If so, how can this be done? Alternatively, would it be desirable to soft pedal partisanship in the Senate, to make it less important than it is now? Such questions are, in fact, little considered. It seems odd that the significance of party in the Senate has not been more widely discussed.

If we use as our standard of partisanship the incidence of "party voting" (roll calls on which a majority of Democrats oppose a majority of Republicans), the Senate of the Ninety-ninth Congress was the most partisan in the last twenty-five years. Just over half of all Senate roll calls so divided the parties. But many of the total number of votes occurred on relatively insignificant issues—for example, legislation prescribing "Made in America Month" or "National Digestive Diseases Awareness Week." If we examine only major legislation—the "key votes" identified by Congressional Quarterly—then the lion's share of Senate votes were partisan. In the Ninety-eighth Congress, more than 80 percent of key votes were party votes, and in the Ninety-ninth Congress, more than three-quarters of the votes divided by party; these represented the highest levels of Senate party voting in the postwar era.

In a partisan Senate, leaders may seek support for a program of legislative action from members of their party and may strive to achieve as much party unity as possible on important issues that come to a vote. Today's Senate leaders, however, have an easier time fostering party voting than did their predecessors of the 1950s. Occasionally Democratic Majority Leader Robert Byrd lectured his colleagues about their partisan obligations. For instance, in 1980, he complained that "there should be more political discipline in this body . . . there has to be party unity. . . . A party has to be held responsible for the governance of a nation." [56] Later that year, Senator Byrd said that he had "tried to bring about a resurgence of feeling of party spirit, party unity, and unity behind the leadership" and that he thought "there [had] been a revival of that spirit."[57]

Robert Dole's leadership performance has been consistently partisan. According to Thomas B. Edsall in the *Washington Post*, as majority leader, Dole "carefully orchestrated the amendment process and the rules under which senators get recognition to effectively prevent Democrats from forcing issues that could be embarrassing to the administration or to the GOP," and now he "relishes the opportunity to do battle with the Democrats as the leader of the Senate minority."[58]

Senate partisanship requires party organization. Once thought to be detrimental to a spirit of party unity among senators, weekly caucuses are now conducted by leaders of both parties. In the case of the Republicans, the policy committee hosts luncheons every Tuesday that all Republican senators attend.[59] The Democrats, Sen. William Proxmire, D-Wis., said approvingly on the Senate floor, "now have regular weekly caucuses where the majority will of our party in the Senate is determined."[60]

Neither the Senate leaders' networks for intelligence gathering nor the dynamics of persuasion are well understood. Apparently leaders depend heavily on the offices of majority and minority secretary to provide the basic intelligence (that is, where senators are and how they will vote) required for effective party leadership. Although both Republican and Democratic Senate whip organizations have been strengthened somewhat in recent years, they remain underutilized.[61] For instance, during Baker's regime as Republican majority leader, whip checks were conducted by the office of the majority secretary and not by whip Ted Stevens, R-Alaska. Sen. Alan K. Simpson, R-Wyo., elected whip when Senator Dole was elevated to the floor leadership, seems to have played a more active role. Senate Democrats have acquired a somewhat more vigorous whip system, and Majority Leader Byrd made some use of the whip organization. He once referred to whip Alan Cranston, D-Calif., as "the best nose counter in the Senate" and indicated that he attended weekly whip meetings.

Other components of Senate party organization have special idiosyncrasies. While the committees on committees contribute much, normally their work is completed after the first two or three weeks of a session. The campaign committees have come to play an enormous role in senatorial campaigns as consultants, staff, fundraisers, and technicians, but this activity remains somewhat separate from the party life of the Senate. The committees of the two parties have little to do with formulating policies or legislative programs. The Republican Policy Committee consists largely of a research staff that provides information and research for individual party members. It also formally sponsors the Tuesday luncheon meetings of Republican senators.[62] In addition to the policy committee staff, the Republicans maintain a sizable conference staff. This conference staff offers a wide range of professional media and communications services to Republican senators. The Democratic Policy Committee is almost entirely a staff operation providing an impressive menu of research and services to members of the Democratic caucus (there has been no separate Democratic caucus staff). Thus, although it is technically correct to speak of Senate organizations as sets of party committees, in fact, the organizational design of the parties does not comport with conventional external expectations. There is, accordingly, room for much discussion of how the Senate parties are and should be recognized.

The Problem of Succession

Some political organizations regularly face serious crises of leadership succession. Not the United States Senate. Most incumbent Senate party leaders are reelected, and contested leadership change is rather uncommon. Yet at times contests and even revolts against the candidacy of established leaders do develop.[63] How can changes in the party leadership of the Senate be accounted for?

One way of resolving the succession problem is to move people up the career ladder to top leadership posts. By and large, this has been the practice in the postwar years among Senate Democrats. Four of the last five Democratic leaders (Scott Lucas, D-Ill., Lyndon Johnson, Mike Mansfield, and Robert Byrd) were promoted to the top post from service as whip. But there have been vigorous contests for Democratic whip in recent memory. Perhaps the most spectacular occurred at the opening of the Ninty-second Congress in 1971, when Senator Byrd, who had been serving as secretary of the Democratic conference, upset incumbent whip Edward Kennedy for the position. When Senator Mansfield stepped down as majority leader in 1977, Byrd was elected unanimously and served as Democratic leader until 1988.

Accession to Senate Republican leadership is a different story. Most Republican whips have not been successful in getting promoted to leader. Hugh Scott of Pennsylvania and Everett M. Dirksen had served very briefly as Republican whips prior to their elevations to leader. One other postwar Republican leader, Kenneth Wherry of Nebraska, had previously served as whip. Between 1935 and 1944, the Senate Republicans did not appoint a whip because of their small numbers. When Senator Dirksen died in 1969, party whip Scott replaced him as leader after a contested election in which he was challenged by Howard Baker, a freshman senator and Dirksen's son-in-law. At the same caucus, Baker lost to Robert Griffin of Michigan for the post of whip. He again challenged Scott unsuccessfully in 1971, but when Scott retired in 1976, Baker was elected leader over Griffin by a single vote, 19-18. When the Republicans took control of the Senate in 1981, Baker was chosen majority leader without opposition.[64]

Senator Baker's decision not to run for the Senate in 1984 precipitated an extraordinary leadership contest. When the Republican conference met in December 1984 to choose officers, there were five serious contenders for the new majority leadership: Senators Robert Dole, Ted Stevens, Richard G. Lugar of Indiana, Pete V. Domenici of New Mexico, and James A. McClure of Idaho. Three conference ballots successively eliminated McClure, Domenici, and Lugar from the contest. In the final balloting, Dole, who had never held a party office in the Senate, defeated Stevens, the incumbent party whip, by a 28-25 vote.

On April 12, 1988, Senator Byrd announced that he would not be a candidate for Democratic leader after the Ninety-ninth Congress adjourned.[65] Well before Byrd's announcement, three senators began to campaign for his post—Daniel K. Inouye, D-Hawaii, J. Bennett Johnston, and George J. Mitchell, D-Maine. Inouye had served as secretary of the Democratic caucus (or conference); Johnston, who had briefly challenged the selection of Byrd as leader in 1986, wielded major influence in the Senate as chairman of the Energy and Natural Resources Committee and as a pivotal player in appropriations politics; and Mitchell had served in 1986 as chairman of the Democratic Senatorial Campaign Committee, helping Democrats regain a Senate majority. Democratic whip Alan Cranston was not in contention to be promoted to the top leadership post.

It was believed to be a close three-way race right to the end; when Democratic senators caucused on November 29, 1988, however, Senator Mitchell won 27 votes on the first ballot. Johnston and Inouye, who garnered only 14 votes apiece, moved to elect Mitchell by acclamation. At the same conference, Cranston was reelected whip over Sen. Wendell H. Ford, D-Ky.; Sen. Alan J. Dixon, D-Ill., was chosen chief deputy whip unopposed; and Sen. David Pryor, D-Ark., was named secretary of the conference over Sen. Patrick J. Leahy, D-Vt. In a break with tradition, Mitchell then designated Sen. Thomas A. Daschle, D-S.D., as cochairman of the Democratic Policy Committee and Senator Inouye as chairman of the Democratic Steering Committee, posts previously held by the leader alone. Mitchell also named Sen. John B. Breaux, D-La., who had been Senator Johnston's campaign manager, chairman of the Democratic Senatorial Campaign Committee.

At the Senate Republican caucus on the same day, Senator Dole was reelected leader and Senator Simpson was reelected assistant leader. In a contest over the campaign committee chairmanship, Sen. Don Nickles, R-Okla., defeated Sen. John S. McCain, R-Ariz., by a 28-17 margin. By the same margin, Sen. John H. Chafee, R-R.I., won reelection as conference chairman over Sen. Frank H. Murkowski, R-Alaska.

The contentiousness, or lack of it, in Senate leadership succession has striking consequences about which we may speculate. For some reason, "revolts" against incumbent party leaders are far less common among Senate Republicans than among Senate Democrats. (House Republicans are, by the way, much more rebellious.) Why is this so? Is effective performance as a Senate leader enhanced by contest for the office? How can the effectiveness of Senator Dole as majority leader be accounted for, given the apparent divisiveness of this election? More generally, what role do contests play in Senate leadership succession? Are contests desirable, or would it be better to strengthen the career ladders in the Senate parties so that there would be regular promotion to the top leadership? Oddly enough, these issues about the health of the system for selecting Senate leaders are rarely subjects of general discussion.

The Problem of the Leader's Role

What actions should Senate party leaders take to be the most effective? How should the floor leader perform? What is the appropriate job of the party whips? What should caucus leaders and other party leaders do? In the Senate, there is considerable leeway in the definition of party leadership posts.

It has been observed that the role of the floor leader can be shaped dramatically by the leader's relationship to the president. If the majority leader and the president belong to the same political party, then the majority leader may feel a responsibility to pilot the president's legislative program through the Senate. A particularly close relationship developed between President Kennedy and Majority Leader Mansfield, but Mansfield's working relationship with President Johnson cooled as their differences widened over the war in Vietnam. Majority Leader Alben Barkley, D-Ky., regarded himself as President Roosevelt's leader in the Senate, but he resigned when a major policy difference developed between him and the White House. Democratic Majority Leader Johnson was able to cultivate a very good working relationship with President Dwight D. Eisenhower, a Republican. However, an even rarer circumstance faced Majority Leader Dole: he commanded a Senate majority and worked with a Republican White House, but he also dealt with a Democratic House of Representatives. Dole was sometimes required to seek modifications in President Reagan's proposals so that they could succeed in the Senate and have some chance of success in the House.

Lyndon Johnson was so commanding and effective as Senate majority leader that all of his successors' performances have been compared with his. Often Johnson's leadership is contrasted with that of Mansfield; for example, Senator Byrd remarked in a Senate debate:

> Johnson and Mansfield employed very different styles of Senate leadership, and it would be hard to find two different men. Johnson

was loud; Mansfield quiet. Johnson was impatient, Mansfield had infinite patience. Johnson twisted arms, Mansfield took a low-key, conciliatory approach. Johnson wanted it to be known that he was totally in charge; Mansfield believed he was simply one among equals and treated all other senators as equals.[66]

The role of the floor leader is quite malleable; it can be shaped to fit extremely different personalities. Perhaps this is so because there exists in the Senate, as John G. Stewart, a former aide to Hubert Humphrey, once put it, a "deficit of institutionalized power which must be compensated for in some fashion."[67]

Certainly today more than ever, the floor leader's role is multifaceted. Majority Leader Byrd once explained that the party leader "has to be a traffic cop, babysitter, welfare worker, minister, lawyer, umpire, referee, punching bag, target, lightning rod [and] . . . the cement that holds his party group together." [68]

There is a kind of symbiotic relationship between the majority and minority leaders of the Senate. The capacity of the Senate to operate as a legislative body indeed depends on the ability of these two leaders to cooperate. Moreover, both are the top leaders of their legislative parties; the jobs are exchangeable, depending on the party majority. Here Senate leadership differs drastically from House leadership, where there is a great status differential between the positions of House minority leader and Speaker.

There are important differences between the roles of majority and minority leader. When the 100th Congress convened, Senator Dole, who became minority leader, admitted that he still found himself "wanting to jump up and get order and do all those things leaders do." [69] The majority leader is much more involved in doing "all those things leaders do." Majority leaders may feel they are responsible for producing a legislative program, while minority leaders may feel their job is merely to lead the "loyal opposition." As Senator Byrd put it, "a majority leader, who is the agent of the majority in the Senate, in effect, does speak for the Senate. He is the leader of the Senate . . . the minority leader speaks for his party. The minority leader does not speak for the Senate." [70]

The definitions of the roles of other Senate party leaders depend largely on the views of the floor leaders. Majority Leader Johnson deprived his whip, Mike Mansfield, of any real function; instead, staff member Bobby Baker handled the function of whip. Similarly, Republican Majority Leader Howard Baker gave his whip, Ted Stevens, only a limited role in nose-counting work. On the Democratic side, several party offices are occupied by the floor leader; on the Republican side, although different senators occupy the party offices, they may be subject to close coordination by the leader. In truth, we know rather little about the roles of Senate party leaders other than that of the floor leader.

The Problem of External Relations

Senate party leadership thrusts senators into the vortex of national policy making and casts them into the limelight of national, and even international, affairs. The linkage between the Senate and the external environment is problematic. Both organizational and environmental constraints can complicate relations between Senate leaders and their counterparts in the House of Representatives. Communication breakdowns can occur, as they did in late 1977 between Senate Majority Leader Byrd and House Speaker Tip O'Neill. How important bicameral problems at the leadership level are we do not know. Senate leaders deal regularly with the White House and with top leaders in the executive establishment. But extensive partisan warfare can develop, as it did for a time during the Nixon administration. There is little existing analysis of the problems inherent in relationships between Senate leaders and the executive.

Again, Senate leaders may have dealings with interest groups, and certainly they are regularly sought out by the media. Leaders may be better insulated from lobbyists than rank-and-file senators are because of their more extensive staffs. Is this a desirable situation? Leaders receive more media attention than most of their fellow senators. Indeed, some senators have criticized Senator Byrd for allegedly being not effective enough as a television personality and not as witty or photogenic as Senator Dole. What should be the role of the Senate leader as a public figure and media performer?

Conclusion

One of the fascinations of Senate party leadership is that it raises a dazzling array of questions and draws attention to various interesting political puzzles. For these reasons, it is fun to talk about the Senate and all the more curious that senatorial politics have not been the focus of more determined historical and analytical study.

That party leadership in the Senate is problematic in various ways is no unkind reflection on the Senate. Within that body, transient personalities and a perennial institution interact creatively. Our preoccupations are often with the personalities, but the institution has a more durable appeal. Lindsay Rogers, fervent exponent of the Senate (and, parenthetically, impassioned defender of the filibuster), said it well six decades ago: "Senators, perhaps, should not be taken too seriously, but the importance of the Senate must not be underestimated."[71]

The Senate of the 1980s was more exemplary than ever. It commendably weathered two changes in political power—in 1981, when the Republicans took charge, and again in 1987, when the Democrats returned to power. The "changing of the guard" in the Senate of the Ninety-seventh Congress transpired very smoothly, and "the absence of major internal changes following this transition suggests the extent to which the contemporary Senate has become institutionalized."[72]

Notes

1. David J. Rothman, *Politics and Power: The United States Senate, 1869-1901* (Cambridge, Mass.: Harvard University Press, 1966), 72.
2. Lindsay Rogers, *The American Senate* (New York: Knopf, 1926), 3-4.
3. Woodrow Wilson, *Congressional Government* (New York: Meridian Books, [1885], 1956), 145.
4. Randall B. Ripley, *Power in the Senate* (New York: St. Martin's, 1969), 21-79.
5. Charles O. Jones, "House Leadership in an Age of Reform," in *Understanding Congressional Leadership*, ed. Frank H. Mackaman (Washington, D.C.: CQ Press, 1981), 117.
6. For a summary of literature on legislative leadership, see Robert L. Peabody, "Leadership in Legislatures: Evolution, Selection, and Functions," in *Handbook of Legislative Research*, ed. Gerhard Loewenberg, Samuel C. Patterson, and Malcolm E. Jewell (Cambridge, Mass.: Harvard University Press, 1985).
7. Christopher J. Bailey, *The Republican Party in the U.S. Senate, 1974-1984: Party Change and Institutional Development* (Manchester, England: Manchester University Press, 1988), 85.
8. For example, see Ralph K. Huitt and Robert L. Peabody, *Congress: Two Decades of Analysis* (New York: Harper and Row, 1969), 182.
9. Ibid., 181.
10. David B. Truman, *The Congressional Party: A Case Study* (New York: Wiley, 1959), 115.
11. See: Charles O. Jones, *The Minority Party in Congress* (Boston: Little Brown, 1970), 39-54; Robert L. Peabody, *Leadership in Congress* (Boston: Little, Brown, 1976), 486; Randall B. Ripley, *Majority Party Leadership in Congress* (Boston: Little, Brown, 1969), esp. 169-187; and Joseph Cooper and David W. Brady, "Institutional Context and Leadership Style: The House from Cannon to Rayburn," *American Political Science Review* 75:423-424.
12. Peabody, *Leadership in Congress*, 484-485.
13. See Ralph K. Huitt, "Democratic Party Leadership in the Senate," *American Political Science Review* 55:331-344; Rowland Evans and Robert Novak, *Lyndon B. Johnson: The Exercise of Power* (Cleveland: World Publishing, 1966).
14. Peabody, *Leadership in Congress*, 401.
15. For example, see Peabody, *Leadership in Congress*, 401; Huitt, "Democratic Party Leadership in the Senate."
16. Cecil A. Gibb, "Leadership," in *The Handbook of Social Psychology*, IV, 2d

ed., ed. Gardner Lindzey and Elliot Aronson (Reading, Mass.: Addison-Wesley, 1969); Cecil A. Gibb, ed., *Leadership: Selected Readings* (Harmondsworth, England: Penguin, 1969), 255-276; Sidney Verba, *Small Groups and Political Behavior: A Study of Leadership* (Princeton, N.J.: Princeton University Press, 1961), 142-184.

17. Barbara Sinclair, *Majority Leadership in the U.S. House* (Baltimore: Johns Hopkins University Press, 1983) 1-3.
18. Quoted in Ripley, *Power in the Senate*, 105.
19. See Jean E. Torcom, "Leadership: The Role and Style of Senator Everett Dirksen," in *To Be a Congressman: The Promise and the Power*, ed. Sven Groennings and Jonathan P. Hawley (Washington, D.C.: Acropolis Books, 1973), 195-219.
20. William S. Cohen, *Roll Call: One Year in the United States Senate* (New York: Simon and Schuster, 1981), 252-253.
21. Richard F. Fenno, Jr., *The Makings of a Senator: Dan Quayle* (Washington, D.C.: CQ Press, 1989), 112.
22. Quoted in Jacqueline Calmes, "Byrd Struggles to Lead Deeply Divided Senate," *Congressional Quarterly Weekly Report*, July 4, 1987, 1423.
23. Ross K. Baker, *Friend and Foe in the U.S. Senate* (New York: The Free Press, 1980), 204.
24. Truman, *The Congressional Party*, 95.
25. Robert L. Peabody, "Senate Party Leadership: From the 1950s to the 1980s," in *Understanding Congressional Leadership*, ed. Frank H. Mackaman (Washington, D.C.: CQ Press, 1981), 74.
26. Donald R. Matthews, *U.S. Senators and Their World* (Chapel Hill: University of North Carolina Press, 1960), 145.
27. Samuel C. Patterson and Gregory A. Caldeira, "Party Voting in the United States Congress," *British Journal of Political Science* 18:111-131.
28. Aage R. Clausen and Clyde Wilcox, "Policy Partisanship in Legislative Leadership Recruitment and Behavior," *Legislative Studies Quarterly* 12:246.
29. Donald A. Gross, "Changing Patterns of Voting Agreement Among Senatorial Leadership, 1947-1976," *Western Political Quarterly* 37:120-142.
30. Randall B. Ripley, *Congress: Process and Policy*, 4th ed. (New York: Norton, 1988), 218.
31. Peabody, *Leadership in Congress*, 483; Ripley, *Power in the Senate*, 84-89.
32. Quoted in Wilson, *Congressional Government*, 135.
33. Bernard Asbell, *The Senate Nobody Knows* (Baltimore: Johns Hopkins University Press, 1978), 413.
34. See Jones, *The Minority Party in Congress*, 47-52; Ripley, *Majority Party Leadership in Congress*, 180-182.
35. See Ripley, *Majority Party Leadership in Congress*, 180; Cooper and Brady, "Institutional Context and Leadership Style."
36. Matthews, *U.S. Senators and Their World*, 123-125.
37. Truman, *The Congressional Party*, 95.
38. Ibid., 115-117.
39. Ibid., 115.
40. Clausen and Wilcox, "Policy Partisanship in Legislative Leadership Recruit-

ment and Behavior"; Gross, "Changing Patterns of Voting Agreement Among Senatorial Leadership, 1947-1976"; Samuel C. Patterson, "Legislative Leadership and Political Ideology," *Public Opinion Quarterly* 27:399-410; and William E. Sullivan, "Criteria for Selecting Party Leadership in Congress," *American Politics Quarterly* 3:25-44.

41. Charles O. Jones, "Joseph G. Cannon and Howard W. Smith: An Essay on the Limits of Leadership in the House of Representatives," *Journal of Politics* 30:617-646.

42. Torcom, "Leadership," 198, 218-220.

43. Wilson, *Congressional Government*, 136.

44. *Congressional Record*, April 18, 1980, S3922.

45. Barbara Sinclair, "Senate Styles and Senate Decision Making, 1955-1980," *Journal of Politics* 48:899.

46. Roger H. Davidson, "Senate Leaders: Janitors for an Untidy Chamber?" in *Congress Reconsidered*, 3d ed., ed. Lawrence C. Dodd and Bruce I. Oppenheimer (Washington, D.C.: CQ Press, 1985).

47. See Christopher J. Deering, "Leadership in the Slow Lane," *PS* 19:37-42.

48. *Congressional Record*, April 18, 1980, S3922.

49. *Congressional Record*, April 18, 1980, S3924.

50. *Congressional Record*, January 6, 1987, S16.

51. *Congressional Record*, October 18, 1986, S17294.

52. *Congressional Record*, August 7, 1987, S11603.

53. For example, see Elizabeth Drew, *Senator* (New York: Simon and Schuster, 1979), 94-95.

54. Glenn R. Parker, "Stylistic Change in the U.S. Senate: 1959-1980," *Journal of Politics* 47:1190.

55. See Bruce I. Oppenheimer, "Changing Time Constraints on Congress: Historical Perspectives on the Use of Cloture," in *Congress Reconsidered*, 3d ed., ed. Lawrence C. Dodd and Bruce I. Oppenheimer (Washington, D.C.: CQ Press, 1985).

56. *Congressional Record*, April 18, 1980, S3924.

57. *Congressional Quarterly Weekly Report*, September 13, 1980, 2699.

58. *Washington Post*, March 9, 1987, A8.

59. See Malcolm E. Jewell and Samuel C. Patterson, *The Legislative Process in the United States*, 4th ed. (New York: Random House, 1986), 131-133.

60. *Congressional Record*, April 13, 1988, S3848.

61. Walter J. Oleszek, "Party Whips in the United States Senate," *Journal of Politics* 33:955-979.

62. For example, see James A. Miller, *Running in Place: Inside the Senate* (New York: Simon and Schuster, 1986), 86-90, 115-117.

63. See Peabody, *Leadership in Congress*; Peabody, "Senate Party Leadership"; and Garrison Nelson, "Leadership Selection in the U.S. Senate, 1899-1985: Changing Patterns of Recruitment and Institutional Interaction," typescript, 1985.

64. Roger H. Davidson and Walter J. Oleszek, "Changing the Guard in the U.S. Senate," *Legislative Studies Quarterly* 9:650-653.

65. See Janet Hook, "Byrd Will Give Up Senate Majority Leadership," *Congressional Quarterly Weekly Report*, April 16, 1988, 975-978.

66. *Congressional Record*, September 8, 1986, S12048.
67. John G. Stewart, "Two Strategies of Leadership: Johnson and Mansfield," in *Congressional Behavior*, ed. Nelson W. Polsby (New York: Random House, 1971), 87.
68. *Congressional Record*, April 18, 1980, S3922.
69. *Congressional Record*, January 6, 1987, S16.
70. *Congressional Record*, May 2, 1980, S4495.
71. Rogers, *The American Senate*, 255.
72. Davidson and Oleszek, "Changing the Guard in the U.S. Senate," 635.

4 ▬▬

Committee and Informal Leaders in the U.S. House of Representatives

Susan Webb Hammond

The contemporary House of Representatives is characterized by structural decentralization and member individualism. Changes in rules and procedures have given members the opportunity and resources to participate in policy making, and changes in norms have encouraged this. The result has been new conditions of leadership.[1] Policy outcomes are less predictable. Party leaders operate by inclusive leadership, with expanded party organizations.[2] Consequently, there are new opportunities for leaders who do not occupy positions of formal leadership within the party structure, or have formal responsibility for coordinating the work of the House, but who shape the House's work as leaders of committees, subcommittees, and groups of members, or through individual expertise or force of ideas. This chapter suggests ways such leadership may be perceived and raises questions that might be explored usefully, particularly regarding informal leadership in the contemporary House.

Identifying Leaders

Some members are leaders of recognized House subunits: committee and subcommittee chairs and ranking minority members; party task-force leaders (formally constituted subunits); and leaders of congressional caucuses or informal discussion groups (informally constituted subunits with varying degrees of organization). The leaders who have an organizational base are termed "leaders with portfolio." Other members, who are active individually as issue leaders, coalition builders, and strategists, are "leaders without portfolio."

In some ways, leaders with an organizational base are like midlevel managers: they must respond to party leaders and be responsive to an in-House constituency of members. In contrast, leaders without portfolio work with or oppose party leaders as individuals and do not have a stable, identifiable constituency to which they are accountable and must be

57

responsive. Some, for example, are self-chosen; they gradually develop expertise and become identified as issue leaders. Others may be chosen by the formal party leadership; these are the close advisers, the brokers who build a coalition as a bill comes to the floor, and the speakers who seek to persuade others by forceful oratory as a floor debate winds down. Other leaders without portfolio are senior staff who are recognized by members as influential in the policy process and who, through expertise or position, may be considered informal leaders of the House.

Both leaders with portfolio, including committee and subcommittee chairs, ranking minority members, ad hoc caucus chairs, and discussion group heads, and those without portfolio, including issue leaders, coalition builders, advisers, speakers, and staff, constitute a leadership network separate from the party leaders that flourishes in the contemporary House of Representatives. Committee and subcommittee leaders operate from positions of authority within the formal structure of the House. The others are informal leaders, without the positional authority of the formal House structure. Our understanding of House leadership is incomplete without consideration of this leadership system, particularly of the role of informal leaders. This chapter describes the context and parameters of committee and informal leadership, suggests a framework for analysis, and proposes questions for further research. What are the constraints of these positions? What are the opportunities? How do members become informal leaders? How do such leaders assist or impede the work of party leaders? What effects do they have on the work of the House?

Committee Leaders

Committee chairs and ranking minority members, chosen by their party caucuses, and subcommittee chairs and ranking minority members, generally chosen by the committee's party caucus, differ from all other nonparty leaders. Members generally view them as part of the formal House leadership. But because they are followers (of party leaders), and also must be responsive to *their* followers, they are similar in many ways to informal leaders.

Some factors that affect party leaders also shape the environments of committee leaders: structure of party hierarchy and of committees; majority or minority status; requirements of agenda issues; and the needs and demands of such followers as subcommittee chairs and committee rank-and-file members. In some instances, leaders may be forced to exert leadership or lose committee function and prestige. Or, because of their position, they may be forced to focus on problems that are not necessarily in their political or personal interests. If committee leaders want success, how do they get it? What are the constraints of committee leadership? The processes of leader selection surely affect leader activity; if today's leaders are more responsive, how does the election process affect committee operations and policy outcomes? Alternatively, how do individual members and informal groups use that responsiveness norm to achieve policy goals?

Although committee leaders do not have a monopoly on issue leadership in the contemporary House, there is clearly some overlap. Committee chairs and ranking minority members are often recognized as issue experts. Issue expertise may be a factor in the election of subcommittee chairs, or serving as subcommittee chairs may give members an opportunity to become issue experts. Sometimes a formal position may force a member to become an issue leader, which was seemingly the case with Sen. Alan K. Simpson, R-Wyo., and Rep. Romano L. Mazzoli, D-Ky., on the immigration bill (PL 99-603) of 1986. The fit between committee assignments and personal interest appears to have increased. Do issue leadership and formal positions of leadership now overlap more? If so, why do there seem to be more, not fewer, leaders in the House?

There is variation in the relationships between committee and subcommittee chairs. Models range from committees where the chairman is the chief contact point for all committee activity to committees with "strong" chairs but relatively autonomous subcommittees to committees with complete subcommittee autonomy, in which there is little oversight by the committee chair and subcommittee chairs work directly with party leaders. In discussing the factors that affect committee and subcommittee leadership, it is useful to distinguish between these possible models.

In their book *Committees in Congress*, Steven Smith and Christopher Deering report that subcommittees in the House are more active since the reforms of the 1970s; most hearings and a majority of markups are held at the subcommittee level. Subcommittee chairs manage about two-thirds of the bills on the floor, an increase of 35 percent from the 1960s. But subcommittee initiative has not necessarily resulted in subcommittee autonomy; subcommittee chairs may not control staff, budgets, or agendas. Smith and Deering conclude that although subcommittee chairs "represent an influential new leadership category in . . . [the] chamber," they are not "sovereign." [3] Nevertheless, an increase in the authority of subcommittee chairs has contributed to a decrease in the power of full committee chairs and has perhaps narrowed the arena in which legislation is considered and marked up. Some observers believe it has helped foster subcommittee entrepreneurship and decreased the brokerage role played previously by committee leaders.

Party leaders affect the work of committee leaders. We know that generally party leaders work directly with subcommittee chairs only at the direction or with the acquiescence of the committee chair. But party leaders' actions affect committee leaders in other ways as well. Increased activity in monitoring committee work, setting specific schedules of floor consideration, directing Appropriations to move ahead without a budget resolution, and meeting with committee and outside interests—as, for example, former Speaker Jim Wright, D-Texas, did on agricultural issues early in his tenure—change the parameters within which committee leaders work. Recent Speakers have been more willing to identify agenda issues and to take issue stands, which also affects committee actions. Party leaders must be responsive to committees, but they can also push them and subcommittees to action.

Congressional Caucuses

In the contemporary House, ad hoc caucuses offer members an alternative structure for leadership and the pursuit of policy interests.[4] For junior members, or for members who do not serve on a relevant committee, caucuses provide an opportunity to gain expertise and to develop issues so that they are put on the formal agenda and given attention by party leaders. For some members, chairing one of the long-established congressional caucuses may legitimize leadership within the broader environment of the House. Alternatively, through caucus activity, a junior member may become identified as a leader and "rising star." There may be, however, unanticipated negative consequences. Although caucuses offer opportunities to develop issue expertise and leadership skills, identification as a leader may tag the member as too ambitious, or too closely tied to an issue position, or too "adversarial," in effect, actually working against later leadership positions. Also, caucus leaders may lose rather than gain prestige if their positions are not well thought out.

Various types of caucuses operate differently. Ad hoc caucuses of intraparty groups (for example, the Democratic Study Group (DSG), the Boll Weevils, the Conservative Opportunity Society, and the '92 Group) work much more closely with party leaders than do other caucuses and have special access to White House and executive-branch officials of their party.[5] Other caucuses are based on personal interest or are constituency related. These are national (for example, the Congressional Black Caucus and the Congressional Caucus on Women's Issues), regional, district (for example, the Rural Caucus), and district-industry constituency caucuses. Personal interest and constituency caucuses work less frequently with party leaders; to do so, these bipartisan caucuses must identify a partisan subset of members and shift to partisan activity.

Congressional caucuses have changed the information/communications system of the House. They provide information and serve as communication-exchange arenas. Many members rely on the Democratic Study Group for legislative information.[6] Other caucuses play a similar, although less extensive, informational role. Caucuses permit members to pool resources and to focus on particular policy interests. They are an alternative structure for scrutinizing issues. No longer is it true that "if you are on a committee, you know [the information], and if you are not on a committee, you find a member you trust and ask advice or vote as he does." [7]

Caucuses can also facilitate integration of issue networks by including viewpoints of adversaries and outside constituencies. They may serve as catalysts for building consensus and bringing together diverse groups of members and, on occasion, diverse constituency interests. From this perspective, they fulfill a conflict management role for the House. As a senior aide noted, caucuses may become more important as informal leadership groups if they can bring together outside constituencies to achieve a policy "everyone can live with." The question is will this be successful only if done on party leaders' terms?

For individual members, caucuses contribute to developing issue expertise and leadership skills and to achieving policy or other goals. Caucus members are included in leadership task forces and strategy meetings, either because of their knowledge or as representatives of groups of members concerned about an issue. A Republican from New Jersey, Rep. Jim Courter's activities on defense procurement issues during the 100th Congress "stem[med] from his co-chairmanship in '83-'84 of the Military Reform Caucus." [8] Rep. Buddy MacKay, D-Fla., was active on budget issues after leading the Budget Study Group of the Class Caucus during his freshman term.

For party leaders, caucuses offer access to blocs of members and can be useful in whip counts and disseminating information. They may assist in shaping long-range issue agendas (and, in this way, fulfill a function similar to official party research groups and task forces). For caucuses, leadership support can help achieve policy goals: during the 1980s, the Arms Control Caucus successfully achieved legislation to limit U.S. activity in Central America with the Foley amendments to Department of Defense (DOD) authorization bills. But caucuses also require responsiveness and increase the number of issue players. Viewed from a party leader's perspective, caucuses can complicate coalition building and oppose the leadership. Activity on the floor may mean opposing party leaders, as was the case when the Northeast-Midwest Congressional Coalition successfully obtained repeal of the requirements of the Maybank Amendment at the end of the Ninety-sixth Congress. Party leaders may prefer to include rather than fight caucuses: for example, the Conservative Opportunity Society eventually helped plan party conferences, and the Boll Weevils achieved desired committee and party appointments. Also, party leaders are sometimes reluctant to rely on caucus leaders in coalition building because too intense a commitment to a position may be a hindrance.

Caucuses intersect at the individual, committee, and party leadership level with other networks in the House. As subunits within the House, caucuses are important in information gathering and exchange, identifying issues, setting agendas, and, on occasion, developing policy. Caucuses may be most important as a bloc when the caucus viewpoint coincides with a regional or ideological stance. For individuals, caucuses serve as an alternate structure for identification as an informal leader and as an alternate route to formal leadership positions. How can caucuses assist formal party leaders? What problems do they present? And what are the opportunities, constraints, and issues for caucus leaders?

Discussion Group Leaders

In an era of decentralization and individualism, and in an institution as organizationally fluid as the House of Representatives, there are very informal groups of members with shared issue concerns. During the 1970s, a small group of DSG members, called "The Group," met regularly to discuss concerns relating to the Vietnam War. A recent example is the arms control group led by Rep. Thomas J. Downey, D-N.Y., which has met regularly, raised concerns at whip meetings, and significantly helped move arms-control issues to priority status within the party leadership.

Discussion group leaders and issue leaders often overlap; a member may initially develop issue expertise and only gradually gather together a group of colleagues to work on the policy interest. An interesting question to pursue is how such leaders become effective in the broader policy arena of the House. How do groups of members with no formal position or organizational base act effectively on major issues? What strategies do members use in dealing with party leadership? How do strengths and weaknesses of committees and committee leadership affect these?

Issue Leaders

In the House, individuals who are recognized as issue leaders often hold simultaneously formal positions of authority—committee or subcommittee chairs or ranking minority member positions. Issue leaders may also lead caucuses or even more informal groups of members. However, individuals with no organizational base may also play a major role in policy making. For example, *Congressional Quarterly* reported on the activities of Rep. Charles Schumer, D-N.Y., in resurrecting the immigration bill in the Ninety-ninth Congress and developing an acceptable compromise proposal on foreign farm workers. CQ concluded that he "used the media brilliantly," could "read the mood of the House" (which wanted an immigration bill), and eventually practiced the politics of inclusion by expanding the drafting group to bipartisan membership, including those from formal committee positions.[9] In this instance, membership on the relevant committee and friendship networks were important factors in undertaking and achieving leadership.

Other members become expert on issues unrelated to their committee work. As a freshman, Rep. Henry Hyde, R-Ill., continually raised and prevailed on antiabortion measures. Many of the "rising stars," or leaders without portfolio, identified in the media are junior or midlevel seniority members who are regarded as experts on particular issues.[10] Party leaders can identify individuals in their party who are issue experts—on drug testing, labor, or trade, for example. What facilitates the development of issue expertise? Are individuals who do not have an organizational base effective mainly on narrow issues? How do individual issue experts intersect with formal committee membership, or with committee or party leadership positions? How do these experts facilitate or impede the work of party leaders?

Coalition Builders

Building coalitions is central to the work of the House. Advisers, brokers, and orators assist in this. The Board of Education of Rep. Sam Rayburn, D-Texas, and the close group of colleagues surrounding other Speakers, serve as advisers to party leaders. Party leaders also choose close associates as brokers, behind-the-scenes negotiators and vote whippers, such as Rep. Richard Bolling, D-Mo., for Speaker Rayburn. Or, depending on the issue, party leaders choose those who can serve as brokers for regional, seniority, or ideological groups within the House. They need individuals who are group members, possess credibility, know the politics of the issue, communicate well, and have the skills to work with a diverse group. Some brokers are valued for their ability to mobilize outside constituency groups. Brokers shift with the issue. They must be good negotiators, and they are inherently compromisers.

Brokers may also be relied on for their skills as vote counters and whippers. Jacqueline Calmes remarked of a leadership aide: "There are very, very few people who can work the House and fewer who like it. But [John] Murtha has energy and nerve, a second skin. He has absolutely no fear of rejection, of going back to members again and again for their votes." [11]

Some brokers are not "chosen" by party leaders and may, in fact, be their adversaries on issue positions. The requisite skills are similar; the results may be coalition defeat, party defeat, or inclusion by leaders in party negotiations. Steven Smith argues that personal goals affect the bargaining strategies of brokers, or "coalition leaders," and that those with strong policy commitments are less likely to compromise than colleagues with the primary ambition to serve as leaders.

Orators are sometimes used as heavy artillery. Valued for their rhetorical ability, they often speak toward the end of floor debates. One colleague described the role of orators in coalition building:

> One of the ways you establish coalitions in this House is you show that
> coalitions are worth belonging to. You have to attract people not only
> because of the politics of the matter, but because of the force of the
> idea. . . . If you don't have a Henry Hyde articulating those views very
> forcefully, very well and with intelligence behind them, it's hard to
> attract people to come over.[12]

To what extent are the activities of brokers and orators officially
sanctioned by party leaders? How do party leaders' styles affect their
choice of assistants? What are the constraints and opportunities of these
roles? How do coalition builders interact with other informal leaders and
their networks? To what degree do these roles overlap?

Staff

A discussion of informal leadership in the contemporary House
should include staff, because although they are not elected and do not
vote, senior staff may significantly influence the policy process. To a
limited degree, this has been the case since the 1946 Legislative Reorganization Act, but in recent years staff members' greater specialization and
increasing expertise have expanded their opportunities to play significant
roles in legislative decision making.[13] Staff who have issue expertise shape
agendas and influence the development of legislation. They filter information, and their expert judgment sets parameters for decision making
and determines the decision details. Also, they serve as information
sources for members and communication links between staffs and
members. Position also determines informal leadership. Members offer
ideas, suggestions, and complaints to staff in senior positions with party
leaders. They want to test ideas, gauge reactions to suggestions, and
perhaps have their complaints passed on to leaders. These staff act as
guideposts and coalition strategists. Senior staff in other positions—party
organizations, committees, caucuses—serve in similar capacities.

What factors affect a staff "leadership" role? Autonomy linked with
seniority and expertise appears to be important. We know that committee
environments and leadership variation affect staff policy entrepreneurship.[14] How does staff leadership differ from informal member leadership? Is expertise more important for staff? How do responsiveness
requirements for these informal leaders differ? How does timing affect
influence—is there more impact in the early stages of policy development
or at the end of a session? How do staff leaders intersect with other leaders
and their networks?

The Context of Leadership

Leaders and Followers

The leaders discussed in this chapter are also followers: all are members of a party; some work directly with party leaders; many must also lead followers on committees or in informal groups of colleagues. What are the incentives to assume a committee or informal leadership role? What are the benefits? What are the costs?

Party leaders operate within the parameters set by the reciprocal relationship between leaders and followers; leaders assess what members want and then attend to these interests. In the contemporary House, where leaders sometimes win their positions by a handful of votes, and where committee chairs can be ousted, responsiveness to followers takes on increased importance. Is this also the case for informal leaders?

Structure

The House structure defines the parameters within which committee and informal leaders work. In a decentralized structure, party leaders must deal with many more "leaders" than previously. Also, the organizational fluidity that characterizes the House permits easy establishment of informal subunits such as caucuses and issue discussion groups, shifting coalitions, and the rise of individual issue leaders.

In much of their work, party leaders typically follow the formal hierarchical system: leaders work with committee chairs or ranking minority members; committee chairs work with their own subcommittee chairs; and subcommittee chairs work with their own subcommittee members. When subcommittee chairs or ranking minority members are brought into leadership deliberations, it is with the concurrence of the full committee leaders. This is an economical operating procedure in an institution of 435 members.

Yet overlaid on this is an informal system involving caucus leaders, issue leaders, and interested and knowledgeable junior members. These members are often brought into party leadership deliberations and strategy sessions; party organizations that offer participation to junior members and informal leaders (for example, the Democratic Caucus Task Forces and the Republican Research Committee Task Forces); and communication arenas—party caucuses, whip organization meetings, and the floor—that allow general discussion and the testing out of ideas. What are the consequences for party leaders of the increased number of subunits? Of the expanded activity of members? What are the consequences for committee and informal leadership? Research on communications channels could shed light on informal leadership and the processes of shaping agendas, establishing priorities, and developing policy. The media's effect on informal leadership in the House also deserves examination.

The House's formal structure offers multiple access points to the outside environment. How does the informal structure affect executive-branch and constituency contacts? Do presidents of the House's minority party, on occasion, go to caucuses or junior members for issue leadership? Same-party or different-party control of the two houses of Congress may also affect informal leadership. At what points do formal and informal leadership networks intersect? At what points should they intersect? These are questions that would be useful to explore.

Party Leaders

For committee, subcommittee, and informal leaders, the personal style and priorities of their party leaders establish constraints and offer opportunities. Former Speaker Thomas P. ("Tip") O'Neill, D-Mass., has been described as waiting for issues to rise to the surface, while Speakers Jim Wright, D-Texas, and Thomas S. Foley, D-Wash., set agendas. What structural, procedural, or stylistic factors affect the inclusion and partici-pation of informal leaders? How does the work of party leaders facilitate or impede the work of informal leaders? Are there cycles in the degree of leadership responsiveness? Under what conditions is there likely to be change?

Party task forces, congressional caucuses, and individual issue leaders can develop new ideas and therefore offer benefits to party leaders. But what are the costs of too many ideas and too many leaders demanding attention? Also, what are the costs of a leadership style, or a House structure, that does not permit this process to occur?

Timing

It is important to examine the effect on informal leaders of the stage of legislation and the time in the congressional session. Various types of informal leaders affect the House's work at different points in the legislative process. Caucus and issue leaders are particularly important in identifying issues, setting agendas, and in the early stages of legislative development. Some committee leaders, issue leaders, and coalition build-ers especially influence the development and processing of legislation at the committee stage. At the floor stage, party leaders are particularly involved, working with committee leaders and choosing informal leaders to assist them as advisers, brokers, orators, and issue experts. Other self-selected issue experts, strategists, and coalition builders also operate at this stage; some cooperate with, and some are adversaries of, party leaders. Does end-of-session timing make informal leaders more influential?

Conclusion

A brief overview of informal leadership in the House can serve primarily to raise questions for further exploration. We can distinguish between leaders who have an organizational base (committee, ad hoc caucus, task-force, and discussion group leaders) and those who do not (issue leaders, brokers, and orators).

We can consider the functions informal leaders perform. The congressional caucus, task-force, and issue leaders are "heralds," who identify issues, shape agendas, and may eventually cooperate with other leaders to develop and pass policy. Committee leaders, holding formal authority positions under House and caucus rules, are "honchos," with major, official responsibility in the policy process. Advisers, brokers, and orators are "henchmen," working on strategy, building coalitions, and shaping debate. They may vary from issue to issue. Often they assist party leaders, but henchmen also use their skills to operate as adversaries of the formal leadership.[15]

A number of questions deserve discussion. What are the opportunities for committee and informal leaders in the contemporary House? What are the constraints on these leaders? What is their relationship to party leaders?

Leaders often hold multiple and overlapping roles. How does this affect informal leadership? Subcommittee or caucus leadership may be strengthened when members are also issue leaders. To what extent do the networks of informal leaders overlap, and how does this affect leaders' activity and influence? Are issue leaders who are also members of the relevant committee, and who chair a task force or discussion group, more likely to be effective? Is there value in both official (research task-force) and unofficial (caucus, discussion group) herald organizations?

Committee and informal leaders are also followers. What strategies do members use to deal with the formal leaders of the House? What factors determine which strategies will be used?

Do some informal leadership positions offer an alternate route to positions of power in the formal structure of the House? When that occurs, does this change the focus or scope of interest? Does it mean new constraints? New opportunities? What is the effect of such a transition?

We might explore what contributes to identification and strength as an informal leader. How can someone who wants to be a leader seize control of an issue, especially when there is often competition for issue leadership? Members can develop issue expertise in caucuses, discussion groups, and on Republican Research Committee or Democratic caucus task forces. Expertise, combined with membership on a relevant committee, positions members for later leadership. Also, informal leadership can be tested and developed within a committee and then expanded to the broader environment of the House. Some leaders combine issue knowledge with adeptness at legislative strategy and coalition building across diverse views. Some leaders have a particular ability to mobilize outside interests. Others, usually with an identifiable ideological and issue commitment, are recognized for their talents in building bipartisan accommodation. An organizational base can be important; party leaders may be responsive to, and want help from, members who represent caucuses, discussion groups, and blocs of colleagues.

What conditions facilitate the work of informal leaders? Some functions must be carried out by formal party leaders. Are there others that are more easily carried out by informal leaders? How do informal leaders work together, and what facilitates their integration into the formal system? What are the consequences of such integration? How can tension between formal and informal leaders be managed? Are there cycles of party leader responsiveness? Under what conditions is there likely to be change? How does conflict in the choice of formal leaders affect informal leadership? Committee and informal leaders are significant in House operations. Consideration and analysis of how the activities, opportunities, problems, and consequences of their leadership affect individuals, party leaders, and the House as an institution can contribute to understanding congressional leadership.

Notes

1. See Frank H. Mackaman, ed., *Understanding Congressional Leadership* (Washington, D.C.: CQ Press, 1981).
2. Barbara Sinclair, *Majority Leadership in the U.S. House* (Baltimore: Johns Hopkins University Press, 1983).
3. Steven S. Smith and Christopher J. Deering, *Committees in Congress* (Washington, D.C.: CQ Press, 1984), 199.
4. Congressional caucuses are voluntary groups of members, without formal recognition in chamber rules or line-item appropriations, that seek to affect the policy process. Discussion in this section draws on research for a project on congressional caucuses, to be published as *Informal Congressional Groups in National Policymaking*, Susan Webb Hammond, Daniel P. Mulhollan, and Arthur G. Stevens, Jr. (Washington, D.C.: American Enterprise Institute, forthcoming).
5. Susan Webb Hammond, Daniel P. Mulhollan, and Arthur G. Stevens, Jr., "Informal Congressional Caucuses and Agenda Setting," *Western Political Quarterly* 38 (December 1985): 583-605.
6. For example, see U.S. House of Representatives, Commission on Administrative Review, "Administrative Reorganization and Legislative Management," *Final Report*, H. Doc. 95-232, 95th Cong., 1st sess., 1977.
7. Quotations not otherwise footnoted are from the author's interview data. All

respondents were promised anonymity.

8. Richard E. Cohen and Burt Solomon, "Congress's Rising Stars," *National Journal*, January 24, 1987, 182.

9. Nadine Cohodas, "Immigration Bill Resurrected," *Congressional Quarterly Weekly Report*, October 11, 1986, 2571-2573.

10. For example, see Cohen and Solomon, "Congress's Rising Stars," 176-189; and Jacqueline Calmes and Rob Gurwitt, "Profiles in Power," *Congressional Quarterly Weekly Report*, January 3, 1987, 11-18.

11. Jacqueline Calmes, "John Murtha," *Congressional Quarterly Weekly Report*, January 3, 1987, 17.

12. Rob Gurwitt, "Henry Hyde," *Congressional Quarterly Weekly Report*, January 3, 1987, 14.

13. For example, see Harrison W. Fox, Jr., and Susan Webb Hammond, *Congressional Staffs: The Invisible Force in American Lawmaking* (New York: The Free Press, 1977).

14. Samuel C. Patterson, "The Professional Staffs of Congressional Committees," *Administrative Science Quarterly* 15 (March 1970): 22-37; and David E. Price, "Professional 'Entrepreneurs': Staff Orientations and Policymaking on Three Senate Committees," *Journal of Politics* 33 (May 1971): 316-336.

15. I am indebted to Roger Davidson and Fred Pauls for suggestions on the nomenclature of functional categories.

5 ▰▰▰▰

Informal Leadership in the Senate: Opportunities, Resources, and Motivations

Steven S. Smith

My image of the Senate is a composite picture of individual senators. In contrast to my image of the House, which is constructed of a mass of more anonymous faces, the Senate image is one of distinctive personalities: Bentsen, Bradley, Byrd, Dole, Gramm, Hatch, Helms, Kennedy, and so on. Many of these senators gained their prominence by virtue of the formal positions of party or committee leadership they held. But many senators gained their political identity through activity not directly connected to formal leadership posts. Rather, they attained prominence because of their leading roles on issues not associated with a committee chairmanship or elective party post. Bradley and tax reform, Gramm and budget procedures, and Helms and abortion are pairings that are quite common in the Senate. Indeed, it is difficult to imagine the Senate without a central place for informal policy leaders.

To speak of informal leaders as a special class in the U.S. Senate requires great care. After all, leadership in the Senate has traditionally come from informal sources. During the Senate's first hundred years, the effective party leaders were not formally elected to their positions. Even today, key powers of formally elected party leaders are not grounded directly in the formal rules of the Senate. The majority leader's right of first recognition, for example, is a matter of precedent rather than written rule, but it is the cornerstone of his power to set the Senate's floor agenda. And Senate committee chairmen exercise far more influence over committee business—setting agendas, hiring staff, working with outsiders—than the formal rules of the Senate or its committees would suggest.

Furthermore, the ability of senators to perform leadership functions on issues not associated with formal party positions or committee leadership depends on many informal practices of the Senate. Dependence on unanimous consent to proceed to the considerations of a bill, while a by-product of the cloture rule, is an informal practice that has enhanced the role of the rank-and-file senator, as has the associated practice of holds. Consequently, to understand the changing role of informal leadership in the Senate requires that we go beyond the formal procedures of the floor and committees.

In this chapter, I consider policy leaders in the Senate whose role is not tied directly to a party or committee leadership position. I do so by noting the context in which all senators operate, reviewing some evidence on motivations for policy leadership, outlining propositions about the conditions under which informal sources of leadership will be more or less important, and considering the frequency of policy leadership in the Senate. I have set aside some obvious points, even certain important ones, to present some less obvious propositions about informal Senate leadership.[1]

The Context of Informal Leadership in the Senate

All senators are actively involved in shaping public policy in some area. The decision of a senator to take up an issue as his or her own is shaped by the nature of the political and parliamentary opportunities, the nature of his or her resources, and the character of his or her political goals. I reserve for the next section a discussion of members' goals and turn now to opportunities and resources.

Opportunities

The opportunities for rank-and-file members to assert policy leadership have increased as members' constituencies and organized interests have increased in number and complexity in recent decades. Nearly every senator and his or her staff receive many requests for taking up a cause of an outside group or constituency each week. Home-state interests are a constant source of demand, but now, due to the great expansion of the interest group community in Washington, there is a scarcity of senators for leadership roles on issues important to organized groups. In contrast, a very large portion of the House does not receive, or receives only very few, requests for a leadership role on issues of importance to groups not connected to their districts.

As a result, the typical senator is asked to take up a cause more often than he or she likes, while the typical representative is asked less often than he or she likes. Members of both the House and Senate are constantly scanning the political landscape for issues that will help them further their political interests. But senators are inundated with requests, forcing them to choose between requesters and sometimes to alienate friends in the process. In contrast, many House members go begging for attention, are constantly on the prowl for some way to get more involved, and are envious of the ability of senators to steal their claim to the leading role on surfacing national issues.

The opportunities created by committee and subcommittee assignments have improved in recent decades.[2] In the 1950s, senators normally had two or three committee assignments and four or five subcommittee assignments. By the mid-1970s, most senators served on four standing committees, and they averaged ten subcommittee assignments. A rule instated in 1977 reduced the number of committee assignments to three and the number of subcommittee assignments to six or seven for most senators, although both committee and subcommittee assignments have risen slightly since then. Furthermore, the large number of committees and subcommittees means that normally every majority-party senator can chair at least one committee or subcommittee—most chair at least two. And the opportunities have increased even more than these numbers suggest, as full committee chairmen generally have given their subcommittees much greater freedom to set agendas than was the case in the 1950s. The typical senator comes into personal contact with a great array of issues in the normal course of events and is likely to have ready-made opportunities to pursue most issues by virtue of committee and subcommittee membership.

For the typical senator, the large number of committee and subcommittee assignments means that there is usually a way to stake a jurisdictional claim on most issues that arise. One observer recently discovered that nearly 60 percent of the Senate sits on a committee with jurisdiction over some aspect of national security policy.[3] The same is true of most major policy fields. As a result, senators see a much broader policy landscape in the course of their regular committee activities than do representatives.

The opportunities created by party practices have improved in recent decades. Party conference and policy committee meetings have become important opportunities for rank-and-file members to influence party and committee leaders' decisions about scheduling, political tactics, and policy substance. Floor leaders have made it easier for members to protect their individual political interests by institutionalizing holds, hot lines, and other practices. And, as in the House, party leaders have occasionally appointed informal task forces, often not following committee memberships and seniority, to devise solutions to tricky policy and political problems on the floor. These party developments have come largely as a product of formal leaders' desire to service the needs of members, but the net result has been to reduce the number of times rank-and-file members forgo a leadership role by default.

Thus, in the Senate of the 1980s and 1990s, even the most assertive majority leader is unlikely to keep a significant issue off the Senate floor. This stands in sharp contrast to the House, where the recognition power of the Speaker, a strict germaneness rule, and special rules that limit amendments make it far more difficult to raise issues *de novo* on the floor. Membership on the appropriate committee is often critical to policy leadership in the House. But in the Senate, the absence of a germaneness rule for floor amendments to most bills, the ability to filibuster, and dependence on unanimous consent to limit amendments and debate empower the individual senator to bring matters to the floor, almost at will.

Nevertheless, the typical senator's policy leadership activity is more likely to be tied to a formal leadership position than that of the typical representative. This is counterintuitive because it is correctly assumed that the House is more committee-oriented than the Senate. However, senators hold more committee and subcommittee assignments and are much more likely than representatives to hold a committee or subcommittee chairmanship or ranking minority post. As a result, their committee assignments are not as confining as are those in the House, and there is a greater probability that an issue of particular interest can be connected to their committee responsibilities. After all, with so much choice in the Senate, senators are usually able to join committees that handle issues connected to their personal and political interests. With so many committee assignments and leadership positions, the creative, aggressive senator often finds a way to connect many, if not most, issues to his or her committee duties in some way. Thus, while the House is more reliant on committees and grants its committees greater autonomy, the probability that individual members' activities as policy leaders are connected to a committee position is higher in the Senate.

Even with the richer variety of opportunities that accompany their committee duties, senators are increasingly developing specialties that do not correspond neatly with jurisdictions of their committees. This is partly a function of the continuing mismatch between national issues and committee jurisdictions. But it is also a function of an increasingly more popular career strategy. Senators' specialties are usually associated with committee jurisdictions. Developing a reputation for work in a particular field can establish a claim to a leadership role on a wider range of issues than committee jurisdictions would allow. Such a specialty sometimes develops incrementally and unintentionally, but members now search deliberately for a field that suits their own backgrounds and circumstances, is not dominated by another member, and will not disappear quickly from the Senate's agenda. The model to whom many senators refer is Sen. Sam Nunn, D-Ga. Nunn chairs the Committee on Armed Services and has been involved in defense issues thus far, but he has extended the reach of his personal involvement to many foreign policy and economic issues that belong to the much larger field of national security policy.

Resources

The dramatic improvement in resources available to rank-and-file senators since the 1960s is widely recognized. Personal and committee staffs, and access to consultants from support agencies, have expanded the capability of rank-and-file members in both chambers. But there are certain aspects of senators' resources that are somewhat less obvious.

While the typical senator's total resources are much greater than the typical representative's, discretionary resources available for policy leadership efforts are often lesser for senators, especially junior senators. Senators representing states of even moderate size must devote tremendous time and resources to constituency service, local press relations, speech writing, and committee duties, all of which are at least proportionately more burdensome for senators than representatives. Compensating committee staff support is usually not available for several years. And, in the view of many senators, the increasing electoral hazards and burdens of fundraising have further reduced discretionary staff resources in the last decade.[4]

A special Senate advantage is the efficiency with which most senators can allocate scarce staff resources. Senators are not management geniuses, to say the least. But they do gain efficiencies that accompany staff size—a more fully developed division of labor within their personal offices and the ability to shuffle staff between personal and committee operations as their needs warrant. Furthermore, even rank-and-file senators benefit from the ability to attract higher quality professionals to their personal staffs than can most representatives.[5] Such staff are less likely to be burdened by case work and letter writing, freeing them to pursue their principals' legislative interests.

A frequently cited advantage of senators is their access to the national media, through which they can publicize themselves and their causes. The best evidence suggests that access to the national media is an important resource, but it is not available to the average senator to the extent often assumed. Donald Matthews noted thirty years ago that time pressures and accuracy compel reporters to depend on the top party and committee leaders as their prime Senate sources.[6] More recently, Stephen Hess has reviewed the evidence for the top national media outlets in 1984 and reconfirmed that senators with senior party and committee positions dominate coverage.[7] Nevertheless, the average senator gets covered more than the average representative, creating opportunities that many senators find useful.

Developments in local media coverage have undermined the traditional distinction between workhorses and showhorses. The expansion of satellite communications has made it possible for local television stations and newspapers to cover Washington events themselves at an affordable cost. Live interviews from the Senate television studio are now common on local television stations. Local station cameras, or those of freelance operators selling services to local stations, are now commonplace in congressional hearings. Even the most serious legislators now head to the Senate television studio or the Capitol steps to talk with local reporters after debating an issue of either national or local importance on the Senate floor. From the local stations' viewpoint, these developments showcase their technology and help create local angles to national stories. And senators, who enjoy far greater name recognition than representatives, are more attractive guests than representatives for local news programs. Such developments may not increase a senator's visibility nationwide, or improve the odds of legislative success, but they increase senators' incentives to pursue policy interests in the public forums the Senate provides.

Good relations with colleagues remain a valuable resource for many senators seeking to shape policy outside of their committee jurisdictions, but establishing good relations with colleagues is no longer a necessary condition for effectiveness in the Senate. In the 1950s and 1960s, the label "maverick" retained some meaning: nonconformity to norms of apprenticeship and deference to committees, floor activism, full exploitation of parliamentary privileges, and low success rates. Today, all of these characteristics, except the last, apply to a large portion of the Senate. In fact, in today's Senate, an unassertive senator risks seriously disadvantaging himself or herself in the competition for space on committee and floor agendas. Knowing restraint is still important, but the boundaries are substantially broader than they were two decades ago.

Finally, the most important resource—a senator's own discretionary time—is becoming ever more scarce. Staff assistance has not kept pace with the increasing burdens on senators' time during the 1980s. No longer can senators studiously attend committee meetings to learn the ropes and gradually ease their way into Senate life. From the start, demands from constituents and outside groups, multiple committee and subcommittee assignments, oversight of the Senate, and other activities force the freshman to identify carefully the highest priority responsibilities and to ignore others. Few members believe that they are able to set their priorities very successfully.

Some senators report that they have adapted by turning over more and more to top legislative aides, providing them with an even larger role in legislative initiation and negotiation. Many senators report (my guess is that it is many more than would have in the 1960s and 1970s) that they have rejected opportunities to start new initiatives; set more restrictive guidelines for staff initiatives; and instituted more formal review and evaluation mechanisms for establishing priorities within their offices. Few offices follow through on established procedures very well and require instead that members and staff put in longer and longer hours. Growth of the congressional office management business, and computerization of correspondence and communications activities, reflect the search for organizational and technological solutions to a political problem.

Table 5-1 Motivation behind Issue Leadership in the Senate

Response	%
Personal policy commitment	68
Constituency/state issue	51
Committee position responsibility	32

Source: Author interviews with Senate legislative directors.

Note: Question: "Why did Senator ——— take the lead on this issue?" Multiple responses possible.

Motivations for Senate Policy Leadership

Unfortunately, we do not have a solid foundation upon which to assess senators' motivations for assuming policy leadership roles, especially over time. We can get some clues from a recent survey of Senate legislative directors on the political motivations of their bosses for taking up particular issues. No staff member can be certain about a senator's private thoughts, although most top aides come to recognize the nature of a senator's interest in the major issues on his or her own agenda. The legislative directors of sixty-five senators in the Ninety-ninth Congress were asked to identify one or two issues on which their bosses assumed responsibility to solicit support from colleagues and were then asked why the senators took up each issue identified. Their responses have been grouped as indicated in Table 5-1.

The responses suggest several important lessons about the motivations for policy leadership. Most obviously, the conventional view of senators—that their legislative efforts reflect a mindless pursuit of electoral goals—is off the mark. Senators frequently have choices about which issues to pursue as their own, and their selections depend heavily on personal policy interests. Most senators value their unique positions in the political system, and most use them to pursue issues that they consider important. Thus, in the Senate at least, it is likely that the leading senator on an issue has genuine policy commitments that motivate him or her beyond the dictates of electoral needs or formal responsibilities.

Furthermore, constituency connections are important in about half of the policy leadership cases, but, overall, they are secondary to personal policy interests as a motivating force for Senate policy leadership. I have discovered only a handful of senators who feel compelled to take up nearly every state issue that comes to their attention. The vast majority finesse a large portion of state issues, sometimes by allowing a House member from the affected district to assume the leading role. This is not to say that senators approach issues mindless of the electoral consequences of their actions. To the contrary, it is likely that many—if not the vast majority—respond to most issues exclusively in terms of electoral costs

Table 5-2 Motivational Combinations for Senate Policy Leaders

Motivations	%
Policy	26
Policy/constituency	22
Constituency	17
Policy/position	15
Constituency/position	8
Position	5
Policy/constituency/position	5

Source: Author interviews with Senate legislative directors.
Note: Multiple responses possible.

and benefits. However, those senators who assume, as policy leaders, the responsibility of soliciting support from their colleagues are not usually motivated by electoral considerations alone.

Only about one-third of the policy leadership cases stem directly from senators' duties as formal party or committee leaders. Obviously, there is good reason to examine Senate policy leadership from sources other than formal committee positions. But the proposition noted above should be kept in mind: this figure is higher in the Senate than in the House, where only 23 percent of policy leadership efforts result from responsibilities as party or committee leaders. Because representatives are less likely than senators to hold a position of formal party or committee leadership, they are also less likely to hold a formal leadership position directly related to their activities as policy leaders.

These conclusions are substantiated by the pattern illustrated in Table 5-2, which provides the frequencies for the various combinations of purposes mentioned by legislative directors. Personal policy interests, by themselves and combined with state constituency interests, account for about half of the policy leadership cases in the Senate. The cases involving only state interests are substantial in number, but they constitute a distinct minority of all cases. And not surprisingly, the responsibilities of formal leadership positions seldom appear as the sole motivation for policy leadership, since personal and constituency interests usually shape assignment decisions in the first place.

Curiously, in the survey of top legislative aides, presidential ambition did not surface as a motivation for policy leadership in the Senate. It is not because there is a lack of interest in the presidency—the aides of eleven senators noted that their bosses have an eye toward the White House. Indeed, the eleven aides were willing to identify their bosses as strongly "oriented" toward running for the presidency in their day-to-day activity. So why the absence of higher-office goals in the responses to my question?

The main reason is that pursuit of the presidency does not require establishing a record of legislative accomplishment. Having a strong legislative record may help a senator gain national recognition, as it has for Sam Nunn. Indeed, being associated with some legislative proposals can be quite important. But once there is a commitment to pursue the presidency actively, most senators find presidential and legislative efforts incompatible. A presidential campaign is so time consuming for a senator and his or her staff that little time is left for serious legislative activity. Moreover, many senators believe that conspicuous presidential aspirations handicap their legislative efforts, primarily because their colleagues begin to second guess their motivations and commitments in legislating. For most senators, it appears that the decision to pursue the presidency means dropping nearly all legislative efforts as he or she reorients his or her priorities.

Conditions for Informal Policy Leadership

Several propositions can be specified about the likelihood that a legislative battle will be led by senators who do not hold a position of formal party or committee leadership associated with the issue. I offer them as informed speculation, although they are consistent with what senators report from their personal experiences.

First, new issues are more likely to involve informal sources of leadership. Old and frequently recurring issues are eventually taken over by committee chairs, as they use their procedural advantages to gain some personal control over issues under their committees' jurisdictions. But new issues offer the informal leader an opportunity to run with issues on which committee chairs may have no experience or expertise. Legislative proposals emerging in response to new issues are often named after informal leaders.

Second, even if the substantive policy questions are not new, issues dividing senators and outside interests in new ways are more likely to involve informal leaders. Emerging coalitions associated with new interests seek informal leaders for their causes when they find senior committee leaders committed to the old coalitions. Entrepreneurial senators often help to identify and stimulate the formation of new combinations of interests when conditions create opportunities to do so.

Third, issues that do not fall neatly within a single committee's jurisdiction are more likely to involve informal leaders. Many of the advantages of committee leaders are neutralized when their jurisdictions do not fit the issues well and they must compete with each other for control over policy outcomes. Such competition gives other senators an opportunity to propose solutions and pursue extra-committee tactics.

Finally, issues that are not central to interparty disputes are more likely to involve informal leaders. Issues recognized as vital to collective party interests tend to fall into the laps of formal party and committee leaders. Such issues create demands for central party leadership and lend great legitimacy to central leaders' efforts. The media tends to turn to such leaders as spokespersons for the contending sides. But when the party connection is weak, informal leaders are often encouraged to assume the burden of managing legislation.

These propositions suggest that informal leaders play a greater role during periods in which new issues arise frequently, issues do not consistently divide the parties, and political coalitions are relatively unstable. On most counts, the 1960s and 1970s fit these conditions better than the 1980s. Since the late 1970s, the dominance of budget issues has suppressed new policy initiatives, clearly divided the parties, and provided for substantial stability in the factional composition of the Senate. As a result, the last decade or so has not provided very fertile soil for the growth of informal leadership in Congress.

The Frequency of Policy Leadership in the Senate

Unfortunately, there is no fully satisfactory way to determine how often senators seek a leading role on issues. Most senators indicate that they solicit the support of colleagues for or against legislation five or six times a year, compared with only two or three times a year in the House, although there is great variance in both chambers. Typically, senators are involved in some lesser capacity far more often. Much of what they accomplish requires no support-building activity, at least on their part. And much of what they push personally is not accompanied by any genuine solicitation. But nearly all senators recognize the special opportunities their chamber offers for policy entrepreneurship and take advantage of it.

One way to assess policy activism is by looking at senators' amending activity on the floor. This bypasses committee activity and efforts in noncongressional arenas but shows us the changing patterns of participation among senators. As Table 5-3 indicates, much more activity has occurred on the Senate floor since the early 1970s than was common in the 1950s and 1960s.

For our purposes, the important aspect of the growth in amending activity is that since the mid-1960s more senators have been involved in contested amending activity. The expanded participation in amending activity and contested amending activity has involved both parties, all levels of seniority, and both members and nonmembers of the committee reporting the legislation.[8] Now open to all members, the Senate floor is a more contentious and active location for decision making.

Rank-and-file amending activity has been accompanied by, and may even be encouraged by, practices developed by recent floor leaders. The

Table 5-3 Amending Activity in the Senate

Congress (year)	Number of amendments	Number of contested amendments	Number of senators offering contested amendments
84th (1955-1957)	590	53	31
88th (1963-1965)	702	109	41
92d (1971-1973)	1261	199	72
96th (1979-1981)	1802	203	77
99th (1985-1987)	1752	182	73

Source: Congressional Record.

Note: Contested amendments are subject to a roll call and result in a 60-40 split or closer.

efforts of Sen. Robert C. Byrd, D-W.Va., in particular, to improve scheduling, provide better notification, and regularize the identification of senators' objections to pending legislation reflect the difficulties of managing the floor given the deluge of amendments from rank-and-file members. At times, the same practices stimulate interest and activity on the part of senators and their staff, creating problems where none would have otherwise occurred.

Senator Byrd and others continue to argue for significant changes in the rules affecting amending activity on the floor. He has recommended changes that would make filibustering the motion to proceed more difficult and imposing a germaneness requirement on amendments easier, and has proposed installing electronic voting and stacking roll-call votes on pending amendments and other motions. Byrd's attempt to attach such rules modifications to the Senate television resolution in 1986 failed to overcome continued opposition from factions and individuals jealous of their prerogatives on the floor. The rules preserve the parliamentary prerogatives of individual senators seeking to affect significant policy decisions on the floor. As a result, the Senate remains unique among national legislative bodies in its opportunities for the exercise of policy leadership by rank-and-file members.

Conclusion

As this chapter reflects, characterizing informal leadership in the Senate is difficult for several reasons. In the first place, informal leadership is a floating pool. By definition, informal leaders come and go with the issues. And the context—institutional, political, and personal—varies greatly from one instance of informal leadership to the next. I close by making some additional observations about the conditions and opportunities of informal policy leadership in the Senate.

The talent of many senators and their staffs for developing and incubating policy innovations is squandered by activities that are, at best, peripheral to their functions as legislators and representatives of their states. In large part, the fault lies with the current system of campaign finance that requires senators and their staffs to spend too much time, throughout their term, raising money for their next campaign. Quite apart from the implications of reform proposals for winning and losing elections, therefore, more serious consideration should be given to the consequences of campaign finance practices for senators' legislative and representative responsibilities.

Senators regularly complain about the lack of quality interaction between members. In some cases, they complain about the infrequency of opportunities to pursue personally and jointly solutions to pressing political and policy problems. Some of the blame lies with larger and more active staffs that create unnecessary burdens for the principals and distance senators from each other. For the most part, however, I see the staff problem as more symptom than cause. Scheduling conflicts are more critical. In addition to the need to set stricter limits on committee and subcommittee assignments, Senator Byrd's proposal to reserve certain days of the week for floor sessions, prohibiting committees from meeting on those days, should be adopted. Recent efforts to have the Senate meet for three weeks and have the fourth week off has helped senators organize their time, but it has also reduced the number of options for committee meetings and hearings, creating more scheduling conflicts and sometimes making it even more difficult to bring senators to the floor.

Senators disagree about the extent to which multiple committee and subcommittee assignments encourage policy innovation and leadership. One side argues that multiple memberships and meetings make it impossible for members to employ their creative talents. The other side argues that multiple memberships open up combinations of opportunities and cross-fertilization essential to creative legislating. Without judging who is right, it is possible to argue that additional efforts must be made to improve scheduling, reduce senators' scheduling conflicts, and collect more senators (committee members, party members, etc.) in one place at one time to improve interaction between senators.

Fostering informal policy leadership is vital to the institutional strength of the Senate. Much of that strength originates in its traditional role as a policy incubator of the political system.[9] New policy ideas can find a foothold and be nurtured to legislative maturity in few places as well as in the Senate. The Senate's place in the political system is weakened when the opportunities, resources, and incentives for individual senators to take a leading role on new issues are limited. During recent decades, many developments within the Senate and the larger political system have encouraged more policy entrepreneurship, but there have been powerful countervailing forces as well. If the Senate is to retain its traditional role and source of institutional strength, it must be attentive to those features of current legislative procedure and political practice that inhibit the germination or undermine the prosperity of informal policy leadership.

Notes

1. The research reported in this chapter is part of a project conducted under the auspices of the Brookings Institution. It is funded by the Ford Foundation and the National Science Foundation (SES8518819). This chapter is based on unstructured interviews with over fifty senators and a systematic survey of senior legislative aides in senators' personal offices.
2. See Norman J. Ornstein, Thomas E. Mann, and Michael J. Malbin, *Vital Statistics on Congress, 1989-90* (Washington, D.C.: CQ Press, 1989), 120; and Steven S. Smith and Christopher J. Deering, *Committees in Congress* (Washington, D.C.: CQ Press, 1984), Chap. 8.
3. Ross K. Baker, *House and Senate* (New York: Norton, 1989), 123-124.
4. The most obvious exceptions to this pattern are senators from states with only one representative. The senators in such cases have far greater discretionary resources than their House counterparts, who must handle the state's business in the House singlehandedly and with a smaller staff and fewer committee posts.
5. This generalization does not extend to committee staff. In general, senators believe that more experienced and expert individuals are willing to work on their personal staffs than is true in the House. This may be due to the widespread view that individual senators are more powerful but more burdened than individual representatives, with Senate personal staff benefiting from the difference. Senate aides are more likely than House aides to exercise discretion on behalf of their principals. The longer Senate terms of office may also provide greater job security and thus be more attractive to more experienced people. Ross Baker also found senators to hold the view that their personal staffs are of higher quality than those of their House counterparts. See Baker, *House and Senate*, 91-92.
6. Donald R. Matthews, *U.S. Senators and Their World* (New York: Vintage Books, 1960).
7. Stephen Hess, *The Ultimate Insiders: U.S. Senators in the National Media* (Washington, D.C.: Brookings, 1986), Chap. 2.
8. Barbara Sinclair, *The Transformation of the U.S. Senate* (Baltimore: Johns Hopkins University Press, 1989); and Steven S. Smith, *Call to Order: Floor Politics in the House and Senate* (Washington, D.C.: Brookings, 1989).
9. See Nelson W. Polsby, "Policy Analysis and Congress," *Public Policy* 18 (September 1969): 61-74, and "Strengthening Congress in National Policy-Making," *Yale Review* 59 (June 1970): 481-497.

6 ▬▬▬▬

Leadership and the Media in the 101st Congress

Cokie Roberts

Question: "What has two legs and is attracted to light?" Answer: "Phil Gramm." That was a popular joke around the Capitol in 1981 when the junior Democrat from Texas was driving his party crazy by collaborating with the White House and Republicans in Congress to fashion the Gramm-Latta budget. The success of that budget spelled a major defeat for the Democratic House leadership, and during the next Congress the caucus retaliated by refusing to reappoint Gramm to the Budget Committee.

A few years later, a new version of the Gramm joke circulated among Capitol Hill correspondents: "Where is the most dangerous place in the Capitol?" "Between Phil Gramm and a camera." By this time, the not-at-all-chastened Texan was a Republican and a senator, managing once again to upset the traditional structure of Congress by rushing through the Gramm-Rudman law to balance the budget.

Phil Gramm figured out early how to overcome his junior status and accomplish matters by using the press to communicate with voters and his colleagues, thereby pressuring Congress into action. Although it is not an uncommon way to proceed in Congress, it is unusual for someone outside of the elected or committee leadership to be able to command such attention.

Media exposure is much easier to come by for congressional leaders, and party chieftains regularly enlist the press in their efforts to set agendas and spark actions. A wide range of both formal and informal activities is encompassed in the symbiotic relationship between the leadership and the press. Almost every legislative day, the majority and minority leaders of the Senate go to their desks at the front of the chamber for "dugout chatter," the only time when the press is allowed on the Senate floor. The leaders announce the schedule and respond to questions about issues of the moment, and they often use the time to make political points or give hints regarding controversial subjects about to emerge.

85

In the House, the Speaker chooses to occupy the arena alone—without the minority leader. The Speaker holds daily press conferences in the formal offices just off the House chamber or, on rare occasions, in the Radio and Television Gallery studio. The majority leader, whip, and other members of the leadership often attend the Speaker's conferences and continue with informal chatter after the Speaker leaves to call the House into session.

These daily gatherings are particularly helpful to the print media because they are one of the few remaining press situations not geared to the disruptive presence of television cameras. They provide handy daily doses of the party line for anyone needing to know what items the leadership is pushing to the top of its priority list.

Members of the House who are not part of the power structure often wait outside the Speaker's rooms to ask the emerging press corps what the leaders have discussed, particularly about subjects on the schedule vital to them.

The House minority leader holds less frequent press conferences that are usually called for a particular purpose—with cameras and microphones more than welcome. In addition, current minority leader Robert H. Michel, R-Ill., is regularly available for conversation in the Speaker's lobby, an area behind the chamber where members and press can meet without interruption from lobbyists or staff. Michel is particularly popular with the press because he is a straight talker, a person who tells the truth or simply says that he cannot talk about it.

Slightly more organized, but still informal, meetings between House leaders and the press occurred during fairly regular lunches with former speaker Jim Wright, D-Texas, and the occasional office briefings for Capitol Hill "regulars" held by then majority leader Thomas S. Foley, D-Wash. He started the practice as Democratic whip, and it was emulated by former Republican whip Trent Lott, R-Miss. Both men were affable and, more important, available. The same was true of the House leaders on the next lowest rung at the time—Democratic whip Tony Coelho, D-Calif., and Republican Conference Chairman Richard Cheney, R-Wyo.

Leadership staff also play a key role in spreading messages through the press, particularly in the Senate, because senators make themselves less accessible than House members. During an active day in the House of Representatives, reporters who station themselves in the Speaker's lobby can talk to dozens of members on a variety of issues. Because roll-call votes summoning Senate members to the chamber come fewer and farther between, reporters frequently wait up to thirty minutes to speak with a senator once he or she comes off the floor. Luckily the press waiting room in the Senate is the beautiful Brumidi fantasy—the President's Room—but the only serendipitous interviews there occur with senators on their way to the "Senators Only" room.

Good press aides can describe both the strategy and the substance behind Senate action, but outside of the leadership, members generally don't take press secretaries into their confidences to create expert aides. Mark Helmke, who was Sen. Richard G. Lugar's spokesperson while the Indiana Republican chaired the Foreign Relations Committee, remembered his days as a journalist when he joined the senator's staff. Helmke recalled that he had spent too much of his time dealing with other press secretaries who knew little. Helmke agreed to do the job only with the understanding that he would participate in the process, have access to and understanding of the office's policy and politics, and possess the writ to convey it to the press. Most press secretaries do not have that kind of knowledge or exercise that kind of latitude.

Helmke became a familiar face in the press galleries, telling eager reporters what his boss thought about South Africa, or the Philippines, or the War Powers Act, and sending messages to the Senate and White House by aiding the press. Now in public relations, Helmke has come to believe that the "spin" put on a story has a lot to do with the outcome of an issue and contributes to the public's perception of the person who hires the press aide.

In terms of staff effectiveness, one rule appears to hold: leaders who are themselves comfortable and forthcoming with the press invite their press secretaries into the inner councils and allow them a good deal of leeway in press relations. Leaders who are wary of the press want to prevent their press secretaries from spilling a few useful beans. Two noteworthy exceptions: Sen. Robert C. Byrd, D-W.Va., does not easily exchange banter or banalities with the press, but he has given his aide, Linda Peek, the mandate to spread his message. Sen. Bob Dole, R-Kan., who is every reporter's dream to interview, has not vested the same authority in his quite capable staff and it seems instead that he would rather be his own press secretary.

Dole has reason to believe that his system is working. Analyses of numbers of network television appearances have ranked him at the top of the congressional list. Dole is attractive, funny, irreverent, and able to speak succinctly. He is ideal for short soundbites on the regular network evening news, a lengthy interview for public television's MacNeil/Lehrer NewsHour, or the Sunday talk shows. According to a study done by Joe S. Foote, chairman of the radio-television department at Southern Illinois University and a former aide to Speaker Carl Albert, Dole appeared almost twice as often on the evening news as any other member of the Ninety-ninth Congress. Foote's study also indicated that those who appear most often on television are members of the leadership.

For the people who put together the news programs, the leadership offers the added advantage of authority to decide the extent of photographic opportunities. The Senate majority and minority leaders determine whether to permit a "stakeout at the Ohio Clock," a term meaning that camera crews may set up equipment behind the center door of the Senate chamber, the site of an elegant old standing clock. A stakeout means pictures and sound while a photo opportunity technically means pictures only, so television, radio, and print media all benefit.

Senators emerging from a meeting with the vice president, for example, stop at the stakeout to wax eloquent on the glorious events that took place in the meeting room. If the session has the earmarks of contentiousness, the stakeout may be denied.

According to Norman J. Ornstein's study of network news coverage of Congress published in *TV Guide*, stories about Congress appear on the evening news much less frequently than they did in the 1960s. More often, members of Congress make cameo appearances in other stories where they react to White House action or comment on a crisis. As the network "hole" for Congress shrinks, those who fill it—the leaders—loom larger.

Leaders also have the ability to organize a formal response to statements from the other party. Every week during the Reagan administration, a Democrat was named designated hitter to follow the president's Saturday afternoon radio address, a job made more or less desirable depending on how much news the president generated. Under any circumstances, however, a colleague is generally grateful to be tapped. Leaders also decide on the response to more formal presidential speeches and have first crack at the air time themselves. If, in the course of a controversial debate a leader ascends to the Radio and Television Gallery, his or her utterances are likely to receive some coverage. Now that the activities of both houses of Congress are broadcast, time on the floor for leadership purposes is more consciously used. In the Senate, the majority and minority leaders use their "morning business" period to make both political and institutional points.

The first leader to take advantage of the House television broadcasts was, in some ways, the least likely. Rep. Thomas P. ("Tip") O'Neill, D-Mass., hardly looks like a typical anchor, but television made him the most well-known, if not the most powerful, Speaker in history. The advent of television in the House of Representatives preceded by a few years Reagan's election, when the White House transferred to Republican hands—and, for the first time in twenty-five years, so did the Senate. The defeated Democratic president lost so ignominiously that the party pretended he had never existed. That left the Speaker of the House to represent the Democratic party, acting as the mouthpiece of the "loyal opposition." O'Neill's visibility was enhanced by his sheer physical bulk and the use the Republicans made of it and him in attacking the Democrats.

For a period of time, O'Neill found that people jeered at him in public, shouting rude remarks sparked by the television campaign against him. Later O'Neill claimed that he felt vindicated by what he insisted were uniformly favorable comments, also stemming from his television image and generated mostly by the House floor. The peculiar circumstances of O'Neill's fame do not have prospects for replay any time soon.

A fall from the top job does not necessarily run a former leader out of the news. Bob Dole's relationship with the press has kept him in the limelight despite his minority status. Granted, he was a candidate for president in 1988, but so was Paul Simon, another Senate member who is hardly the subject of regular coverage.

Someone who lost his leadership position altogether while keeping a high press profile is Richard Lugar. Lugar was not only deposed as chairman of the Foreign Relations Committee when the Democrats attained a majority in the Senate in 1986, but he was also denied ranking member status by the Republican caucus. His colleagues opted instead for the safer seniority system even if, for many of them, it meant looking the other way as they voted for Sen. Jesse Helms, R-N.C. The networks still call Lugar when a major foreign-policy story breaks, especially one about the Philippines or South Africa.

Former press secretary Mark Helmke argues that there is a "round-up-the-usual-suspects" mentality on the parts of network producers, most of whom are in New York, and that it is hard for Capitol Hill correspondents to introduce new faces to bosses who know nothing about Congress. There is also a tendency for producers to ask, "Who will be on tape?" If the correspondent can name someone the producer has heard of, the piece has a better chance of "making air."

When Lugar first became chairman of the Foreign Relations Committee, Helmke made a conscious effort to approach first the major national newspapers based in New York—the *New York Times*, the *Wall Street Journal*, and, to a lesser extent, the *Washington Post*. Helmke knew that if he could get Lugar mentioned often enough in those outlets, network correspondents would find it easier to sell the Foreign Relations Committee chairman to their producers. Helmke contends that such New York network bias kept Sen. Daniel Patrick Moynihan of that state on talk shows at a point when he had virtually no power in the Senate.

Other leadership aides argue that more of a celebrity system exists at the network level, where there is no greater Senate celebrity than Edward Kennedy. And while substantial resentment over the depiction of Kennedy as spokesperson for the Democratic party exists—both for personal and political reasons—the Massachusetts senator has acquired a considerable degree of respect as an institution within the institution, thus increasing his celebrity position.

Achieving national recognition is still possible even for those who have no celebrity status and no press secretaries to pitch their institutional significance to the major media. If an important story breaks and any given member of Congress is a genuine expert on it—and at all intelligible—that member is likely to be tapped. Generally an expert especially eager for exposure will do everything possible to face the camera at the right time. Rep. Stephen J. Solarz, D-N.Y., became a familiar face during the Philippine elections. Rep. Edward J. Markey, D-Mass., pops up any time a nuclear accident happens, whether it be Three Mile Island or Chernobyl. For quite a while in the mid-1980s, any story about Central America brought forth the amiable young face of former representative Michael Barnes, D-Md., chairman of the appropriate House subcommittee. More important, however, Barnes was well versed in how to handle television and well known to the *Washington Post*, since he did represent an essentially home-town district. Joe Foote's study of the Ninety-ninth Congress showed Barnes as ranking eighth in the House in appearances on nighttime network television programs—higher than 423 colleagues, almost all of whom were his seniors.

Substance still counts for the "long-format" programs such as Sunday talk shows, the MacNeil/Lehrer NewsHour, and National Public Radio's news magazines. Members need to know what they are talking about in order to be asked to return. But how well they communicate is also important.

The impulse is always there to feature a person who says completely outrageous things, accounting for why the two Democratic sheriffs in the House receive more air time than most of their colleagues. Representatives James A. Traficant, D-Ohio, and Tommy A. Robinson, R-Ark., take advantage of the time at the beginning of every legislative day to give "one-minute speeches" of sometimes dubious taste but often delightful humor. Joe Foote's study calculated that as a freshman in his first term, Robinson was on the network news more than 405 other members of the House. During this period, the dean of the House and immensely powerful chairman of the Appropriations Committee, Rep. Jamie L. Whitten, D-Miss., did not appear at all. (Perhaps the networks were concerned that they would need to run subtitles; Rep. Whitten is famous for slipping things by in a mumbled drawl that most of his colleagues find difficult to decipher.)

When presented with a funny, smart person who actually has some standing inside the institution, the temptation to use him or her repeatedly is almost irresistible. I sometimes fear that representatives Henry J. Hyde, R-Ill., and Barney Frank, D-Mass., will become permanent debaters in my stories.

For "short-form" news, which defines most broadcast formats, the master of the fifteen-second soundbite wins the prize. That was a problem for Speaker Jim Wright, considered an orator of some talent but never accused of short-windedness. For other older leaders, failure to fashion the soundbite is simply a question of technique. For example, sometimes when Minority Leader Robert Michel delivers diatribes against despicable Democratic deeds, the person presiding over the House will be appalled by the general lack of decorum in the chamber. The presiding officer, often Rep. William H. Natcher, D-Ky., the soul of decorum himself, will gavel the House to order right in the middle of a mellifluous Michel phrase, and the entire Radio and Television Gallery will groan, "He ruined the bite." Michel, accustomed to giving speeches for the members in the chamber, simply picks up where he left off, whereas younger, more media-conscious members always begin the sentence again—they know how to keep each statement cuttable for the discrete soundbite.

That was one of Phil Gramm's many media talents as he went about his institution-rattling business. The deficit, and the law to reduce it, now constrain everything that Congress does, and the law was the brainchild of a senator ranking ninety-ninth in seniority. Gramm had been hatching his budget-balancing law for years, knowing that the Senate would face a debt-limit bill and figuring that an amendment which called for erasing the red ink would look especially attractive when voting for a more than two-trillion-dollar debt. In the old days, institutional pressure could have defeated Gramm's genius: the measure didn't go through the committee process, and the role of Congress was sharply reduced. But Gramm anticipated those objections and overwhelmed them by bringing in outside pressure through the media. Any rebuttal to Gramm's refrain, "We've got to balance the budget," seemed petty at best, profligate at worst.

The press knew that the deficit genuinely concerned the Congress and, to some degree, the public, and it recognized the radical nature of the legislation, which made the issue well worth covering. Since thoughtfully addressing a complex question in ninety seconds on the television evening news is virtually impossible, Phil Gramm's message emerged through other channels, and the senator was ready and willing to espouse it any place, any time. Need to send a crew to Gramm's office? Fine. Like him to come to the Radio and Television Gallery for some questions? How soon? Would a telephone call at home over the weekend be useful? That is fine too. No camera, microphone, or notebook could be too inconveniently located for Phil Gramm, who never seemed to tire of saying the same thing over and over and over again. As Gramm himself put it, "It's not my Cabbage Patch doll face that attracts them." Eventually the strength of the media barrage, and the institutional imperatives of the debt-limit bill, achieved Phil Gramm's end.

Others in Congress have taken advantage of the institutional forum of hearings to make their mark. Most of the 'made for television' hearings don't win their stars anything more than fifteen seconds in the spotlight on the evening news, such as the day Sen. John C. Danforth, R-Mo., staged a video spectacular by listening intently as outrageously attired rock stars opposed the labeling of record albums with alleged pornographic lyrics. But some lawmakers have succeeded in turning these one-shot hearings into something of a steady diet. Sen. Al Gore, D-Tenn., managed to become a master of what's known as "recess press," that is, the scheduling of hearings on interesting but not earth-shaking topics at a time when nothing else is going on. The Capitol press corps tends to stay on the Hill, to avoid downtown offices, even when Congress is not in session. At slow times any excuse for a story is welcome.

But stars are really born at the hearings of national import. Estes Kefauver and Joseph McCarthy learned that in the early days of television. Senators Sam Ervin, D-N.C., and Howard Baker, R-Tenn., saw it reaffirmed during Watergate. Sen. George Mitchell's already fixed place in the Democratic firmament shines brighter as a result of his glistening performance during the Iran-Contra hearings. Senators like Mitchell and his Maine colleague William S. Cohen not only used the formal hearings to make impressive points to home audiences, but they also accepted every offer to show up at camera positions outside the hearing rooms, or at radio microphones at the press tables, to give their interpretations of the information revealed through the long days of testimony.

Oddly enough, the Senate Judiciary Committee hearings on the confirmation of Judge Robert Bork to the Supreme Court produced no similar stars. The only person who made a strong public impression there was Bork himself, and according to public-opinion polls, his time in the Senate Caucus Room worked against him.

Live broadcast of hearings where a sizable portion of the public sees the Congress without filter for long periods of time can help or hurt the participants. Generally newspaper stories and radio and television pieces make people look and sound better than they otherwise would. Newspaper reporters correct grammar, and broadcasters eliminate non sequiturs, lengthy pauses, "uhs" and "ahs," and leave out the boring or stupid bits altogether. Without that tidying up by the press, some lawmakers would look scruffy indeed.

Now, almost daily, an unfiltered, lint-covered Congress appears on television, as C-SPAN broadcasts, both chambers and countless hearings, providing opportunities for direct address to the cable-television audience. In the early days of House broadcasts a group of young Republicans put together regular political programs from the House floor. For hours at a time, in the after-business sessions known as "special orders," these Republicans attacked the Democrats as big spenders, big taxers, soft on defense, and soft on crime. Due to close-up camera angles, the lone Republican in the room seemed to speak to a full House, until a particularly cantankerous exchange between Speaker O'Neill and Rep.

Newt Gingrich, R-Ga., over the content of the special orders resulted in cameras panning the chamber to show its emptiness.

Ironically, the Democratic leadership had initially outlawed any shots in the House other than those of the person at the microphone; it did not want to be embarrassed by public perception of the House not at home. For a time, Democrats planned to organize some sort of special-orders speeches of their own but found themselves unable to agree on what their message would be.

These after-hours sessions have created some unlikely C-SPAN heartthrobs. Prime among them is Rep. Robert S. Walker, R-Pa., whose chief role in the House is that of gadfly to the majority. Newt Gingrich also takes advantage of the technology to achieve more notice than a junior member of the minority party might expect, but Gingrich uses the media advantageously in a variety of other ways as well. That, in many respects, led to his election as House minority whip in the 101st Congress.

Most Americans see Senate and House floor debate in snippets on the evening news, and savvy members of each chamber try to accommodate the network schedule. In the flap over the scheduling of floor debate on the already-defeated nomination of Robert Bork, the underlying issue was simply: for how many nights would it play on television? Then-majority leader Robert Byrd refused to call up the nomination until he got a firm commitment from the minority leader as to when a vote would occur. Byrd was determined to avoid three or four nights of Democrat bashing on prime-time television.

Broadcasting of Congress not only aids some members but it is of incalculable assistance to the media. For television, it means that the drama of debate, which sometimes actually is dramatic, tells its own story, rather than a reporter encapsulating floor speeches using "voice-over" chalk drawings. For radio, it means that a tape recorder can document debate while the reporter actually reports—or eats lunch. And for print, it means an exact record of what is said on the floor rather than the "revised and extended" version that appears in the *Congressional Record.*

Other new technologies could affect congressional leadership in the future. Satellite transmissions make it possible for local television stations to pick up signals from Washington at any time, including live broadcasts. Local television stations make a fortune from local news, and as the programs become longer, the stories to fill them do not necessarily keep pace. Stations in New York and Chicago might have plenty to keep them occupied at City Hall or, more likely, the courthouse, but that is not true in New Haven, Connecticut, or Wichita, Kansas. As a result, stations often hire Washington stringers, who generally report for several different stations; or, alternatively, a group of stations will form a consortium to hire reporters to cover the delegations representing their areas. This proliferation of local coverage has swollen the ranks of the Radio and

Television Galleries to more than 2,200 members (plus more than 200 technicians). In 1980, the number was 855; nine years earlier it was 469. The emergence of local television has made some members of Congress media stars in their home towns and has done more to protect incumbency than any ranking privilege or newsletter ever could, simply because television is a more pervasive media than print.

When members realized that local television stations could make them household faces, many wasted no time in obliging reporters who were in search of stories. What the home-town viewers tune in to can be pretty silly stuff. Beauty queens from state and county fairs parade across the Capitol grounds then pose, tiaras well-fixed, by the side of a smiling senator or representative at the House Triangle or at "swampsite" spots on the campus. These are places where cameras can set up at any time and get good shots of the most familiar "face" of all—the Capitol dome.

Various members of Congress declare "days" at the Capitol, such as catfish day, chili day, or ice cream day. Members from different states challenge each other as to the superiority of their products—Texas sweet onions versus Georgia Vidalias, for example. One member arrives annually from Arkansas with the "World's Largest Watermelon." All of these activities exist solely for the benefit of local television, which dutifully records them. And that evening, the constituents back in the district see their representative at work in Washington (clearly at work—the Capitol dome is in the picture), promoting a local product and exuding the image of an all-around nice person, a pleasure to have in the living room.

Some local programs do contain a thoughtful look at legislation, and some members of Congress do provide a useful service in interpreting the issues of the day or in explaining their relevance to the district. But in all honesty, most members' statements are presented without criticism, and the gathering of comment might make P. T. Barnum blush. On the night of the 1987 State of the Union address, for instance, in addition to network cameras in Statuary Hall for "instant react," there were some twenty other camera positions set up where representatives of 118 local stations conducted 458 interviews—not exactly a situation conducive to penetrating analysis.

In addition to local news organizations pursuing more-than-willing lawmakers, many House members and even more senators send out electronic press releases. These are sixty- or ninety-second video clips of the representative or senator that are shipped by satellite to local stations too poor or too cheap to hire Washington reporters. Many stations put the packages directly on the air, in the same way that small-town newspapers often reprint written press releases word for word.

The effects of increased television exposure on congressional leadership decisions are yet to be seen, but two thoughts come to mind. First, if the air time aids incumbents, then regular television coverage probably helps produce safe seats, giving members more time inside the institution of Congress, more time to devote to overall legislative and party-oriented concerns. Secondly, the ability to perform well on television has clearly become a criterion in selecting leaders. Members explicitly discussed this when Rep. Les Aspin, D-Wis., was first elected chairman of the Armed Services Committee. Democrats wanted someone who could go on the Sunday talk shows to debate with Defense Secretary Caspar Weinberger. They knew that the elderly and ailing incumbent, Rep. Melvin Price, D-Ill., was not that person, and they did not think that his next in line, Rep. Charles E. Bennett, D-Fla., was either. Rep. Richard A. Gephardt, D-Mo., became Democratic caucus chairman and later House majority leader for many of those same reasons.

Richard Cheney's elevation to Republican Conference chairman went unchallenged in part because he had appeared so many times as a party spokesperson in newspapers, on radio, and on television. And in Bob Dole's election as majority leader, many Senate Republicans expressed the desire for an able articulator of the interests and concerns of the party's congressional wing to balance some of the rhetoric coming from the second-term White House.

Sen. J. Bennett Johnston, D-La., tried to make the pitch that he would present a better Democratic party image when he ran against Robert Byrd for majority leader in this Congress. Among many other liabilities, Johnston was never able to convince the press to invest him with "an aura of electability." People in leadership positions will say that the most important thing a columnist or commentator can do, other than spell your name right, is predict victory. In victory, Robert Byrd took Johnston's lead, hired a media consultant, and put his mind to the business of improving his television image. Even more important, from a leader's perspective, he opted to spread the goodies around, allowing the member recommended by the caucus to be the party spokesperson on a given issue.

The majority leader scores some points with his or her willingness to share the television wealth, since senators tend to show resentment when they see one of their colleagues on television too often. Members wanting to move into the leadership must be careful not to cross the line between being "a good sport to speak for the party" and being "a real hotshot who I see every time I turn on the tube." Not only are some congressional egos unable to withstand one member steadily outshining another, but the old distinctions between workhorses and showhorses still carry some weight inside the caucuses.

As a new generation takes over in Congress, that distinction becomes more blurred. The Democrats in the Senate classes of 1984 and 1986 and, to a lesser extent, the Republicans in the classes of 1978 and 1980, entered the Senate via television, feel comfortable with the medium, and are ready to use it in their ascent within the institution. Many of the new Democrats in the Senate came from the House of Representatives, where they had looked comfortably into the cameras for years as they shrank their messages to accommodate the medium.

These are politicians who grew up with television sets in their homes, entered politics as Americans watched a war and an impeachment in their living rooms, and elected the candidates who came on during commercial breaks. As this generation moves forward in Congress, the question of who performs well on television will fade—they all will be good. But the technology will continue to change. Members of Congress who stay on top of it, who keep up with the satellites and fiber optics and computers as they convey their messages from the Capitol, are likely to be the most successful in the future inside the seemingly timeless marble halls.

7 ▬▬

Congressional Leadership:
A Review Essay and a Research Agenda

Barbara Sinclair

Journalists and political scientists frequently assess congressional leaders as successful or unsuccessful, strong or weak, without specifying their criteria for judgment. Underlying these evaluations often seem to be quite different notions about what leaders should and can do. Furthermore, agreement on who should be considered a leader is also absent.

We need to clarify what it is we expect leaders to do. Certainly that is necessary before we can gauge whether they have led successfully. An approach that seems particularly appropriate here is to derive leadership functions from the functions we expect Congress to perform in the political system. We are interested in congressional leadership because we believe it affects the ability of Congress to carry out its functions successfully. Beginning from congressional functions also helps us to identify and classify leaders other than those formally designated. Members of Congress who take the lead in activities that contribute in a major way to Congress's performance of its functions are worth our research attention.

The Framework

Although there is no one "correct" way of conceptualizing congressional functions, there is broad general agreement that the chief congressional function is lawmaking, "the promulgation of authoritative commands to the citizenry," [1] and that Congress should carry out that function in a way that is sensitive to its representational base. In slightly different words, we expect Congress to make laws that are responsive to the views and needs of a majority and to do so in a way that allows the full range of significant views to be heard. (That function or set of functions will be referred to as democratic lawmaking.)

For the institution to perform this function, what tasks or subfunctions must be carried out? Democratic lawmaking as defined above (and real-life approximations to it) is a complex process.[2] A useful and reasonable analytic simplification identifies three aspects:

1. The identification and focusing of attention on a problem or issue (agenda setting)
2. The formulation of (possibly competing) policy responses
3. The building of a winning coalition behind some policy response

These are not discrete steps but often merge into each other. Nor is the process necessarily a linear one. Interest groups, specialists, or individual members of Congress who manage to focus media attention on a problem are engaged in agenda setting. So, too, is the formal congressional leader who decides that Congress will place an issue on its active legislative agenda. Coalitions may need to be constructed at a number of stages of the legislative process and outside Congress as well as within.

Clearly, given this conceptualization of lawmaking, members of Congress are not the only participants in the process, nor are they the only leaders. Certainly the president and interest groups are often major participants in all three aspects. However, to the extent that outsiders regularly take the lead in any of the three aspects to the exclusion of members of Congress, Congress's potential role in the political system is reduced. The degree to which we believe that Congress should engage in all three aspects represents a judgment about the type of political system we favor. What should the relative roles of the president and Congress be in setting the agenda, for example?

The most basic questions we would like to answer are:

1. Which of these functions are various formal congressional leaders engaged in performing? How do they go about doing so?
2. Have the functions they perform and how they perform them varied over time? If so, how?
3. Have or do other members regularly take a lead in performing any of these functions?

In our traditional understanding of Congress, which is heavily based upon research in the period since World War II, party leaders are associated primarily with coalition building, especially at the floor stage; committee leaders are associated with the formulation of policy responses, that is, with the work of actually writing legislation, though that also involves building a winning coalition in committee. Much of modern scholarship sees the president as the primary agenda setter. Recent work, however, has also focused on the role of individual members—often called policy entrepreneurs—in the publicizing of problems.

Although democratic lawmaking can be posited as the central congressional function, there are two other functions that are preconditions to its success over the long run. The first of these we can label party maintenance, that is, keeping peace in the family or holding the protocoalition together.[3] If it were necessary to build a winning coalition from scratch on each issue, the congressional lawmaking process would be, almost certainly, unacceptably slow. In fact, the political parties form the basis for most successful coalitions. However, numerical majorities do not necessarily translate into policy majorities within the American party system. Party maintenance activities promote cooperation among party members. What those are, in concrete terms, at any given time will depend on the character of the membership—on what members want from their stay in Congress and on how complementary or conflicting members' goals are.

Institutional maintenance is the second prerequisite to Congress's ability to perform its central function effectively. The determinants of institutional effectiveness are extremely complex and cannot be fully explored here.[4] How well Congress performs its legislative function depends, in part, upon how it is organized. Does Congress have the resources to perform its tasks? Does the structure of decision making promote reasonably responsive, reasonably coherent, and reasonably expert lawmaking? Though only partially a function of organization, do members have incentives to perform the necessary legislative work and do it well? Do members have sufficient incentives to engage in the various aspects of lawmaking, develop expertise, and be responsive to the citizenry?

How Congress responds to particularly critical legislative challenges and to encroachments on its role in the political system also influences what that role will be in the future. The president has been Congress's primary competitor as chief lawmaker.

Clearly, no inventory of institutional maintenance activities is possible. Those activities that influence Congress's decision-making processes so as to promote democratic lawmaking, and those that affect Congress's response to critical challenges in such a way that the institution maintains rather than contracts its role, contribute to institutional maintenance.

What, if anything, motivates members of Congress to engage in the various functions or in activities that further these functions? Predicting behavior requires some simplifying assumptions. We can assume that political actors, including congressional leaders and other members, have goals and that their behavior will be directed toward achieving those goals. We can further posit that in formulating behavioral strategies for advancing their goals, members of Congress (and other political actors) will attempt to satisfy the expectations of those whose decisions will significantly affect the chance of goal attainment.[5] Using these propositions requires knowledge about the various actors' goals. In many cases, this is not a major problem; we know enough to make reasonable assumptions. Thus, it is reasonable to assume that retaining their leadership position is a major goal for party leaders. Since leaders are chosen by their party members, satisfying those members' expectations should be a top priority. Member expectations should be a critical determinant of leadership behavior. For example, the building of winning coalitions at the floor stage is a function members have expected of their party leaders throughout the post-Civil War period. Expectations about leadership roles in other stages of the legislative process seem to have varied. What party maintenance entails certainly varies over time. In the postreform Congress, for example, given even junior members' expectations of high levels of participation in the legislative process, party maintenance requires that leaders promote member participation and eschew coalition-building strategies that reduce participation opportunities.

While members may agree that leaders should perform functions such as coalition building, they may not agree on priorities or policy stands. Even a consensus on what leaders are generally expected to do does not necessarily translate into behavior by members conducive to leadership success. Party leaders' styles and strategies (and their probability of success) are a function of the extent to which members, for their own reasons, are inclined to do what the leaders want and need them to do and of the resources leaders have for inducing compliant behavior.

The extent to which members of Congress are inclined without coercion to do what leaders want is a function of the characteristics of the members. The most important stem from the nature of the link between members and their constituencies because, just as congressional leaders need to satisfy their members to retain their positions, members of Congress need to satisfy their constituents to retain theirs. Thus, reelection is a prerequisite to the attainment of other goals. Leaders' resources for inducing compliant behavior, on the other hand, are a function of the institutional environment and how it distributes resources among various participants.

To this point, I have argued that to understand congressional leadership, we must understand the key relationship between party leaders and their members. These are not, however, the only important actors, nor is theirs the only important relationship. When we ask who the primary actors are, our question is not about reality but about fruitful conceptualization: what are the most useful initial categories for classifying past research findings and for developing interesting questions for future research? The categories below make both intuitive and analytic sense. That is, these actors are situated differently in terms of key institutional and contextual variables.

Within each chamber, we will distinguish between majority party leaders, majority committee leaders, majority rank-and-file members, minority party leaders, minority committee leaders, and minority rank-and-file members. Significant actors external to the chamber are the president, members of the other chamber, and various groups.

The External Context

Character of the Party System

We have hypothesized that the nature of the link between members of Congress and their districts is critical to understanding their behavior vis-à-vis party leaders. The most important determinant of the character of that relationship is the character of the party system.[6] A great many studies make clear that for congressional party leaders (and for the president), the number of fellow partisans and their ideological cohesiveness are the strongest determinants of legislative success.[7] Cohesiveness is, in considerable part, a function of the character of the link between the member and his or her district and of the districts' homogeneity or heterogeneity, both of which are functions of the party system. So, too, is the number of Democrats and Republicans in Congress. A full exploration of the character of the American party system—how it has changed over time and its impact on Congress—would take us too far afield, so an outline of the key variables and of some relationships among them must suffice. A discussion of their impact on Congress—what we know, what we hypothesize, and what needs further research—follows.

Character of the Party System (key variables)

A. Social, Economic, and Ideological Characteristics
   1. The distribution of party support (for example, geographical, class, etc.) and its consequences in terms of homogeneity or heterogeneity
   2. The extent of elite ideological agreement within each party. The historical literature on American parties supports the proposition that when a party's mass base is relatively homogeneous, its elites are likely to exhibit considerable ideological agreement, and, conversely, a heterogeneous mass base makes for ideological conflict among elites.

B. Party Strength
   1. "Absolute"—Strong vs. Weak Parties
      a. Role of party organizations in the recruitment and election of members of Congress
      b. Elite beliefs about party government
      c. The strength and pervasiveness of party identification as a determinant of voting behavior vs. other determinants (for example, familiarity of incumbent members, various

short-term forces in presidential elections)
2. Relative—Democrats vs. Republicans

Building on an extensive literature base on parties, Brady and Cooper demonstrate a relationship between the distribution of party support and "absolute" party strength.[8] That is, when each party's mass base is homogeneous and the mass bases differ across parties, strong parties are likely to result.

When parties are strong—playing an important role in the recruitment and election of members, or when party identification is the primary determinant of voting behavior—members of Congress are linked to their constituencies via party and are dependent on party success for their own reelection. Both the homogeneous mass base and the strong organizational role (for example, in recruitment) of such parties contribute to a congressional party membership that is ideologically like-minded. Cooper and Brady, and Sinclair argue that party strength influences what members of Congress expect of their leaders and the powers and resources they are willing to give those leaders.[9] Because the congressional majority party membership is like-minded and because reelection depends on party success, members place great weight on successful coalition building and are willing to give their leaders the resources necessary to that task. Thus, party strength also influences institutional structure.

When the party system weakens and parties play a lesser role in elections, the link between members of Congress and their constituencies becomes direct. Individual efforts and personalized appeals become more important to members' reelection than party success. These generalizations emerge clearly from the vast literature on House elections and incumbency effects. There are, nevertheless, a number of unanswered questions. A more precise delineation of the decline in party organization, for example, would make possible a better understanding of its effects on member behavior and on institutional structure. The revolt against Speaker Joe Cannon in March 1910 deserves attention; especially interesting is the impact of the spread of the primaries. Nelson W. Polsby once estimated that in the 1950s, half of the House members were still products of party organizations. Can that be verified, and the decline and its impact precisely traced?

Most of the congressional-elections work has focused on the House, little on the Senate. The literature suggests that the informational environment of House and Senate elections are very different. Voters tend to have more specific information about senators (and nonincumbent Senate candidates) than about their House counterparts, and that information is more likely to come from sources independent of the candidates (for example, from free media rather than newsletters and campaign mailings).[10] As a result, senators appear to be more electorally vulnerable. There are a variety of hypotheses about the effect of this on senators' behavior; it has been suggested that senators, like House members, now campaign continuously.

A weak party system in which the link between members of Congress and their constituencies is less dependent on party success is less likely than a strong party system to produce congressional party memberships that are ideologically like-minded. To the extent that the weakness of the party system is a function of heterogeneous party mass bases, ideological heterogeneity of members will be the obvious result. In addition, the lesser role of the party organization in recruitment increases the chances of ideological diversity. Also, party system weakness begets intraparty district heterogeneity. If party identification is sufficiently weak as a determinant of voting behavior to allow, say, a Democrat who won a Republican seat in a particularly good Democratic year to hold on to that seat subsequently, the result over time will be that the districts within each party become more heterogeneous.

Members who perceive their reelection to be primarily dependent on their own efforts and less so on party success will often expect leaders to facilitate their district-pleasing endeavors, even if this comes at the expense of coalition-building success. Such members may be leery of giving leaders great powers and resources for fear that they might be used in behavior not conducive to maximizing their individual reelection chances. The extent to which this describes contemporary members of Congress, and whether the Reagan years have modified members' perceptions, deserves research attention.

Relative party strength in the electorate (that is, the number of Democratic identifiers vs. the number of Republican identifiers) is the most important determinant of relative party strength in Congress (that is, the number of Democrats vs. the number of Republicans). Although the recent congressional-elections literature concerns itself primarily with understanding other determinants, it shows that the relationship between party identification and the congressional vote is still quite strong, especially in open-seat contests.

It is generally agreed that the number and the cohesiveness of party contingents are the most important determinants of legislative success. The literature suggests that these variables also affect leadership styles and strategies. A number of hypotheses deserve more systematic investigation: how ambitious leaders' coalition-building efforts are likely to be should depend on their memberships' size and cohesion. How leaders go about coalition building should be influenced by party cohesion. For leaders of a cohesive majority, the task should be primarily one of mobilization. If the membership is less cohesive and the majority not especially large, more persuasion should be required. The leader of a badly factionalized party may find that most possible coalition-building efforts are precluded by strong opposition from one faction or another. Building winning coalitions may not only become impossible, but the effort may be exorbitantly expensive in terms of party maintenance.

Short-term Forces

A variety of issues, problems, and crises can affect election results without having a long-range effect on the party system. Following the Center for Political Studies, we call these "short-term forces" and conceptualize election outcomes as a joint function of the distribution of party identification in the electorate and of short-term forces specific to a given election. Short-term forces account for the fluctuation in the ratio of Democrats to Republicans in Congress around the ratio one would expect based solely on the distribution of party identification in the electorate.

A vast body of literature examines the effects of economic conditions on congressional election outcomes.[11] There is controversy about the nature of the link; Jacobson and Kernell argue that elite expectations for a good or bad year for their party play a critical role,[12] whereas Uslaner and Conway, in their study of the 1974 elections, demonstrate a more direct linkage.[13] The existence of such a relationship is not, however, contested. When economic conditions are poor, the president's party loses seats in Congress.

Some research suggests that such issues can affect party cohesion within Congress. Ripley and Sinclair have found new majorities to be more cohesive and more legislatively successful, specifically in enacting legislation related to central election issues.[14] The new Republican majority in the Senate and the significantly increased Republican House minority in 1981 were unusually cohesive on Reagan's economic policy legislation. This research suggests that when an election seems to revolve around a particular salient issue, and one party gains a significant number of seats, the members of that party are likely to perceive themselves as mandated. They believe that their constituents want them to act on the issue and consequently feel that their reelection is tied to a satisfactory response.[15]

Relative party strength and short-term forces together determine the party of the president. Although we know a good deal about the determinants of presidential voting, that literature is at best tangentially relevant here and thus will not be reviewed. However, two points should be made. Party identification has been declining as a determinant of voting in presidential elections with the result that divided control of Congress and the presidency is a commonplace. Second, the short-term forces that influence presidential voting can be roughly divided into candidate characteristics (character, competence, etc.) and issues, broadly defined. We can hypothesize, and it follows from the previous discussion of the effect of perceived mandates on congressional behavior, that the character of the short-term forces viewed as critical in a president's election will be key in determining the nature of presidential/ congressional relations. Some journalists, notably David Broder, have attributed Reagan's lesser success with Congress after his 1984 landslide— in contrast with his bare 50-percent majority in 1980—to such differences; 1980 was an issue-based election and the victory carried a mandate, whereas the 1984 election was not.

Finally, problems, crises, and highly salient issues can arise between elections and significantly influence the context of decision making. The Iran-Contra scandal weakened the president by reducing his popularity, which had been a major resource for Reagan. The stock-market crash of October 19, 1987, is another example. Such short-term forces are much too diverse to generalize about their effects. However, those that produce a consensus on the need for a speedy legislative response, as did the stock-market crash, tend to strengthen the hand of central leaders—congressional party leaders, the president, or both.

Other Contextual Factors

There are many other factors that may have some influence, but they are too numerous to deal with here. A number of the more important ones work through the party system and need not be considered independently. There are, however, several factors or trends that should be singled out because of the magnitude of their impact and because they require further study.

A highly complex set of socioeconomic changes in the nineteenth and twentieth centuries altered what Americans expected of their government and significantly increased the congressional workload. Much, though not all, of this was mediated by the political parties, but, in any case, an attempt to explain the process is greatly beyond the scope of this chapter. It is important to remember that the size and scope of the congressional workload is largely a function of the external environment. The impact of the increased workload on party leadership has received little research attention.

Two recent, secular trends in the politically relevant environment deserve special attention because they seem very important and yet their effects are not well understood. The first is the changing role of the media in American politics; the second is the growth in the number, diversity, and activity level of interest groups active in Washington.

The impact of television on American electoral politics has received considerable scholarly and journalistic attention.[16] While there are certainly many points of disagreement, the consensus is that television has further weakened parties by making it possible for candidates to communicate with voters directly. Most Senate campaigns are media campaigns with television being a major component.[17] House campaigns cannot necessarily make effective use of television; it depends on the fit between the district and the media market. Yet those House members who cannot use television are not necessarily disadvantaged and may, in fact, be more fortunate. The free media coverage they do receive—by smaller newspapers, for example—tends to be uncritical, and they have available a variety of other ways of making themselves known.[18]

Technological advances have changed the character of local television coverage in recent years. Many stations now have regular Washington coverage, and some House members as well as many senators appear regularly, thus becoming local celebrities.[19] Stephen Hess's study of this phenomenon sheds light on its impact on member behavior.

Beyond election effects, the media's role in the policy process also appears to have changed. Certainly the last thirty years or so have seen a multiplication of the Washington press corps and a great increase in coverage of Washington generally and of Congress specifically.[20] A number of scholars have hypothesized that in the more open and less party-dominated political system that developed in the 1960s and 1970s, there is greater and more open competition to set the agenda and shape debate on issues. The media are extremely useful tools in that competition and can also be employed to pressure decision makers to action.[21]

It would seem to follow that such a change would advantage those participants with the greatest access to the media. Some scholars have hypothesized that junior members could gain independent influence by being adept television performers or by irresponsible grandstanding. Studies of who gets covered by the national newspapers and by television network news and who appears on the prestigious television interview programs revealed, however, that leaders, party and committee, appeared much more frequently than rank-and-file members and, as expected, senators more than House members.[22] Nevertheless, the data did show that senators who are neither party nor committee leaders have considerable opportunities to appear.[23] The expansion in news interview shows— with the MacNeil/Lehrer NewsHour first, and then CNN and C-SPAN— also increases opportunities for House members.

The impact on member behavior is not yet clear and deserves further research. Certainly members of Congress have become more media conscious and attempt to use the media to advantage in furthering their policy goals.[24] For almost all members other than party leaders (and presidential candidates), media access depends on being associated with an issue that the media considers worthy of coverage. For House members, but not for senators, that almost always requires membership on the appropriate committee, though not necessarily the committee or even subcommittee chairmanship. Consequently, in the House, the increased media role would seem unlikely to undermine specialization or provide a source of influence truly independent of institutional position.

Leaders' access to the media appears to present them with an important resource. How they use it is little explored and deserves serious attention. That access, combined with the changed role of the media, has, according to a popular hypothesis, altered what members expect of their leaders. Members of Congress expect their leaders to perform well on television, to present the party and its positions effectively. Much of the criticism by Democrats of Speaker Thomas P. "Tip" O'Neill, D-Mass., during the early Reagan years, and of Senate Democratic leader Robert C. Byrd, D-W.Va., throughout Reagan's tenure, bears this out but, again, this is a hypothesis worth systematic research.

The second important secular trend is the great growth in the number, diversity, and activity level of interest groups in the national political process.[25] The impact on member and leader behavior is not well understood. Do the interest groups compete with leaders for the time, attention, and allegiance of their members? Do they tend to complicate coalition building? And, if so, how has the leadership reacted?

To summarize, external contextual variables are primary determinants of membership characteristics, which are themselves, as we shall see below, critical determinants of congressional leadership styles and strategies. The number of Democrats and Republicans in Congress, and the extent to which the members of each party are ideologically like-minded (for example, naturally cohesive), are functions of party-system characteristics and of short-term forces such as economic conditions. The character of the link between a member and his or her constituency, which strongly influences the kind of behavior the member will perceive as conducive to reelection, is a function of party-system strength.

The more intrusive role of the media and the increase in interest groups put demands on and offer opportunities for various of the key actors identified earlier, thereby changing the policy process. Some impacts are relatively clear. The development of television advantaged former president Reagan vis-à-vis other elected officials. But, as the questions raised above indicate, much research remains to be done.

The Institutional Environment

The resources of leaders and those of other congressional actors are largely a function of the institutional environment. How, at any given time, the institution organizes itself for task performance (the character of the division of labor and of coordination mechanisms), and its distribution of influence, which is largely a function of that organization, are the most important aspects of the institutional environment for current purposes.

The literature suggests that the character of the workload (its size and complexity, especially) and the strength of the party system are the primary determinants of changes in task organization and distribution of influence over time.[26] Chamber size seems to explain best the differences between the House and Senate at a given point in time.

In this section, I will survey what the literature says about the institutional environment and how and why it has changed over time. The emphasis will be on the distribution of resources among party leaders, committee leaders, and rank-and-file members, and on the relationships among them. Because they are very different institutions, the House and Senate will first be treated separately and then compared.

First, however, the historical development of party leadership offices in Congress will be examined. If our understanding of institutional development were more nearly complete, this discussion would be integrated into that which follows. Given the lacunae in our knowledge, clarity dictates separate discussion.

Development of Party Leadership Offices

The Speaker, majority leader, majority whip, minority leader, and minority whip are the core party leaders in the modern House of Representatives. Of these positions, the only one mentioned in the Constitution and the only one that holds office in the House is the Speaker. Because the Constitutional Convention did not debate the nature of this office, we do not know what the framers envisioned. Mary Follett argues persuasively that the Speaker was intended to be a political leader, not simply an impartial moderator.[27] The early Speakers, according to Follett, were "keen guardians of party interest" but not "real party leaders." [28] Henry Clay, who served six terms as Speaker between 1811 and 1825, was the leader of his party and established the Speakership position as a legislative leader. "As a presiding officer Clay from the first showed that he considered himself not the umpire but the leader of the House: his object was clearly and expressly to govern the House as far as possible. . . . He made no attempt to disguise the fact he was a political officer." [29] Most of the Speakers between 1825 and the Civil War did interpret the office as a political one, but not all were leaders of their party or faction. The political turmoil surrounding slavery frequently made choosing a Speaker difficult, with the consequence that "second-rate men" or "tools in the hands of the real leaders" were sometimes chosen.[30] Since the Civil War, the Speaker has been considered and almost always has been, in fact, the leader of his party in the House.

That Mary Follett's book, as good as it is, remains our primary source on the early development of the office of Speaker points out a need for further research. Published in 1896, Follett's study does not use modern analytic categories. However, Ronald Peters's forthcoming work may begin to fill the void.

We know a good deal more about the development of the office from 1869 to 1899, an era of growing Speaker powers.[31] During this period, through parliamentary rulings (especially those making the Speaker's power of recognition absolute and not subject to appeal), rules changes (especially the Reed rules concerning dilatory motions and the disappearing quorum), and other procedural innovations (especially the development of special rules from the Rules Committee to bring legislation to the floor), Speakers fashioned the tools that gave them control of the flow of legislation to the floor.[32]

Since floor scheduling is such an important leadership task in the modern Congress, understanding its origin is important. The combination of a rapidly increasing workload and the strong party system of the time, which resulted in the willingness of members to give their party leaders substantial new powers, seems to account for this development.[33]

The other party offices emerged rather late. During the nineteenth century, the chairman of the Ways and Means Committee apparently was usually considered the majority floor leader, probably because his committee handled so much of the major legislation. In 1899, Rep. Sereno Payne, R-N.Y., became the first officially designated majority leader and, at the same time, chairman of Ways and Means. The offices remained cojoined until 1919, when they were separated, and the majority leader now gives up his or her committee positions upon assuming the party office.[34]

Just what duties devolved upon the majority leader during the early years is not at all clear. Very likely this varied depending on the Speaker's wishes. In the last several decades, the position has become at least partly institutionalized. The routine aspects of scheduling are handled by the majority leader's office, which is responsible for the smooth flow of business on the floor. Service as the majority leadership's representative on the Budget Committee has probably become a permanent part of the job. Nevertheless, much of what the majority leader spends his or her time on is determined by the Speaker. And, as late as the 1950s, a strong Speaker with a highly personalized leadership style left the majority leader with an extremely limited job—at least according to some close observers.

According to Ripley, "since 1883, the candidate for Speaker nominated by the minority party has clearly been the minority leader." [35] We know little about the development of the office and much less than we would like about how it functions currently.

Ripley reports that the first whip was appointed by Speaker Thomas B. Reed, R-Maine, in 1897 to help him keep track of the whereabouts of party members at the time of important votes. "The creating of the formal office was the product of hard-fought party battles in the late 19th century."[36]

The Democratic party also designated its first whip around the turn of the century. The whips were only sporadically active until the 1930s. During the 1930s, both parties developed relatively large and elaborate whip systems.[37] The 1970s and 1980s have seen a further major expansion of those systems.[38] Although the resources the whip has available have increased greatly over time and the activity level of the whip has varied with the styles of the higher ranking party officers he or she serves (Rayburn, for example, made little use of the whip system), the whip's basic function has remained constant. He or she is expected to be a vote mobilizer.

The Senate lacks a counterpart to the House Speaker, and the development of party leadership in the Senate is not well understood. According to Ripley, the pre-Civil War Senate lacked both easily identifiable floor leaders and formally elected party leaders.[39] Since the committees were not yet entrenched power centers, evidently this was a period of informal leadership. The many biographies of leading senators might fruitfully be reexamined as the basis for an analysis of how such a system works.

According to Ripley, Peabody, and Rothman, the development of Senate floor leadership began in the mid-1880s, with the election of a relatively permanent caucus chairman and the consolidation of leadership in the hands of a group of Republican Committee chairmen led by Nelson Aldrich and William Allison.[40] A relatively permanent and formally designated floor leader did not emerge in either party until the twentieth century. According to Floyd Riddick, Senate parliamentarian emeritus, the Democratic Conference voted in 1920 for the first time to elect "a leader," who also served as conference chair, while the Republicans first voted for a leader in 1925. This person also served simultaneously as chair of the conference, but in 1945, the Republicans separated the two positions.[41] The first formally designated whips date from the same period.

The majority leader's right of first recognition, the primary procedural "power" on which his or her ability to schedule legislation for floor consideration is based, is not a rule but a precedent and only dates from the 1930s. And according to Riddick, the dominant role that party leaders now play in floor scheduling was an even later development.[42] Though it is a little researched or understood area, presumably increasing workloads were an important contributor to this development. In any case, the majority party leader's control over the flow of legislation to and on the floor is much less than that of the Speaker. His or her institutional powers are much more meager and that of rank-and-file senators much greater.

House Regimes—Circa 1890 to the Present

Certainly by the end of the 1860s, the party system and committee system provided the twin organizational bases for leadership of the

House of Representatives. The relationship between those systems has, however, varied over time.

The Strong Speakership Period—1890-1910   By 1890 a very powerful speakership had developed. The Speaker appointed the members and chairmen of all committees and was little constrained by seniority in doing so. He chaired the Rules Committee, which gave him control of the flow of legislation to the floor. His augmented powers as presiding officer also increased the Speaker's considerable control over floor activities and results.

Speakers were clearly the preeminent leaders; committee chairmen as Speakers' appointees were not independent. To a very high degree, the party and committee systems were melded; the chairmen of the most important committees were the Speakers' top lieutenants; they were, in fact, party leaders.[43]

"During at least part of the nineteenth century the congressional leaders of the majority party defined the chief legislative needs for the country," Ripley points out. "Only occasionally were they confronted with a President who had any clearly conceived and articulated legislative goals."[44] The Speaker as the preeminent congressional leader thus appears to have taken a lead role in agenda setting and also influenced the substance of policy on major legislation during this period.[45]

Cooper and Brady argue that the Speaker's powers derived from how his formal powers and his party leadership role reinforced each other within the context of a strong party system.

> The existence of a stable party majority ensured the Speaker's ability to implement his formal powers and gave him a degree of maneuverability and control that the rules alone could not give him. Similarly, the rewards and sanctions the rules placed in the Speaker's hands gave party regularity a degree of priority it would not have possessed if it had rested merely on the extent of agreement among party members or their devotion to the doctrines of party government.[46]

Rank-and-file members were without substantial resources. Although average tenure was beginning to lengthen, many members had a very junior status, and staff resources were almost nonexistent. Yet the great power leaders had and exercised vis-à-vis their membership did not produce widespread member discontent until late in the period. Cooper and Brady and Sinclair argue that members supported the development of the strong speakership and its full exercise because, during a period of great party strength in the country, such centralization of power in the hands of the party leader enabled him to meet member expectations about policy outcomes.[47] When party success is a prerequisite to members' reelection and tends to be synonymous with members' attaining their policy goals, members are willing to give their leaders the powers necessary to assure legislative success. And, as the workload grew in the second half of the nineteenth century, the minority found it increasingly easy to use House rules to thwart the legislative will of the majority.

The strong speakership system greatly diminished the power of the minority. Reed is supposed to have said that the rights of the minority are to draw its pay, and its function is to make a quorum.

The strong speakership era came to an end with the revolt against Speaker Joe Cannon and its immediate aftermath from 1910 to 1911. The power to make committee and chairmanship assignments was taken from the Speaker, and he was removed from the Rules Committee. There is a considerable body of historical literature on this key episode.[48]

There are, nevertheless, some differences among scholars about the root causes of the change. In his famous piece on the institutionalization of the House, Nelson Polsby seems to see both the centralization and the discretionary use of power that characterized the strong speakership regime as antithetical to an inevitable process of institutionalization.[49] More concretely, he emphasizes members' lengthening tenure and their consequent desire to exert greater control over what were now becoming careers in the chamber. Price's explanation is similar except that he accounts for the increasing tenure in terms of the 1896 realignment having produced large numbers of safe seats.[50] Cooper and Brady and Sinclair put much more emphasis on the weakening of the party system.[51] "When electoral polarization began to decline, the centralized internal structure also began to come apart," Cooper and Brady write.[52] Sinclair also notes that with the spread of primaries, the relationship between members and their districts changed. Many of the insurgent Republicans who joined with the minority Democrats in the successful revolt against Cannon were products of primaries and, having won their seats after policy-based contests with regular Republicans, saw their own reelection as dependent on passing legislation opposed by the Republican party leadership in the House.

Committee Government—1920-1970   By about 1920, seniority had become the sole criterion for the attainment of committee chairmanships, which consequently became independent positions of power. Although party leaders retained influence on initial assignments, they had no power of removal. The committees became increasingly autonomous—of both the party leadership and the majority party membership.

The reduction in the Speaker's formal powers was followed by a disintegration of party control mechanisms. Cooper and Brady write:

> If it is true that factionalism in the party system led to the decline of party control mechanisms, it is also true that the decline of these

mechanisms had the further effect of allowing party factionalism greater expression. The result of these developments was to heighten the power and independence of the individual member and of key organizational units in the House. Denied the power they possessed over the individual member under Czar rule or caucus rule, party leaders began to function less as the commanders of a stable party majority and more as brokers trying to assemble particular majorities behind particular bills. Denied the power they possessed over the organizational structure under Czar rule or caucus rule, party leaders began to function less as directors of the organizational units and more as bargainers for their support.[53]

When, in the late 1930s, the Speaker lost control of the Rules Committee to a conservative coalition of southern Democrats and Republicans, the magnitude of the power shift from party to committee leaders was clearly evident. The sphere of the Speaker's responsibility contracted. In the mid-1960s, Ripley wrote that party leaders are "now concerned with the flow of legislation rather than its detailed contents. Seldom do they take a part in framing legislative language and in initiating legislation. They assume that either the executive branch or the relevant congressional committees will do these jobs." [54] Thus, the Speaker's policy role was, to a considerable extent, redefined to consist almost solely of building winning coalitions on legislation written by autonomous committees. Party leadership intercession in committee to shape legislation and even to expedite it appears to have been considered illegitimate and to have occurred seldom.

Committee leaders, especially committee chairmen, were the primary beneficiaries of this distribution of influence. Their procedural and organizational powers within their committees—over the agenda, staffing, budget, and organization—in interaction with the committee's legislative autonomy made the chairmen very powerful vis-à-vis rank-and-file members, the party leadership, and actors outside the chamber who wanted something from the committee, including the president. John Manley's study of Wilbur Mills provides a particularly good illustration of the bases and consequences of this distribution of influence.[55]

Rank-and-file members seem to have gained two important benefits from the system. It enabled them to vote their districts and pay little to no penalty if that dictated voting against party majorities.[56] Second, members were given the opportunity to ascend the seniority ladder to committee power secure in the knowledge that no leader or faction could block them. Members who increasingly perceived their electoral fates to be dependent on their own efforts and not on party success or party organization valued independence in voting behavior, especially as the split in the Democratic party deepened after World War II.[57] Members increasingly dedicated to House careers valued an automatic mechanism for advancement, again especially within the context of a split party. The system also gave minority party members a much greater opportunity to influence legislation, particularly but not solely in committee.[58]

An extensive body of literature on the causes and processes of change exists.[59] To summarize, the large number of liberal northern Democrats that entered the House in the late 1950s and 1960s found the system ill-suited to attaining their goals. Conservative southern committee chairmen thwarted the policy goals of these Democrats by blocking liberal legislation and squelched their desire to participate meaningfully in the legislative process by the often autocratic way the chairmen ran their committees.[60] In the late 1960s and early 1970s, reform-minded members succeeded in instituting a series of changes in House and party rules.

The Postreform House Circa 1975 A constellation of rules and norms changes transformed the House. The rules changes can be summarized under four rubrics: sunshine, potentially decentralizing, potentially centralizing, and resource expanding.

A series of sunshine reforms opened up most committee markups and conference meetings to the media and public. Although the consequences of sunshine have not been carefully studied, hypotheses abound. It is thought that open meetings give rank-and-file members an incentive to grandstand, and they make compromise more difficult; they reduce the influence of internal leaders—committee especially but also party leaders—on rank-and-file members' decisions and increase the influence of interest groups. A recent trend toward closing more meetings deserves study. Are leaders the initiators of this trend? And why are members willing to go along with it?

Potentially decentralizing rules changes shifted influence from committee chairmen to subcommittee chairmen and rank-and-file members. The subcommittee bill of rights removed from committee chairmen the power to appoint subcommittee chairmen and gave it to the Democratic caucus of the committee; it also guaranteed subcommittees automatic referral of legislation and an adequate budget and staff. Members were limited to chairing no more than one subcommittee each.

Some of the rules changes of the 1970s had centralizing potential. The requirement that committee chairmen and the chairmen of appropriations subcommittees win majority approval in the Democratic caucus was intended to make them responsive to a party majority, and that has, in fact, occurred. To the extent that the party leadership speaks for the majority, committee chairmen's dependence on the caucus redounds to their advantage. Giving the Speaker the right to nominate Democratic members of the Rules Committee subject only to ratification by the caucus has made the committee an arm of the leadership again.[61] The majority party leadership now truly controls the flow of legislation to the floor. With the shift of the committee assignment function to the new Steering and Policy Committee that the Speaker chairs and a number of whose members he appoints, the leadership increased its influence in the making of committee assignments. The new multiple referral rules gave the Speaker authority to set a deadline for reporting when legislation is referred to more than one committee. The budget process also has centralizing potential.[62] These various rules changes either directly augmented the party leadership's resources or gave it new leverage.

The 1960s and early 1970s also saw a major expansion in the supply of resources available to Congress and its members and a broad distribution of these resources among members. Staff, committee assignments, office resources, including access to sophisticated new technologies, and money for trips to the districts all increased and became available to members on a fully or nearly automatic basis.[63] As a result, members are very well equipped for tending their districts, a necessity, members believe, given the decline in party identification and organization. Many scholars believe that effective and intensive use of the perquisites of office, old as well as new, has produced the increased incumbency advantage and has insulated members from electoral tides.[64] Although some of these scholars have hypothesized that such tending of their districts increasingly absorbs members' time and attention, to the detriment of legislative activities, these resources make legislative activity by junior members much more feasible and seem to have stimulated such involvement. (Just as with resources for tending the district, this consequence was intended.) Staff are a particularly important prerequisite to meaningful participation in the legislative process, and the fact that all House members now have a substantial staff has multiplied the number of potentially significant actors in the legislative process.

These rules changes were accompanied by changes in norms.[65] By the late 1960s, the norm of apprenticeship had passed from the scene, and the norm of deference to senior members had been severely weakened.

There is consensus among scholars and journalists that these changes reduced the power of committee chairmen and increased that of subcommittee chairmen and rank-and-file members. Much of the work on the consequences of these reforms in the 1970s concluded that the party leadership had also been weakened. Some journalists based their conclusions on a highly distorted view of Rayburn (as a benign Czar Reed). Most scholars argued that the dispersion of legislative decision-making power to the subcommittees had resulted in a fractured process that the leadership lacked the resources to coordinate.[66] The broad and largely automatic distribution of resources among members was also seen as weakening the leadership by depriving leaders of rewards they could dole out to compliant members and by making independent activity on the part of rank-and-file members much more feasible.

It was hypothesized that the increased media coverage altered members' career incentives. Members could become media stars of sorts. According to Ornstein, "more outside incentives meant less inside leverage for leaders." The expansion of the interest-group universe was also hypothesized to have weakened the leadership; the large number of diverse and active groups was a formidable competitor for the leadership.

In her study of the Democratic House leadership in the late 1970s and early 1980s, Sinclair found a leadership that was more active than that of the 1960s; that made moderately aggressive and quite innovative use of its formal powers and resources, old and new; and that, during the Carter years, was quite successful at building winning coalitions.[67] She argued that as a consequence of the reforms and of external contextual changes, the leadership operated in a much more unpredictable environment than it did under Rayburn. However, the leadership's new formal powers and resources, when used skillfully, make effective leadership possible so long as the external political context is reasonably favorable.

A reassessment of the impact of the changes of the 1970s on party leadership is beginning.[68] Sinclair argues that the importance of the party leadership's having regained control over the flow of legislation to the floor has been underestimated. Even Rayburn could not assure that committee-reported legislation got past the Rules Committee and to the floor; current leaders can not only bring legislation to the floor, but they can do so at the time and under the ground rules they believe most favorable to coalition-building success. Furthermore, full control over scheduling gives leaders leverage vis-à-vis committees that Rayburn lacked.

It is the multitude and complexity of the 1960s and 1970s changes in rules, norms, and external contexts that make their impact upon party leadership difficult to assess. Some clearly strengthened the leadership's hand; others just as clearly weakened it; the net impact is, however, not clear. It seems to me that this is the result not simply of the complexity but also of the contingent nature of the impact. The impact of the changes depends on the state of other variables.

The rules changes moved resources from the committee chairmen to the party leadership and back down to subcommittee chairmen and rank-and-file members. External contextual changes such as the increased media role and the expansion of the interest-group universe opened up the process and made it more complex. They also made available new resources to whoever is capable of using them. The media and interest groups can give rank-and-file members a base independent of inside leaders. On the other hand, the party leadership can use the media and friendly groups in its legislative efforts, and it has much greater access to both than an average member does.

Compared with the committee government era, both party leaders and rank-and-file members gained influence at the expense of committee chairmen. Individual rank-and-file members also gained influence vis-à-vis the party leadership on balance. However, just where the balance is at a given point in time, with its implications for leadership strength, depends on political contextual variables, particularly those that determine how much emphasis majority members put on policy outputs compared with other values.

Thus, Speaker Jim Wright and his leadership team exercised strong and successful leadership during the 100th Congress.[69] Wright took a lead role in agenda setting and involved himself in the substance of policy. Such leadership was made possible by the weakening of President Reagan as a result of the Democrats' taking control of the Senate; the Iran-Contra scandal and Reagan's lame-duck status; the consequent belief among Democrats that policy goals stymied for six years by the Reagan administration were now attainable; and the Democrats' desire to build a record to take into the 1988 elections. Also contributing to the strong active leadership role was the increased use of very large omnibus vehicles (that is, reconciliation bills and continuing resolutions). As the only entity that can legitimately speak for the party as a whole and that possesses integrative capability, the party leadership perforce gets involved in such broadly encompassing legislation.

Was the stronger, more policy-oriented leadership of Wright only a function of ephemeral political conditions and thus likely to be short-lived? Or are there more permanent changes in the external context and the political environment that might provide the basis for sustained stronger leadership?

It can be argued that permanent changes in House processes, especially the budget process and multiple referral, have made a coordinating, integrating entity essential if the House is to function.[70] Given current structures, only the party leadership has the institutional resources and the legitimacy to serve as that entity.

Will majority party members, almost certainly Democrats, allow their leadership to continue playing that role? That depends on the extent to which they value legislative outputs over values such as independence and on the extent to which they agree on the character of the desired legislative outputs.

It is hypothesized that some contextual changes do, in fact, provide the basis for stronger leadership. Although no party realignment occurred during the Reagan years, the period did see some resurgence of party feeling, at least among elites, and a strengthening of party organizations, particularly the congressional campaign committees. With control of the chamber seemingly in question for the first time in decades, members of Congress realized that achieving their own goals was not independent of party success. Even if their reelection was under their own control, members' power in the chamber depended on their party's attaining a majority and organizing the House.

Although the fear (and hope) of a switch in party control of the House has receded, its impact may linger. This is particularly so as the constituency basis for intraparty factionalism among Democrats has been declining. With the increase in black voting and growing Republicanism in the South, the electoral constituency of most southern Democrats is not radically different from that of their northern party colleagues.[71] The increase in party voting in the House in recent years is the result of this change in constituency bases and of members' perception of a greater stake in party success in interaction with the character of the issue agenda.

The Senate

We know much less about the historical development of the Senate than of the House. Ripley has suggested three models of power distribution in the Senate: centralization, in which the party leadership is powerful and aggressive and committee leaders are loyal to party leaders; decentralization, in which committee chairmen are powerful and independent; and individualism, in which power has devolved to the individual senator. There is a clear parallelism between Ripley's categories and the House regimes discussed earlier. There is also some limited similarity in periodization. Thus, during much of the strong speakership era in the House, power in the Senate was centralized in the hands of Senators Aldrich and Allison. They "controlled the Republican party in the Senate and through it the entire Senate by influencing the committee assignment process, decisions made by the principal standing committees and scheduling decisions made by the Steering Committee." [72] Ripley maintains that during much but not all of the period of committee government in the House, a similar decentralized distribution of power existed in the Senate. He dates the advent of individualism in the Senate to 1961.

Ripley's chronology shows much more frequent change in the Senate's distribution of influence than the generally accepted House chronology presented earlier. Change is explained by two processes. "Every senator's instinct is to seek power and the way to power lies in maximizing individualistic tendencies in the Senate." [73] Change may also be generated by pressures from the Senate's environment. Ripley explains two of the periods of centralization as being a response to strong public pressure for legislative action.[74]

If Ripley's explanation and his chronology are accepted without revision, we would conclude that party system strength, which appears to be such a powerful determinant of House institutional structure, has much less importance for the Senate. Given the differences between the chambers in size and, during a part of the period under discussion, in method of election, that argument could be made. First, however, Ripley's chronology should be reexamined, as he himself invites. Unlike the House, changes in the distribution of influence in the Senate are not so clearly or closely associated with rules changes. Consequently, long-term change and short-term interruptions of a trend are not easy to distinguish.

The literature on the Senate of the 1950s depicts a body characterized by a relatively unequal distribution of influence and constraining norms; it was a committee-centered, inward-looking, and relatively closed institution, dependent on member expertise. The typical senator of the 1950s was a specialist who concentrated upon the issues that came before his committees. His legislative activities were largely confined to the committee room; he was seldom active on the Senate floor and did not make much use of the media. He was deferential to his seniors, loyal to the institution, and highly restrained in the use of the powers Senate rules confer upon the individual.[75]

In the Senate of the 1980s, influence was much more equally distributed, and members were accorded very wide latitude; the Senate had become an open, staff-dependent, and outward-looking institution, in which significant decision making took place in multiple arenas. The typical senator no longer specialized; he or she became involved in a broad range of issues, including ones that did not fall under the jurisdiction of his or her committees. Although he or she served on more committees than senators of the 1950s did, he or she did not confine his or her activities to the committee room. He or she was also active on the Senate floor and often made use of public arenas as well. He or she was less deferential to anyone and much less restrained in using the powers granted to him or her by the Senate rules.[76]

A good deal has been written on the process of change. In addition to Ripley, Ornstein, Peabody, and Rohde, Foley and Sinclair have contributed to the area.[77] The consensus view is that at least some of the change is the result of pressure from the new liberal northern Democrats who entered the chamber in large numbers between 1959 and 1965. A number of these scholars also place considerable emphasis on external contextual changes, especially the pervasive media role and the expansion of the interest group universe. Sinclair, for example, argues that the new policy system that emerged from such contextual changes offered opportunities to senators to pursue their goals in new ways and in new arenas. Taking advantage of those opportunities required senators to change not only their behavior but also institutional arrangements—for example, by expanding committee positions and staff resources.

The formal powers of the Senate majority leader were little altered by this change. The office has always been deficient in formal powers, and, in the early 1950s, its prestige was at a low point. Two majority leaders in succession had been defeated at the polls after less than glorious tenures. Lyndon Johnson, D-Texas, took the meager bits of formal power, combined them with what influence he could derive from his party positions, and, through formidable energy and skill, made the office into an influential one.

In the process, he may have significantly altered the character of the office. That Johnson made the majority leader a much more central figure in legislative scheduling is a proposition worth exploring. Johnson did not, however, increase the power of the office in any obvious way that lasted beyond his own tenure. Nor has there been any such change since then.

Senate party leaders in the 1950s had to contend with sixteen or so powerful committee leaders over whom they had little control; now they must contend with almost one hundred powerful senators inclined and able to involve themselves broadly in the legislative process and little restrained in using the powers granted to them by the Senate rules. Leaders face that task without any increase in their scant institutional resources.

House and Senate Differences

Throughout their histories, and especially since the latter part of the nineteenth century, the House and Senate have operated under very different rules, which have extremely important consequences for party leadership. A number of the differences have been mentioned already and their implications will be discussed further when leadership strategies are later analyzed, but their importance warrants a separate treatment here.

The House gives much more power to its presiding officer and to majorities than the Senate does. The presiding officer has considerable discretion over recognition on the floor, debate is limited, and amendments must be germane. Given this set of rules, if the majority party leadership controls the Rules Committee, it can control the flow of legislation to and on the floor. As long as the majority party leadership commands a procedural majority, the rules give the minority party leadership little leverage. Conversely, the rules give the majority party leadership not only the capacity to affect policy outcomes directly (by using carefully constructed rules to structure the choice situation members face on the floor, for example) but also the capacity to do a variety of favors for members (scheduling a subcommittee chairman's legislation at a favorable time, for example). How aggressively majority party leaders can use the powers inherent in House rules varies, depending on factors beyond the rules themselves. Yet certainly since the institution of the Reed Rules, which deprived minorities of the ability to obstruct, House rules have provided the potential for strong majority party leadership.

In contrast, the presiding officer of the Senate has little discretion over recognition, debate is unlimited, and, in most cases, amendments need not be germane. By precedent, the majority leader is recognized first when several senators simultaneously seek recognition; this is the only institutional advantage the majority leader has to aid him or her in the floor scheduling of legislation.

The majority leader lacks the rule-based control over the flow of legislation to and on the floor that the House majority party leadership possesses. By using nongermane amendments, individual members can bring up issues the majority leader would prefer to postpone or avoid altogether; by unlimited debate, they can delay or obstruct his or her legislative program. The extent to which rank-and-file senators have been able and willing to exploit fully the power inherent in the rules has varied over time. Certainly during most of this century, the minority party leadership has been much more influential vis-à-vis the majority leadership in the Senate than in the House, primarily because of the rules differences.

Whereas the House works by majority rule, the Senate operates by unanimous consent. Strong majority party leadership, to the extent that it has existed in the Senate, has emerged despite the chamber's rules that militate against such leadership.

Leaders and Leadership

Leadership Selection

A House officer, the Speaker is formally chosen by vote of the entire membership of the House. The other top party leaders (the floor leaders and whips) are chosen by the members of their party in their chamber. In actuality, the Speaker, too, is the choice of the caucus of the majority party in the House. The vote in the full House is a formality, as now it is always a straight party-line vote. The Republican House whip has been elected by the conference since 1965; prior to that time, he was chosen by the Republican committee on committees and subject to ratification by the conference. House Democrats allowed their top leaders—the Speaker, if they were in the majority, and the floor leader—to appoint the whip until the 100th Congress (1987-1988), when the post became elective.

As Robert Peabody, the preeminent student of congressional leadership selection, points out, leadership stability and not leadership change is the norm.[78] In his examination of party leadership change in both chambers from 1955 to 1974, he found that challenges to incumbent leaders are rare except among House Republicans.[79] Peabody explains House Republicans' tendency to be more conflict prone than the other three congressional parties largely in terms of the frustrations of minority status combined with specific electoral disasters. Thus, Halleck deposed

Martin in the wake of the 1958 elections and was himself defeated by Ford after the 1964 electoral debacle.

When a leadership position becomes vacant, the most important variable determining succession appears to be whether an established pattern of succession exists.[80] Of the sixteen people who have served as Speaker since 1899, thirteen, including the twelve most recent, first served as their party's floor leader.[81] When such a pattern exists, members expect the floor leader to become Speaker, and that expectation changes the decision calculus of potential challengers and of members whether or not a challenge develops. Most frequently, succession occurs without challenge. The potential challenger must persuade his or her colleagues not just that he or she is preferable to the heir apparent, but that the heir apparent is so lacking that the various possible negative consequences of attempting to oust him or her are worth risking. Brown and Peabody's discussion of why several potentially strong challengers for the speakership in 1986 decided not to take on heir apparent Jim Wright illustrate this calculus.[82]

None of the other top leadership positions has such a clear ladder of succession developed. Among House and Senate Democrats, the whip has an advantage in becoming floor leader.[83] John McCormack, D-Mass., Carl Albert, D-Okla., Thomas Boggs, D-La., "Tip" O'Neill, D-Mass., and Thomas S. Foley, D-Wash., all moved from whip to majority leader. John McFall, D-Calif. (and John Brademus, D-Ind., who was defeated for reelection) are recent whips who did not move up, while Jim Wright, majority leader from 1977 to 1986, had not previously served as whip. The election of whip will change the dynamics of succession contests and most likely will result in future House Democratic whips, who will have shown themselves capable of winning an open contest for the position, moving up to majority leader. Democratic floor leaders in the Senate from Johnson through Sen. Robert C. Byrd, D-W.Va., moved up from whip, but Sen. George J. Mitchell, D-Maine, Byrd's successor, had not served as whip.

Among Republicans in the Senate, no leadership ladder has developed. Senators Robert A. Taft, R-Ohio, and William Knowland, R-Calif., had served as chairmen of the policy committee; senators Everett M. Dirksen, R-Ill., and Hugh Scott, R-Pa., had been whip; and the two most recent leaders, Senators Howard Baker, R-Tenn., and Robert Dole, R-Kan., had held no lesser party office.[84] In the House also, Republicans have established no clear pattern of advancement to the position of minority leader. Michel served as whip before becoming minority leader, but in the mid-1980s knowledgeable observers expected a fight between then-whip Trent Lott and Republican conference chairman Dick Cheney to succeed Michel. That expectation may have influenced Lott's decision to run for the Senate in 1988. If Michel decides to retire soon, current whip Newt

Gingrich will almost certainly face a challenge for the position.

When there is no, or only a weak, pattern of succession, what variables determine the character of the contest and the outcome? Peabody has identified twenty variables falling into four clusters that may explain leadership change: individual personalities and skills; variables such as the level of the position sought by the candidates; institutional characteristics, such as those related to House-Senate differences; and external variables, including aggregate election results.[85] From his case studies he concludes that internal conditions are the primary determinants; of the external variables considered, only congressional election results were important.[86] No such definitive statements were possible about the other variables; some contests brought many of the variables into play; in others, one or two variables appeared to be critical.[87]

Peabody's work makes clear that leadership selection in Congress is a complex process affected by a broad range of variables some of which have their roots in the distant past. This complexity, combined with the relative infrequency of leadership change, may preclude a more powerful theory of leadership selection.

Several areas deserve research attention. As one participating member in the Dirksen-CRS seminars said, members make their decisions among competing contestants for leadership positions on the basis of "what can he do for me." More research attention should be paid to ascertaining what it is members want their leaders to do for them and what they realistically expect them to do. Both scholars and journalists have hypothesized that members increasingly expect their leaders to be good media performers. It has even been suggested that this ability has become a lead criterion of choice. Brown and Peabody's study of the 1986 leadership changes in the House indicates that to be an exaggeration. They conclude: "Success in late 20th century contests calls for an insider strategy that makes increasing use of what may be considered 'outsider' skills, most particularly, raising money and generating favorable publicity for House Democrats." [88] A survey of member expectations concerning their leaders would also serve as a baseline from which change over time could be measured. Of great interest is whether a change in member expectations results in perceptibly different patterns of leadership selection (for example, a different type of leader selected or revolts against leaders who do not meet the new expectations).

Also worth further exploration is the developing tendency among House Democrats to wage long and elaborate campaigns for lesser leadership positions. That the first contest for the elective whip position would be vigorous was to be expected, although just how early Tony Coelho, D-Calif., the eventual winner, started and how sophisticated a campaign he ran were probably not. Several members ran similarly long and sophisticated campaigns to succeed Rep. Richard A. Gephardt, D-

Mo., as caucus chairman in 1989. The position of chairman of the House Budget Committee, which, in many ways, is part of the House Democratic leadership, has also occasioned vigorous and lengthy contests.

These contests combined with members increased desires for whip positions appear to reflect an increase in the value members' put on being part of the even broadly defined party leadership. For top leaders this may prove to be a mixed blessing. Service as caucus chair and as chairman of the House Budget Committee is limited. Do members who have successfully won these positions against stiff opposition tamely return to rank-and-file status when their allowable terms end, or do they challenge higher leaders?

Characteristics of Leaders

Are there characteristics that distinguish leaders from other members? Are there characteristics that bar a member from becoming a leader?

The attempts that have been made to define leadership in personality terms and to delineate the personal characteristics that distinguish a leader have not been very productive in the social sciences. In congressional studies, there exists a consensus on the contextual rather than the personal perspective as being most productive for the understanding of congressional leadership.[89] As Lester Seligman writes, "Leaders are always, covertly or overtly, 'preselected' by their supporters according to the situational needs of the group." [90]

Since the turn of the century, members have always chosen a senior member as Speaker. Some nineteenth-century Speakers were very junior—Rep. Henry Clay of Kentucky was elected his first day in the chamber—but today high seniority appears to be a necessary though certainly not sufficient condition for choice.[91] The development of a leadership ladder tends to produce senior Speakers. Although most floor leaders in both parties and chambers were established members when they won those positions, they were not necessarily highly senior and a few, such as Lyndon Johnson, were quite junior.

Perhaps the best-known hypothesis about characteristics of leaders is the ideological middleman hypothesis. Truman long ago suggested that the congressional parties are likely to choose ideological middlemen or moderates as their leaders.[92] Hinckley has hypothesized that, in addition, high party support in voting behavior is a prerequisite to leadership selection.[93]

William Sullivan's careful test of these hypotheses casts doubt on both. Examining the voting behavior of the top leaders (floor leaders and whips) of both parties in both chambers during the period from 1955 to 1973, Sullivan found that only in the case of House Republicans were leaders moderates in terms of the spectrum of their congressional party.[94] He concluded, "The selective process appears to exclude only those members who are the most extreme ideological mavericks in the congressional party . . . extreme Democratic conservatives and extreme Republican liberals."[95] Sullivan did find that when leaders were compared with their party colleagues with similar seniority and from the same region, leaders tended to be more moderate.

Sullivan found little support for the high-party-support hypothesis. "The selective process does not recruit in any systematic manner congressmen exhibiting high levels of party support in roll-call voting," he wrote. "It also fails—at least in the Senate—to bar entry into the leadership arena to those members with less than even moderately supportive voting behavior."[96]

For the Democratic party, with its important and often conflicting northern and southern wings, regional balance in the leadership team has been considered important. In the House, the two top positions have usually been split between the regions. Rayburn (Texas)/McCormick (Mass.) was followed by McCormick/Albert (Okla.), and Albert/Boggs (La.) but with O'Neill (Mass.) as whip, next by Albert/O'Neill and then by O'Neill/Wright (Texas). When Wright became Speaker, Tom Foley of Washington faced no real opposition in moving up to majority leader although both positions would then be held by members from west of the Mississippi. Regional balance was an issue in the campaign for whip, but Tony Coelho won despite being from California and thus further unbalancing the leadership team. In 1989 there was no southerner among the top leadership. "Regional considerations still count in leadership races, but with waning force," Brown and Peabody conclude.[97] Regional balance was an important consideration in Speaker Wright's choice of Rep. David E. Bonior, D-Mich., as chief deputy whip. It is assumed that Speaker Foley will appoint a southerner to that or another position. Among Senate Democrats, the two top positions also have usually been split between north and south.

In sum, seniority, ideology, and region at most narrow the pool from which leaders are selected.

Party Structures

The four congressional parties are relatively elaborate but each somewhat different in organization. The organization of all party members in the chamber is called the caucus by House Democrats and the conference by the three other groupings. Each congressional party also has a number of party committees, most of which have existed for a considerable period of time. The mere existence of an entity does not necessarily mean it is important or active. We know that some of these committees at some times have been mere paper entities, the Steering Committee under Rayburn, for example.

The various party structures may be valuable tools of the leadership; the House Democratic whip system, for example, plays a critical role in coalition-building efforts. These structures may provide leaders with resources; thus, as chair of the Steering and Policy Committee, the Speaker controls a sizable staff. The Speaker appoints some members of Steering and Policy, and he or she and the other top leaders appoint a sizable number of at-large whips. These appointments are a resource for the leadership; since the positions are desirable, leaders can bestow them as favors. The decisions made by these entities can sometimes shape the leadership's tasks. The committee-assignment decisions of the congressional party's committee on committees, for example, influence the legislative output of committees and that, in turn, affects coalition building at the floor stage. A number of these entities provide arenas for interaction among members and between members and leaders. As such, they can provide valuable information for leaders as, for example, the weekly Democratic whip meetings and the periodic meetings of the Democratic caucus do. The structures can provide a mechanism through which leaders give members opportunities for meaningful participation as, for example, Democratic whip task forces and caucus committees do. Those headed by members other than the top leaders, the Republican Policy Committees, for example, provide potential sources for the recruitment of leaders. Some of these entities also provide an arena for intraparty conflict and a forum for possible competitors to the leadership. Rayburn, for example, opposed meetings of the Democratic caucus because he believed that, by providing an arena in which warring northerners and southerners could confront each other directly, such meetings would only exacerbate intraparty conflicts.

Understanding how these entities function, and especially the relationship between these various entities and the top party leadership on the one hand and the membership on the other, is a prerequisite to understanding party leadership.

We know a good deal about House Democratic party structures—much more than about any of the three other congressional parties. That literature indicates that starting in the late 1960s, party structures were revitalized, first under the impetus of reform-minded members. In the 1970s, party leaders expanded and made greater use of party structures as part of their attempt to cope with the consequences of reform. Since the 1980s, the whip system, the Steering and Policy Committee, and the caucus have played an important role in the leadership's efforts to reconcile member demands for participation with the dictates of coalition building.[98]

Ripley provides an overview of how House Democratic party structures functioned in the mid-1960s as well as some historical background.[99] Sinclair analyzes their functioning in the late 1970s and early 1980s.[100] The old committee on committees and its decisions are analyzed by Masters and Shepsle.[101] Ripley, Dodd, and Sinclair describe the whip system and how it has changed over time.[102] Wolfensberger discusses the changing role of the party caucus.[103] With the exception of the Democratic Congressional Campaign Committee, which will be discussed below, we have a relatively satisfactory description and analysis of House Democratic party structures. To be sure, these entities are not static, and thus descriptive information can soon become outdated. Nevertheless, the other three congressional parties deserve priority.

Our knowledge of House Republican party structures and how they have developed over time is woefully inadequate. Jones and Ripley provide considerable but still incomplete information for the mid-1960s;[104] Jones thoroughly analyzes the functioning of the Policy Committee in the early and mid-1960s;[105] and Peabody, as a by-product of his studies of leadership change, casts some but limited light on various of the party structures.[106] No scholarly treatment of the more recent period exists, although two young scholars, Jack Pitney and Bill Connelly, were working in that area.[107] Before we can assess the role these structures play in the relationship between leaders and members and in the exercise of leadership, some basic descriptive information is required.

We need to know how the various entities are organized and staffed, what they do, how frequently, and with what consequence. Reports of a revolt against the party leader in the Committee on Committees suggests the decision-making process as a focus of study and reminds us that while we know a great deal about that process among House Democrats, we know little about how it works across the aisle.

Rohde, Ornstein, and Peabody have analyzed the changing character of the membership of the Senate Democratic Steering Committee;[108] Bullock has given us some insights into its decision making;[109] Oleszek has provided some information on the whip system;[110] and a number of scholars—Peabody, Ornstein, Huitt, Davidson, and Patterson—in the process of discussing leadership more generally have shed light on various leaders' inclinations to use the conference or to rely upon the whip and their varying roles in the committee-assignment process.[111]

These leadership structures are less intrinsically important in the Senate than in the House. Nevertheless, we should know more about them than we do. Until recently, the Democratic leader, unlike his or her Republican counterpart, chaired the conference, the Steering Committee, and the Policy Committee. At least potentially, these positions fulfilled the needs of a leader with meager institutional resources. George Mitchell, however, dispensed some of these positions to other Democrats with consequences that were not apparent as of 1989.

The Policy Committee might well be the most fruitful first target of a research effort aimed at describing and analyzing Senate Democratic party structures. Under Byrd, the committee provided the Democratic leader with a very sizable staff. Legislative scheduling, the negotiating of unanimous consent agreements for the floor consideration of legislation, some issues research, and press relations all appeared to be carried out primarily by this staff. Thus, as the leader used the staff to carry out the tasks most central to party leadership in the Senate, the staff provided an excellent vantage point on the functioning of Senate leadership.

Among Republicans, a different senator chairs the conference, the Committee on Committees, and the Policy Committee. This arrangement has had an impact on leadership selection—several floor leaders have moved up from the Policy Committee. Its impact on the functioning of leadership is less clear; some scholars have characterized Republican leadership as more collegial as a result. Whether that is, in fact, still the case is a question worth pursuing. Within the context of the very broad distribution of influence in the contemporary Senate, and Senate floor leaders' consequent need to deal with any senator who decides to participate in a given legislative battle, this organizational difference between the parties may pale into insignificance. On the other hand, the existence of these various entities, each with a different chair and a significant staff free from the floor leader's control, raises the possibility of conflict. Has that occurred and, if not, how has it been avoided?

The existing literature on Senate Republican party structures is scant. In the 1950s, Jewell and Bone wrote about the Policy Committee, and other information is embedded in more general discussions of party leadership.[112]

These party structures are best treated as part of a broader study where their relationships to other structures and leadership functions can be fully analyzed. Unfortunately, most of the broader studies do not provide even a full description of the structures. While broad-gauge analytic studies of the three neglected congressional parties that placed the structures in context would be most desirable, narrower descriptive studies would also be useful. An advantage of a narrower focus would be the greater attention that could be devoted to discovering or developing quantitative indicators. To assess stability or change over time with confidence, we need such indicators.

The four campaign committees have received little attention from congressional scholars. Political scientists who study elections and campaign finance have remarked on their development over time and have done some analyses of giving patterns. Comprehensive studies of the growth in size, function, and technological sophistication of the committees and of their changing patterns of giving are still lacking, although Herrnson's work represents an excellent start.[113] Certainly the committees deserve more attention from those interested in congressional leadership.

To some unknown extent, they perform public-relations functions for their party; for example, in the summer of 1987, when Reagan traveled around the country blaming the deficit on congressional Democrats, he was greeted in many cities by large newspaper advertisements saying, "It's Your Deficit, Mr. President," paid for by the Democratic Congressional Campaign Committee. If, as many scholars have hypothesized, congressional leadership increasingly involves communicating with the public and attempting to influence public opinion, the role of the campaign committees warrants further research. A more difficult but important question concerns the effect of election aid from the party on members' behavior in Congress. Does it make those members more inclined to support party positions? Kayden and Mahe suggest that the help on issues that the Republican and, increasingly, the Democratic committees provide their candidates may produce greater homogeneity on issues among party members.[114] They argue that during the course of a campaign, a candidate is required to express a position on a great many issues on which he or she, in fact, has little information or interest. If candidates rely on the issue briefs from the campaign committees, often the easiest course, the result will be party homogeneity.

Interactions and Interrelationships Among Key Actors

How well or poorly Congress performs its central function of democratic lawmaking is largely a by-product of the complex of interactions and interrelationships among the political actors identified earlier. How are those interrelationships patterned? Is there some analytic key to understanding their complexity? Our framework is based on the assumption that members of Congress and other political actors, in formulating behavioral strategies for advancing their goals, will attempt to satisfy the expectations of those whose decisions will significantly affect their chances of attaining their goals. Congressional party leaders, for example, should be especially concerned with meeting the expectations of their party members in the chamber because the leaders depend on the members for their positions. That assumption dictates that to understand the complex of interactions and interrelationships among the key actors, we need to know what the key actors expect of each other; what capabilities various actors have to enforce their expectations; what resources they have to meet the expectations of other key actors; and how the key actors go about doing so, that is, the behavioral strategies they develop for advancing their goals while meeting the expectations of other key actors.

An examination of all the logically possible relationships among the key actors would go a long way toward providing a comprehensive understanding of Congress. That is, however, too big a task, so we will concentrate on those that seem most important to understanding party leadership.

Party Leaders/Party Members   The relationship between party leaders and their members is, by consensus, the most critical relationship to understand. As leaders are chosen by members, leaders must at least minimally satisfy member expectations to keep their positions. Consequently, leaders should be more responsive to the expectations of their members than to those of any other actor.

What do members expect of their leaders? It seems reasonable to hypothesize that member expectations are a function of their own goals and of their assessment of leaders' resources and capabilities. Members probably expect their leaders to help them advance their individual goals to the extent that leaders are seen as capable of doing so. That leaders will not thwart members' goal-advancing efforts is probably an even stronger expectation. The extent to which members expect leaders to advance the party as a collectivity even if it means hurting some individual members—or tolerate leaders doing so—is an open question. So, too, are member expectations about leaders' institutional maintenance activities.

Member expectations of their leaders should vary over time as member goals, the institutional environment, and the external context vary. Cooper and Brady and Sinclair have argued that House members in the latter part of the nineteenth century expected strong, policy-involved party leadership.[115] Such leadership was considered necessary for legislative party success, which, in turn, was perceived as important to electoral success for the party and consequently for the individual member. Polsby and many other scholars contend that as more and more members in the early twentieth century began to see service in the House as a career, their expectation of their party leaders changed.[116] Leaders were now expected to defer to the committees, which were the basis of member influence; they were expected primarily to help committees, if they needed it, pass their legislation at the floor stage. One major impetus to the reforms of the 1970s was a desire on the part of rank-and-file members for more opportunities for meaningful participation in the legislative process. In the postreform Congress, members expect their leaders to facilitate and not thwart such participation. There is some evidence suggesting that House Democrats' expectations of their leaders have changed in recent years.[117] They still expect their leaders to consult broadly and facilitate participation, but they also appear to expect them to assume a more aggressive policy role, especially in agenda setting.

Jones argues that for the minority party, the ultimate goal is majority status.[118] Certainly for most minority party members, the attainment of majority status would contribute immeasurably to the advancement of all their goals. Yet the extent to which the minority party leadership can influence aggregate election outcomes is limited; what strategies are likely to be most effective is in dispute; and some strategies that may be effective in the long run are costly to member goal advancement in the short run.[119] A strategy of confrontation rather than compromise, for example, is likely to cost minority party members district projects and limited policy victories. Given this situation, what are the expectations minority members have of their leaders? Is there less consensus among minority than majority party members? Are the expectations ones that leaders can hope to meet?

Ripley and Davidson suggest that member expectations of leaders may be different in the House and Senate.[120] The resources of rank-and-file senators are considerably greater than those of rank-and-file House members, while those of the House majority leadership are significantly greater than those of the Senate majority leadership. The consequence may well be that senators expect less of their leaders than House members do and will not tolerate as strong leadership.

Thus, we know a good deal about the leader/member relationship from indirect evidence. There are a number of interesting hypotheses concerning the relationship and how it varies with majority versus minority status and chamber. Yet direct evidence is sparse. Ripley tells us something about how House members and senators regarded their leadership in the 1960s.[121] Loomis provides a perspective on junior House members' perceptions in the 1970s.[122] None of these studies, however, was based on random samples.

Given the importance of the relationship, it is worth serious and systematic investigation. An exhaustive study of Congress members' expectations of, perceptions of, and interactions with the party leadership (and committee leaders) should be a top priority. A random sample stratified by party, seniority, and, for Democrats, region should be taken in both the House and Senate. Serious thought should be given to supplementing this with a sample of committee leaders. Their expectations of party leaders are clearly important and may well be different from those of other members. Rank-and-file members should also be questioned about their relationships with committee leaders, because those relationships are intrinsically important and will provide a basis of comparison for their responses about their relationships with party leaders.

Such a survey would allow us to test a number of interesting hypotheses and would provide a baseline against which future change could be measured. Some of the questions such a study would allow us to answer are: How do members themselves formulate their expectations of the leadership? What can the leaders do for and to their members, as perceived by members? How do members rank the importance of various possible leadership functions/tasks? What are the bounds of legitimate leadership activity?

Is there a consensus on leadership functions? If not, how do expectations of the leadership vary with member characteristics such as seniority, ideology (especially whether the member is in the party mainstream or not), electoral situation (safe seat or not), institutional position (does the member hold a committee leadership position? Does he or she hold a lesser party position such as appointed whip?), and, most important, minority or majority status and chamber?

Do member expectations provide the basis for relatively strong, policy-oriented majority party leadership in either chamber?

Are member expectations of leaders different in the House and Senate? Is there, in fact, a basis for stronger leadership in member expectations in the House?

Are the expectations of minority party members, especially in the House, inherently unmeetable?

As members define leadership, is it primarily an in-house job (as we believe it used to be), or are members now expecting leaders to represent their party and chamber to the public? (Has the changing role of the media, especially television, in American politics changed what members expect leaders to do?)

Party Leaders/Committee Leaders   This relationship is important because it determines who sets the party's policy positions and priorities, at least within the chamber. We know a good deal about this relationship for the House majority party but not much for either the Senate or the minority.

During the strong speakership era, the melding of the party and committee systems resulted in committee chairs being party leaders under the Speaker and the Speaker having the capability, which he regularly employed, of determining priorities and the substance of legislative proposals.

During the period of committee government, party leaders became primarily concerned with the flow of legislation rather than its content.[123] Strong, autonomous committees were resistant to leadership intervention and involvement in substance. If the president was of the same party, he set party priorities, although committees did not always go along with them. If not, party policy was the result of the independent legislative efforts of autonomous committees. Party leaders lacked resources to play a more active role vis-à-vis committee chairs.

In the postreform House, the election of committee chairmen by the Democratic caucus has altered the power balance. Other reforms, including multiple referral, have reduced committee autonomy. As a result of a constellation of changes, now committee leaders frequently depend heavily on the party leadership's help in passing their legislation, and the most prestigious and desirable committees often need the most help. The party leadership has a greater opportunity to get involved in priority setting and in substance—an opportunity of which it is increasingly taking advantage.[124] Is the thick line demarcating the party system and the committee system blurring? Is the party leadership's greater role in policy a temporary or a permanent change?

We know less about the relationship between committee and party leaders in the House minority. Committee leaders are often faced with the choice of playing a meaningful legislative role on their committee that involves bargaining and compromise or simply opposing. The former seems to bring them into conflict with party members who interpret this as selling out, and perhaps also with party leaders. This is worth exploring as part of a study of minority party leadership, and also as part of the study of member expectations.

Again, we know less about those relationships in the Senate than for the House majority. Drawing upon the literature, we can hypothesize that Senate committee leaders are now less powerful vis-à-vis rank-and-file senators than they were in the 1950s but possibly only marginally less powerful vis-à-vis party leaders (what they have lost as chairs, they have gained as individual members).[125]

Senate party leaders' roles in priority setting and in substantive policy making require more careful study.[126] The literature suggests that given the extremely open and fluid policy process in the Senate, party leaders can sometimes play an important role. They have resources that give them advantages over other senators, but the role party leaders play may often be different only in degree and not in kind from that of other senators.

When applied to congressional history of the 1980s, our framework suggests a hypothesis worthy of further study: the decline in committee autonomy, combined with resources of the House majority leadership for passing legislation at the floor stage, has made committee chairmen much more dependent on party leaders than they used to be and has fundamentally changed the character of that relationship. It is closer, more consultative, and more frequently concerned with policy substance. In contrast, among the other three congressional parties, party leaders lack the resources—especially institutional ones—to help committee leaders to nearly the same extent, and consequently committee leaders remain more independent.

By including a sample of committee leaders in the study of members' expectations of their leaders, valuable information on the committee leader/party leader relationship could be obtained. Data on the frequency and content of interactions would make possible some tentative conclusions about the relative roles of these two key participants in the various stages of the legislative process. How the House majority leadership's more aggressive policy role is perceived and evaluated by committee leaders is of great interest. And since we know so much less about the relationship in the three other congressional parties, the data from the study would provide a basis for some tentative conclusions about the validity of the major hypothesis discussed earlier and a basis for further hypothesizing.

Party Leaders/President　The key variable in determining the character of the relationship between the president and the congressional majority party leadership is whether they are of the same party. Chamber does not appear to be important.

There are instances of close working relationships between an activist president and his party leaders in Congress that date back to Jefferson. It was during the presidency of Franklin Roosevelt, however, that the expectation that party leaders serve as chief legislative lieutenant to a president of their party became pervasive in the political community. In Congress, among members and leaders, leaders' obligations to their own members are perceived as primary and overriding those to the president if there is a serious conflict.[127] Such instances, however, are relatively rare, and all the major actors—the president, members of Congress, interest groups, and leaders themselves—expect the party leadership to devote much of its efforts to building winning coalitions on the president's program. Since the leaders' reputation with other political actors and with the press depends heavily on how successful they are in passing the president's top priorities, they have considerable incentive for doing so. Furthermore, an appreciable proportion of their own members and some important groups allied with the party are likely to have a direct interest in the passage of each major item on the president's program.

The relationship between a majority party leadership and a president of the other party is much less defined by stable expectations. A range of strategies is available to both actors; the likelihood of success of a given strategy will depend on the resources available to each, especially the president's popularity and the majority's size and cohesion. The president's popularity is important because it influences how members want their leaders to react. If a president is perceived as highly popular, especially with a member's own constituents, that member is more likely to want his or her leadership to support or at least compromise with the president. (The range of strategies and their determinants will be further discussed in the section on leadership strategies.)

The relationship between a minority party leadership and a president of the same party appears to be primarily a by-product of the relationship of that president with the majority. Because the president is of its party, the minority leadership is expected to support his program; yet because it does not command a majority, the minority party leadership is incapable of passing that program without help. If the minority is large and the majority split, the minority party leadership may itself be able to build winning coalitions for the president's priorities. More frequently, however, the president will bargain with segments of the majority party on his own and sometimes with the majority party leadership itself. This, Jones suggests, is likely to lead to demoralization of the minority party.[128]

The study of member perceptions and expectations should include questions probing members' expectations about the relationship between their leaders and the president. The relationship itself can be systematically studied by relying primarily on the public record, supplemented by interviews.

Majority Party Leaders/Minority Party Leaders This relationship differs fundamentally in the House and Senate. The institutional environment is the critical determinant. The House is a majority-rule institution, and so long as the majority party leadership commands a majority on organizational and procedural questions, it need not consult the minority.[129] In the Senate, individuals have much greater resources to delay and obstruct, and a sizable minority can bring the chamber's business to a halt. Consequently, the majority and minority leaders work together on an almost continuous basis.[130] This relationship would be well worth studying systematically. A study of Senate floor scheduling would need to deal with the relationship between these leaders and might provide an excellent vantage point for further study.

House Party Leaders/Senate Party Leaders We know some about the (relatively infrequent) contacts between the House and Senate majority party leaders during the Carter years.[131] Contact was more formalized, more frequent, and warmer in the 100th Congress, but problems of coordination stemming from leaders' imperfect control over their party memberships and from differing institutional contexts remain.

A careful analysis of the mostly journalistic literature on relationships during the period of split control of the chambers combined with interviews (which should be done soon before memories fade) would provide some needed descriptive material and might shed light on the interrelationships of institution, majority status, and party. It is not direct interaction between leaders that is of primary interest here, but the impact one chamber's actions (actual and anticipated) had on the actions of party leaders in the other chamber. The president's role needs to be considered simultaneously.

Party Leaders/Groups   Only incidental evidence exists in this area, although a Ph.D. dissertation on group access to the leadership was under way as of 1989 by Diedra Sullivan Free of the University of Wisconsin. The relationship might be studied fruitfully in the context of case studies of coalition building.

Other Relationships   Other relationships that are important to the exercise of leadership are the rank-and-file member/committee leader relationship and the rank-and-file member/group relationship. Both committee leaders and groups can be either competitors of the party leadership for the allegiance of Congress members or allies of the leadership. These relationships are too complex to be totally incorporated into a study of party leadership. Nevertheless, some questions about member expectations of committee leaders should be included in the survey discussed earlier. We want to know whether member expectations of committee leaders hinder or help the party leadership in carrying out its tasks. The systematic case-studies project proposed below will shed light on both of these relationships.

Leadership Strategies

As an analytic starting point, we can posit coalition building (if understood to include agenda setting and policy formulation under some circumstances) and party maintenance as the primary functions of the congressional party leadership. (The various studies proposed in this chapter should lead to a refinement of that assumption.) This section will summarize what we know, what we hypothesize, and what we still need to learn about leadership strategies for performing these functions.

House Majority Party Leadership   Both the descriptive and the analytic literature on House majority party leadership is considerably more extensive than that on the other three congressional parties. An overview of the generalizations and hypotheses that emerge from that literature should reveal the dimensions scholars have considered important in describing leadership styles and strategies and the variables they have focused on as determinants.

Such a review reveals no agreement among students of congressional leadership on the most fruitful conceptualization of leadership styles and strategies. In fact, careful and comprehensive analytic consideration of the concepts of congressional leadership is lacking. What are the most useful dimensions of style? What is the range of possible strategies? These are questions that deserve attention.

Majority party leadership during the strong speakership era is usually described as centralized and powerful.[132] Certainly power in the House was centralized in the Speaker. His institutional resources combined with his role as leader of the majority party during a strong party era made it possible for the Speaker to dominate the House. Because party success was a prerequisite to reelection, the dictates of party maintenance and those of coalition-building success were usually in harmony. Speakers were expected to play a policy role. They could concentrate on mobilizing an existing majority; usually it was not necessary for them to create a majority through persuasion. In sum, an institutional structure that vested great resources in the Speaker, and a strong party system that made such an institutional structure possible and directly affected what members expected of their leaders, resulted in a leadership style that was centralized, mobilization based, and policy oriented.

The style of Sam Rayburn, the most highly regarded Speaker of the committee government era, however, is described as persuasion based and less policy oriented.[133] The possessor of much more meager institutional resources and leader of a factionalized party during a weak party era, Rayburn usually deferred to powerful committee chairmen on policy. He had to build coalitions and, given his limited resources, do so through persuasion and not command. The need to persuade dictated that Rayburn be heavily involved in doing favors for members.

Rayburn's style is also described as highly personalized. He made little use of party structures such as the whip system, party committees, or the caucus. Rather he relied on an informed network of colleagues for information and, in coalition building, he himself bargained with the key actors. Rayburn believed that the deep North/South split in the Democratic party could be best controlled by a personalized style that denied factions a forum, such as the caucus, for open conflict. The decentralized but highly unequal distribution of influence in the House that resulted in a very limited number of key actors made Rayburn's style possible. In sum, an institutional structure that limited the Speaker's resources and gave great powers to committees and their chairmen and a badly split party seem to account for Rayburn's personalized, persuasion-based, and service-oriented leadership style.[134]

The leadership styles of the Speakers of the postreform era are much less personalized than Rayburn's was; they continue to be persuasion based, and they are service oriented but also increasingly policy oriented.[135] The change in institutional structure that multiplied both the number of significant actors and member expectations of meaningful participation have dictated much more use of both formal and informal party structures for information gathering and coalition building.[136] Although leaders gained significant institutional resources, their impact on members' reelection continues to be marginal, and, consequently, leaders must persuade and not command or simply mobilize. The need to persuade to build winning coalitions, and rank-and-file members' resources for legislative participation, dictate a leadership style oriented toward providing services and favors for members. At the same time, however, the leadership is becoming increasingly policy oriented. The decrease in the power of committee chairmen and the increase in the leadership's institutional resources, particularly its gaining control over the Rules Committee and the institution of multiple referral, made possible greater party leadership involvement in policy—both in setting priorities and in the substance of policy. Democratic members' desire for policy successes vis-à-vis President Reagan accounts, in part, for the extent to which Speaker Wright took advantage of the possibility from 1987 to 1988.

Attempts to analyze the leaderships of Reed, Cannon, and Rayburn are limited by a far from complete factual base. Consequently, the characterizations of leadership styles have tended to be broad global ones of the sort discussed above. Using data obtained from participant observation and interviews, Sinclair has attempted to describe the component strategies of the O'Neill-Wright leadership style of the late 1970s and early 1980s.[137] A heavy reliance on positive inducements is one component; the leaders were engaged in the provision of services to their members collectively and of favors to them individually. Second, the leadership employed its formal powers and influence to structure the choice situation so as to advantage the outcome it favored. Third, the leadership attempted to include as many Democrats as possible in the coalition-building process. These three strategies were attempts to deal with the problems of coalition building within an unpredictable environment; structuring the choice situation through the use of restrictive rules, for example, reduces uncertainty. The strategies were also aimed at reconciling the dictates of party maintenance and coalition building. The strategy of inclusion, for example, provides members with opportunities to participate in the legislative process, which they covet, but channels that participation so that it benefits the party effort.

Sinclair's analysis thus provides further evidence for the importance of member expectations and of institutional structure and the consequent distribution of resources as central determinants of leadership styles and strategies.

To this point, our emphasis has been on leaders' styles and strategies vis-à-vis their members. A second important set of questions relates to leaders' strategies vis-à-vis the president.[138] If the president is of the same party, the majority party leadership is restricted in its choices; as discussed earlier, it is expected to build winning coalitions based on the president's legislative priorities. If the president is of the other party, however, the range of possible strategies is much greater: the congressional leadership can oppose the president's program; it can work with the president toward mutually agreeable policy outputs; or it can attempt to pass its own program over the president's objections. The intermediate compromise strategy actually consists of a family of strategies ranging from support of the president to hard bargaining.

What variables determine the strategy chosen? The literature, scholarly and journalistic, suggest that among the most important are the president's political strength, the ideological distance between the president and the majority party, and the size and cohesion of the majority and minority parties.

A politically strong president—one who is popular and politically adept—may refuse to compromise significantly, believing that he can sway enough majority party members to pass his own program, as Reagan did in 1981. The majority party leadership must then decide whether to support or oppose. We can hypothesize that the majority leadership's decision will be influenced by its party's ideological distance from the president and by the size and cohesion of its membership. Thus, in 1981, the Democratic leadership could not support Reagan's program because, for many of its members, that program was anathema to their notions of good public policy and to the interests of their constituencies. By contrast, Rayburn, faced with a popular president in the 1950s, pursued a strategy of compromise weighted often toward support. The small size and weak cohesion of his majority influenced his choice of strategy. Eisenhower's generally moderate policy stances presumably made the strategy choice possible. In 1987 and 1988, a weakened president and a sizable majority made a strategy of policy initiative on the part of the House Democratic leadership possible. Democratic members believed that policy initiatives stymied during the first six years of the Reagan administration had a real chance of passage, and they wanted a record of legislative accomplishment to bring to the 1988 elections. Those expectations made the aggressive policy-oriented leadership of Speaker Jim Wright possible. In general, the variables identified above not only have a direct effect on strategy choices but often appear to exert at least an equally important indirect effect through their impact on member expectations. Leaders must be sensitive to member expectations, and those expectations will influence strategy choices.

Although we know a good deal about majority party leadership styles and strategies, more research remains to be done. If a sufficient historical record exists, more detailed comparative analyses of majority leadership strategies in the past would be useful.[139] The frequency of divided control in the post-World War II period dictates more attention to leadership strategy choices under those circumstances. Of special interest is the leaderships' attempt to develop media strategies to counter the president.[140] In an age where the terms of the debate are often framed through the media, the congressional leaderships' attempts to challenge presidential domination are worthy of study.

House Minority Leadership   The most comprehensive work on House minority leadership is by Jones, although Ripley and Peabody have also contributed to our knowledge.[141] This work, however, is now descriptively dated, and, as mentioned earlier, research on how the minority party and its various organs function is very much needed.

In his book on the minority party in Congress, Jones concerns himself with the strategies open to the minority party in the process of majority building; with the conditions or variables that determine the range of choices; and with the choices actually made. He concludes that when the presidency is held by a politically strong president of the other party, and the national party unity of the minority is weak and its size small, the strategies available to the minority party are restricted. When the minority party controls the presidency, its strategic options are also limited; it is expected to participate in majority building. When the minority party faces a politically weak president of the other party and the minority is relatively large and cohesive, its strategic options are greatest.[142]

From an examination of several twentieth-century Congresses, Jones concludes that "the overall record of the minority party in this century is not impressive if one uses productivity under ideal circumstances as a measure. The minority party frequently failed to take advantage of such circumstances." [143] That the minority party frequently does not employ the more creative and positive strategies open to it seems due, in considerable part, to the lack of a direct payoff for doing so. "These strategies will probably not contribute significantly to electoral success for the minority party," adds Jones.[144] To the extent that the majority party can grab the credit, minority party innovation and cooperation may, in fact, have the counterproductive effect of keeping the majority party in power.[145]

Differences of opinion over the role the minority party should play in the policy process have been important in House Republican leadership contests and in other intraparty conflicts. Rep. Joe Martin, R-Mass., was deposed as minority leader in 1959 in part because he was seen as insufficiently aggressive and too inclined to cooperate with Rayburn. A desire for more positive strategies, particularly policy initiation, was critical in the defeat of Charles Halleck, R-Ind., by Gerald R. Ford, R-Mich., in 1965.[146] The conflict between younger and more ideological Republicans, many of them members of the Conservative Opportunity Society (COS), and more senior and pragmatic Republicans centers on such strategy questions. To simplify, the COS advocates presenting alternatives that are in sharp contrast to majority party programs, using all means to publicize its differences with the majority, and refusing to cooperate or compromise with the majority. In this case, as in the others, the argument hinges in large part on what strategy is most likely to contribute to the goal of majority status.

That the minority party leadership has a great deal more difficulty meeting the expectations of its members seems clear. Its resources are more meager than those of the majority leadership, and its members' ultimate goal is one they can little affect. Yet minority leaders are not routinely deposed nor is there any lack of candidates for leadership positions. The study of member expectations outlined above would shed light on how minority members adjust their expectations to unpalatable reality and on how tenuous that adjustment is.

A real understanding of minority leadership strategies ideally would be based on participant observation. How do the leaders themselves formulate their functions? What are the resources leaders possess, and how do they use them on a day-to-day basis to carry out their functions? To what extent do conflicting expectations among their members influence their choice of strategies? To what extent do unmeetable expectations have that effect? Are time, energy, and resources diverted to activities actually undertaken for party-maintenance reasons (highly visible but futile floor battles, for example) that could be better used elsewhere? More generally, how does the Republican House leadership deal with its competitors (Robert Bauman, R-Md., and others in the late 1970s, the COS in the early 1990s), and what are the consequences for the exercise of leadership?

By studying minority party leadership in the House from the dual perspective of member expectations and leadership activities, an understanding may emerge of the problems of a permanent minority for both the party and Congress. Jones argues that a minority party pursuing aggressive, positive strategies can make important contributions to the policy process but that the incentives for the minority to play that role are at best ambiguous. If the Democrats were to regain control of the White House, the House Republican minority might well pursue a highly aggressive strategy combining the advocacy of policy alternatives with noncooperation in the legislative process. The consequences would be interesting to behold.

Senate Majority Leadership No Senate leader, majority or minority, has been as extensively chronicled as Lyndon Johnson.[147] All accounts agree that Johnson took a position with meager formal powers and made it one of substantial influence. Most suggest that in addition to his formidable personality, Johnson's influence was the result of his centrality in the Senate communications network and in Senate bargaining. Neither came to him simply by virtue of the position he held. Rather he worked at being better informed than anyone else, and that information then made him better equipped than anyone else to broker many agreements. Thus, Johnson knew what other senators wanted and what they needed. Huitt emphasizes Johnson's sensitivity to helping other senators "maximize their effectiveness in playing their personal roles in the Senate" as critical to the success of his leadership.[148]

Compared with that of Johnson, the leadership of Mike Mansfield was low-keyed and permissive.[149] While differences in personality contributed to their different leadership styles, so, too, did changing member expectations. The large liberal Democratic class of 1958 wanted bolder policy initiatives than Johnson pursued and broader opportunities to participate in the legislative process than the Senate then provided junior members.[150] Johnson's last two years as leader are generally considered less successful than the earlier part of his tenure. Mansfield's style seems to have been suited to these new member expectations. Certainly his style maximized individual senators' leeway to participate in the legislative process and to pursue their own policy preferences. It seems likely, however, that the White House's heavy involvement in coalition building during the 1960s, which made the tremendous legislative successes of the Great Society possible, was an important contributor to Democrats' satisfaction.[151]

The majority leaderships of Byrd, Baker, and Dole have been insightfully discussed by Peabody, Ornstein, and Ornstein, Peabody and Rohde.[152] Taken in conjunction with the work on Johnson and Mansfield, that literature points to the need for a better delineation of the dimensions of style and, very clearly in the case of the Senate, for further research to be accompanied by some basic empirical work. Sinclair's study of House leadership strategies shows how closely those strategies are tied to the institutional and party tasks leaders perform.[153] Thus, some of the most important favors leaders can do for members and many of the tactics they use in coalition building stem from their floor-scheduling responsibilities. Almost certainly the same is true for the Senate majority party leadership. Consequently, we need a much more detailed understanding of what the Senate majority leader does on a day-to-day basis. Because it is the key task delegated to the leadership and one that affects all senators, floor scheduling should be the focus of such a study.

The position of Senate leader appears to be less institutionalized and consequently more variable with personality than the position of Speaker.[154] Nevertheless, many of the same variables systematically affect leadership styles and strategies in both chambers. Most of the generalizations and hypotheses about congressional leadership strategies vis-à-vis the president apply to both houses. Clearly, variations in institutional resources and in member expectations will affect strategies in both the Senate and the House. Senate rules are such that the potential for strong party leadership is considerably less than in the House. The expectations of members also seem to place greater constraints on Senate leaders.[155] The study of member expectations proposed earlier would provide data to test the hypothesis that member expectations in the Senate are such that the dictates of party maintenance conflict with those of coalition building to a greater extent than in the House, independent of the ideological heterogeneity of the party membership. For example, senators seem to expect that their individual convenience will be considered highly in their leaders' scheduling decisions, which presumably makes strategic scheduling much more difficult.

Senate Minority Leadership   Jones's study of minority party leadership covers both the Senate and the House, and his conclusions summarized earlier apply to both chambers. Differences in institutional structure do have some effect. "The structure and norms of the Senate seem more accommodating to creativity among individual minority party members and less accommodating to creativity within the minority party as such," he writes.[156] Because Senate rules and norms make it possible for the individual senator, whether of the minority or the majority, to exercise considerable influence in the policy process, senators have even less incentive than their House counterparts to make the party into a positive policy instrument.[157]

To go beyond Jones in our understanding of Senate minority leadership strategies, we need a similar basic descriptive work for the majority. Because Senate rules are so permissive, the minority leader is much more involved in floor scheduling in the Senate than in the House. His or her role in floor scheduling and floor leadership might well be the most productive focus for an initial study. Ideally, participating observers located in the majority and minority leaders' offices would study floor scheduling and floor leadership simultaneously. By cooperating, the two could develop a much more complete picture of how these tasks are carried out on a day-to-day basis since considerable consultation between the leaders appears to be involved. More important, a leader's strategy choices in the Senate almost certainly depend on the choices of his or her counterpart in the other party. Having the perspective of both offices would aid immeasurably in an attempt to disentangle such complex interrelationships.

A particularly interesting but difficult question to answer definitively concerns the impact on leadership strategies of the alternations in partisan control in the Senate. Does the Senate minority or the Senate majority act differently as a result of having recently held the other status, or as a result of the prospect that the status may change again? We know that new majorities tend to be more cohesive.[158] The new Republican majority in 1981 clearly fit this pattern, and the new Democratic majority in 1987 did also, although because a new president was not brought in, the impact on policy was less. Davidson and Oleszek's study of the impact of the switch from Democratic to Republican control combined with the journalistic literature on 1987 suggests no dramatic effect on majority party behavior beyond the impact on cohesion.[159] Whether there were more subtle effects on member expectations and leadership strategies would be worth examination. The impact on the minority is of greater theoretical interest. Both the Democrats' response to unexpected minority status after 1981 and the Republicans' much more aggressive response in 1987 and 1988 deserve study. We can compare Republican behavior and leadership strategies in the House and Senate, but differences cannot all be attributed to the change-in-status variable. If Senate Republican members and leaders behave differently from their House counterparts, their having recently been the majority may be, in part, responsible. However, the differences in institutional structure certainly are also a determinant. For example, Minority Leader Dole's strategy of aggressively using the filibuster to block Democratic initiatives in 1987 obviously depended on Senate rules.

Other Leaders

Democratic lawmaking, Congress's chief function, can be conceptualized as consisting of the identification and focus of attention on a problem or issue; the formulation of a policy response; and the building of a winning coalition to back the policy response. This conceptualization is a simplification for analytic convenience. Nevertheless, it captures enough of the complexity of democratic lawmaking to highlight the need to consider those other than party leaders if we are to understand the process. As pointed out earlier, the literature suggests that the extent to which party leaders have been involved in the three aspects has varied over time and varies with majority or minority status, party of the president, and chamber. Committee leaders' involvement has also varied, depending on institutional structure, particularly the distribution of influence between party and committee leaders, the president's party and legislative role, and a host of variables that distinguish committees from one another.[160]

If a member of Congress who takes the lead in performing one or another of these functions on a particular issue is defined as a congressional leader, then clearly party and committee leaders are not the only significant congressional leaders. We can find examples throughout history of other members taking a lead role in publicizing a problem, formulating a policy response, or building a winning coalition on a particular piece of legislation. Scholars agree that the changes in congressional structure and in the distribution of resources during the late 1960s and the 1970s greatly increased the opportunities for ordinary members to play leadership roles.

As a phenomenon of the postreform period, the informal leader or policy entrepreneur has received some research attention. Uslaner did some early work identifying the phenomenon.[161] Loomis's research on the House class of 1974 deals with both informal issue leadership and self-promotion within a group considered particularly important to the development of the phenomenon.[162] Sinclair and Smith discuss informal leadership in the Senate;[163] both argue that the rules and norms of the contemporary Senate provide vast opportunities for individual members to take the lead on particular issues. Stevens, Mulhollan, and Rundquist, and Hammond et al. examine congressional caucuses as one aspect of the phenomenon.[164] Sinclair and Baker analyze party leadership strategies of inclusion as a response to the phenomenon.[165]

A number of scholars and many journalists have questioned whether the activity observed is really policy leadership or simply self-promotion.[166] That the modal representative or senator is more active now than in the 1950s or even the 1960s seems clear, but is this activity genuinely aimed at publicizing a problem, shaping debate, formulating solutions, or building coalitions? Or is it empty grandstanding aimed solely at reelection?

Hammond contends that "our understanding of House leadership is incomplete without consideration of the informal leadership system." She defines informal leaders as "those members who do not occupy positions of formal leadership within the party structure and do not have formal responsibility for coordinating the work of the House, but who shape the work of the House as leaders of committees, subcommittees, and groups of members, or through individual expertise or force of ideas." She then divides informal leaders into "leaders with portfolio"—those having an organizational base as committee or subcommittee leaders, caucus chairs, or discussion-group heads—and "leaders without portfolio"—issues leaders, coalition builders, or strategists who do not have an organizational base. (See Chap. 5.)

An understanding of informal leadership in Congress requires answers to these questions: How frequently do members who are not party (or committee) leaders take a lead role in some aspect of the legislative process? Does this vary with the stage of the process? For example, is informal leadership more likely in publicizing issues and shaping debate than in coalition building? Does frequency vary with the nature of the issue? Smith hypothesizes, for example, that new issues, less partisan issues, and issues that cut across committee jurisdictions are more likely to highlight informal leaders' involvement. (See Chap. 4.) How do the opportunities for informal leadership vary with majority versus minority status, party of the president, and chamber? How do members become informal leaders? What are the most typical bases or credentials for informal leadership? Is this related to the stage of the legislative process? That is, do informal leaders who publicize problems have different characteristics than those engaged in coalition building?

Is informal leadership more frequently undertaken in cooperation or in competition with the party leadership? More generally, how do such leaders assist or impede the work of party leaders?

To answer these questions, we must be able to identify legitimate informal leaders and distinguish them from the grandstanders. Whether or not we include committee leaders among informal leaders as Hammond does, her definition and categorization of these leaders make clear the broad variety of possible bases and the ambiguity of possible credentials—for example, issue expertise and forceful oratory. These problems suggest a research strategy that begins not with the leader but with the issue and the act of leadership. While it cannot be done with absolute precision, determining who is taking a lead role on an issue may nevertheless be done well enough to satisfy most scholars. Consequently, a study of informal leadership should begin by identifying issues and proceed to identifying leaders on those issues. Starting there would make the questions asked above much more tractable. Steven Smith's study of policy leadership proceeded in somewhat this fashion and can serve as a model. (See Chap. 5.)

Legislative Success and Leadership Success

Legislative success is the most commonly employed criterion of congressional leadership success. As building winning coalitions is a central leadership function, legislative success is certainly a reasonable criterion. Defining legislative success, however, is not without its problems. In his study of majority party success from 1901 to 1966, Ripley bases his judgment on the measurement of output versus the requests and expectations of the president and the majority party leaders themselves and on the standards of those in a position to judge the activities of the Congress at the time it met.[167]

From a detailed examination of ten Congresses, Ripley concludes that truncated majorities—those facing a president of the other party— were least likely to be successful.[168] Not surprisingly, split control tends to produce relatively unsatisfactory results for the minority party and the president as well.[169] The Reagan presidency, especially in 1981 and 1982, could be cited as a major exception, but the president's party did control one chamber and that control was critical to Reagan's significant legislative success in those years.

In addition, Ripley finds that if control is united and the president is a legislative activist, then the larger the majority, the greater the chances for legislative success. Also a new majority is more likely to be legislatively successful than an established majority. A president involved with the majority leadership in the planning of legislative tactics and a majority leadership that is innovative similarly contribute to legislative success.[170]

Other work suggests that party cohesion is also a critical variable.[171] Voting cohesion may be impacted by the majority party leadership; persuasion efforts and strategies to influence the choice situation members face are aimed at doing exactly that.[172] Yet these efforts affect only the margins. Party cohesion is basically a function of the members' ties to their districts and of the homogeneity or heterogeneity of those districts. This constituency-based party cohesion frequently varies across issues and, consequently, voting cohesion in the Congress will depend on the congressional agenda.[173]

Relatively few of the determinants of legislative success are under the control of the majority party leadership. The president, and the size and "natural" cohesiveness of the majority and minority, are largely beyond the leadership's control. The leadership will have somewhat more, although by no means total, control of the congressional agenda, and we would expect a skillful leadership to adjust the agenda to conditions. Under favorable conditions, a more ambitious agenda should be laid out, but whatever the conditions, issues that maximize natural cohesion should be emphasized and those that split the party avoided. We would expect the president to make similar calculations.[174]

If, in fact, agendas are thus adjusted, using the requests and expectations of the president and the majority party as the basis for judging legislative success presents obvious problems. That approach should not simply be abandoned, however; instead, we should study how those requests and expectations developed.

Legislative success is not the only criterion of leadership success commonly employed. Scholars, journalists, and Capitol Hill insiders all rank Sam Rayburn and Lyndon Johnson as more successful leaders than Mike Mansfield and John McCormack, D-Mass. Yet if legislative success were the only criterion used, the leaders during the highly productive Congresses of the mid-1960s would necessarily outrank those of the much less legislatively productive 1950s. The majorities Johnson and Rayburn led were small and rent with factions, and the presidency was controlled by the other party. During the most productive Congresses of the 1960s, in contrast, the Democratic majorities were very large, and a skillful and activist Democrat was president. The consensus judgment thus must rest upon how well a leader performed given the circumstances confronting him. To systematically make and substantiate such relative judgments requires more analytic sophistication and perhaps more empirical data than we now possess, but it is a worthy goal.

In sum, the literature suggests that skillful congressional leadership is neither a necessary nor a sufficient condition for legislative success. Conditions can stack the deck against highly skillful leaders; conversely, a strong and skillful president may provide leadership when the congressional leadership is weak.

That the impact of the party leadership is constrained by circumstances does not make it unimportant. We know that the majority party leadership in the House plays a central role in coalition building and is increasingly more involved in agenda setting and in policy substance. The changes the House underwent in the 1970s have made a stronger integrative party leadership role necessary if the institution is to carry out its key function of democratic lawmaking. Although our understanding is far from complete, the Senate majority party leadership seems to have been less successful in coping with change. Given its meager institutional resources, the Senate majority leadership seems to play a lesser role in all aspects of the legislative process than its House counterpart. On the other hand, the current Senate is extremely well suited to the policy entrepreneur; rules, norms, and the distribution of resources give the individual senator broad opportunities to play a leadership role.

A definitive assessment of the contribution of congressional leaders to the performance of the key congressional function of democratic lawmaking awaits answers to the myriad of questions posed above. As this review has made clear, we already have considerable although spotty knowledge about various congressional leaders' direct contribution to agenda setting, policy formulation, and coalition building. Our knowledge of leaders' party maintenance activities is less but has received some research attention. In contrast, institutional maintenance has received almost no attention—especially as a consideration in leadership decision making.[175]

A final suggestion for future research is that this critical question be given some attention: To what extent are various leaders aware of the possible institutional consequences of their actions? Which leaders, if any, take such consequences into account in making their decisions and to what effect?

Congressional Leadership— A Proposed Research Agenda in Summary

Within the American political system, the U.S. Congress is expected to make laws that are responsive to the views and needs of a majority of the citizenry and to do so in a way that allows the full range of significant views among the citizenry to be heard. How close Congress comes to meeting this ideal of democratic lawmaking depends, at least in part, on congressional leadership. Yet whether defined narrowly as party leadership, or more broadly to include committee and informal leadership, congressional leadership is a far from exhaustively studied phenomenon. Before we can assess its contribution to democratic lawmaking, considerable empirical and analytic work needs to be done.

Congressional scholars agree that congressional leadership is best understood from a contextual perspective. The external context and the institutional environment shape and constrain leadership styles and strategies. Since party leaders are chosen by their members, the expectations of those members should be a primary determinant of leadership behavior. Those expectations seem strongly influenced by the character of the link between members and their constituencies, which is itself a function of the character of the party system. The character of that link— whether it is mediated by strong party loyalties and organization or is direct and personal—along with the homogeneity or heterogeneity of party members' districts, largely determines the party membership's ideological like-mindedness; that, in turn, affects what leaders can do and very likely what their members expect them to do. The size of the party membership is another critical contextual variable, also affecting leaders' capabilities and probably members' expectations. How the institution distributes resources through rules and how it conditions the use of resources through norms strongly influence the relationship between leaders and members and consequently leadership styles and strategies.

By consensus, the relationship between party leaders and their members is the most critical relationship to understand. We know a good deal about this relationship from indirect evidence. Thus, the character of the link between members and their constituencies and the institutional environment are believed to be important determinants of that relationship and how it has varied over time. There are also a number of interesting hypotheses about how the relationship varies with majority versus minority status and chamber. Yet direct evidence of members' perceptions and expectations of their leaders is sparse. The first of the two large-scale studies proposed herein seeks to remedy that situation.

A systematic study of members' expectations of, perceptions of, and interactions with the party leadership (and committee leaders) should be undertaken. A random sample stratified by party, seniority, and, for Democrats, region should be taken in both the House and Senate. Serious thought should be given to supplementing this with a sample of committee leaders. Their expectations of party leaders are clearly important and may well be different from those of other members. Rank-and-file members should be questioned about their relationship with committee leaders as well because that relationship is intrinsically important and will provide a basis of comparison for their responses about party leaders.

Such a survey would allow us to test a number of interesting hypotheses and would provide a baseline against which future change could be measured. Some of the questions such a study would enable us to answer are: How do members themselves formulate their expectations of the leadership? What can the leaders do for and to their members, as perceived by members? How do members rank the importance of various possible leadership functions/tasks? What are the bounds of legitimate leadership activity?

Is there a consensus on leadership functions? If not, how do expectations of the leadership vary with member characteristics such as seniority, ideology (especially whether the member is in the party mainstream or not), electoral situation (safe seat or not), institutional position (does the member hold a committee leadership position? Does he or she hold a lesser party position such as appointed whip?), and, most important, minority or majority status and chamber?

Do member expectations provide the basis for relatively strong, policy-oriented majority party leadership in either chamber?

Are member expectations of leaders different in the House and Senate? Is there, in fact, a basis for stronger leadership in member expectations in the House?

Are the expectations of minority party members, especially in the House, inherently unmeetable?

As members define leadership, is it primarily an in-house job (as we believe it used to be), or do members currently expect leaders to represent their party and chamber to the public? (Has the changing role of the media, especially television, in American politics changed what members expect leaders to do?)

If we are to understand congressional leadership, we must explore the interrelationships and interactions among the significant actors in the legislative process. As the most important, the leader/member relationship requires study from both leadership and membership points of view.

Yet party leaders and rank-and-file members are clearly not the only significant actors. Within the chamber, committee leaders are also likely to be important, and, according to both scholars and participants, informal leaders are now often important as well. Outside the chamber, the president will usually be a significant actor, and interest groups will sometimes be considered significant.

We expect that the character of these interrelationships and interactions, including the behavioral strategies employed by the various actors, will depend on variables such as majority or minority status, chamber, and the party of the president. Thus, the strategies of the majority and minority party leaderships and of Senate and House party leaderships should differ because their resources differ. Institutional arrangements give the House majority leadership much greater resources vis-à-vis its membership and the minority than the Senate majority leadership has. Both minority and majority leadership strategies are likely to depend also on whether a fellow partisan is president. The relationship between party and committee leaders may well be different when the president is of their party than during periods of divided control. Current knowledge also leads us to expect variations across issues. On certain types of issues—

those considered especially critical to the party or its core constituencies, for example—party leadership involvement should be extensive; other types of issues should provide more opportunities for informal leaders.

Given the expectation of variation across issues, the problems in identifying informal leaders, and the sheer complexity of the interrelationships and how they vary, a focus on instances of leadership may be more productive for a major study than a focus on leaders. The second major study proposed here would begin with the selection of a number of issues or policy controversies. Care should be taken to represent a range of issue types, although those expected to elicit controversy, to proceed through at least a significant part of the process, and to stimulate significant coalition-building efforts would be overrepresented. A team of researchers large enough to gather data on the full set of actors and relationships would follow the issue from inception to conclusion during a Congress. At each noteworthy point in the process, the researchers would gather information on the activities and perspectives of the majority and minority party leaderships, the majority and minority committee leaderships (House and Senate where appropriate), and other actors (members and groups) identified as significant. (Some reading on the perspective of both majority and minority rank-and-file members would be invaluable, but systematic data would be prohibitively expensive to obtain.) At the core of these interviews should be a standard set of questions, which would be supplemented by questions that varied with the respondent's position and with the issue and circumstances.

Properly done, such a study would provide comparable data on a number of instances of leadership. It would provide a much sounder basis than currently available for answering the complex and sophisticated questions about congressional leadership that the literature suggests.

There are a great many smaller studies appropriate for the individual researcher that would contribute significantly to our understanding of congressional leadership. Hypotheses and research topics are scattered throughout the text. Only those deemed most important are repeated here.

We know vastly more about the House Democratic leadership than about the three other congressional parties. Good descriptive work on the House Republican leadership and both party leaderships in the Senate is needed. That work should include examination of the various party structures (for example, the whip system, conference, committee on committees, and policy committee). A focus on these structures would be especially productive in the House, where they are more likely to be critical to the functioning of party leadership. In the Senate, the single best perspective might focus on floor scheduling. Floor scheduling is the key task delegated to the party leadership; it affects all members and involves both majority and minority leaders. The task is very much affected by Senate rules and norms (unlimited debate, nongermane amendments, members' willingness to exploit unlimited debate, expectations that leaders accommodate individual senators), and also how the task is performed affects outcomes.

Before we can progress much further in explaining why leadership styles and strategies vary, we need analytic work to clarify the advantages and disadvantages of various conceptualizations of leadership styles and strategies. Currently, global characterizations lacking clear theoretical derivations or empirical referents are often used. In other cases, the conceptualization is more clearly spelled out but discusses only one or two dimensions.

Such analytic work is most likely to be fruitful if it progresses in conjunction with the sort of empirical work recommended above. Researchers doing empirical studies should be sensitive to the analytic task but also to the need for indicators, preferably quantitative, of the conceptual dimensions at which they arrive. To take an obvious but important example, the activity rate of leaders in the legislative process is central to leadership style and presumably has varied across leaders. An activity rate properly defined lends itself to measurement. Yet no systematic work on developing quantitative indicators has been undertaken.

Notes

1. Robert L. Peabody, "Leadership in Legislatures: Evolution, Selection, Functions," *Legislative Studies Quarterly* 9 (August 1984): 441.
2. See Roger Davidson and Walter J. Oleszek, *Congress and Its Members*, 3d ed. (Washington, D.C.: CQ Press, 1989); Charles O. Jones, *The United States Congress: People, Place and Policy* (Homewood, Ill.: Dorsey Press, 1982); and John W. Kingdon, *Agendas, Alternatives and Public Policies* (Boston: Little, Brown, 1984).
3. Barbara Sinclair, *Majority Leadership in the U.S. House* (Baltimore: Johns Hopkins University Press, 1983).
4. Joseph Cooper, "Congress in Organizational Perspective," in *Congress Reconsidered*, ed. Lawrence C. Dodd and Bruce I. Oppenheimer (New York: Praeger, 1977).
5. This follows Richard Fenno, *Congressmen in Committees* (Boston: Little, Brown, 1973).
6. See Joseph Cooper and David W. Brady, "Institutional Context and Leadership Style: The House from Cannon to Rayburn," *American Political Science Review* 75 (June 1981): 411-425; and Gary C. Jacobson, *The Politics of Congressional Elections*, 2d ed. (Boston: Little, Brown, 1987).
7. David Brady, Joseph Cooper, and Pat Hurley, "Legislative Potential for Policy Changes: The House of Representatives," *Legislative Studies Quar-*

terly 4 (August 1977): 385-398; Aage Clausen, *How Congressmen Decide* (New York: St. Martin's, 1973); George C. Edwards, *Presidential Influence in Congress* (San Francisco: W. H. Freeman, 1980); Charles O. Jones, *The Minority Party in Congress* (Boston: Little, Brown, 1970); Randall B. Ripley, *Majority Party Leadership in Congress* (Boston: Little, Brown, 1969); and Barbara Sinclair, *Congressional Realignment* (Austin: University of Texas Press, 1982) and *Majority Leadership in the U.S. House* (Baltimore: Johns Hopkins University Press, 1983).

8. David Brady, *Congressional Voting in a Partisan Era* (Lawrence: University of Kansas Press, 1973); and Cooper and Brady, "Institutional Context and Leadership Style."

9. Ibid. Barbara Sinclair, "Party Leadership and Policy Change," in *Congress and Policy Change*, ed. Gerald Wright, Leroy N. Rieselbach, and Lawrence C. Dodd (New York: Agathon Press, 1986).

10. Jacobson, *Politics of Congressional Elections*; Barbara Hinckley, "The American Voter in Congressional Elections," *American Political Science Review* 74 (September 1980): 641-650; and Michael J. Robinson, "Three Faces of Congressional Media," in *The New Congress*, ed. Thomas E. Mann and Norman J. Ornstein (Washington, D.C.: American Enterprise Institute, 1981). The 1988 Senate election study component of the National Election Study should soon fill some of the lacunae in our knowledge.

11. See especially Gerald H. Kramer, "Short-Term Fluctuations in U.S. Voting Behavior, 1896-1964," *American Political Science Review* 65 (1971): 131-143; and, for a selection of recent literature, Richard G. Neimi and Herbert F. Weisberg, eds., *Controversies in Voting Behavior*, 2d ed. (Washington, D.C.: CQ Press, 1984).

12. Gary C. Jacobson and Samuel Kernell, *Strategy and Choice in Congressional Elections* (New Haven, Conn.: Yale University Press, 1981).

13. Eric Uslaner and Margaret Conway, "The Responsible Electorate: Watergate, the Economy and Vote Choice in 1974," *American Political Science Review* 79 (1985): 788-803.

14. Ripley, *Majority Party Leadership in Congress*; and Barbara Sinclair, "Determinants of Aggregate Party Cohesion in the U.S. House of Representatives, 1901-1956," *Legislative Studies Quarterly* 2 (1977): 155-175.

15. Barbara Sinclair, "Agenda Control and Policy Success: The Case of Ronald Reagan and the 97th House," *Legislative Studies Quarterly* 20 (1985): 291-314; and Darrell West, *Congress and Economic Policymaking* (Pittsburgh: University of Pittsburgh Press, 1987).

16. Doris A. Graber, ed., *Media Power in Politics*, 2d ed. (Washington, D.C.: CQ Press, 1989); Austin Ranney, *Channels of Power* (New York: Basic Books, 1983); and Richard L. Rubin, *Press, Party and Presidency* (New York: Norton, 1981).

17. Richard Fenno, *The United States Senate: A Bicameral Perspective* (Washington, D.C.: American Enterprise Institute, 1982).

18. See Robinson, "Three Faces of Congressional Media."

19. See Bob Benenson, "Savvy 'Stars' Making Local TV a Potent Tool," *Congressional Quarterly Weekly Report*, July 18, 1987, 1551-1555.

20. See Robinson, "Three Faces of Congressional Media."

21. See Norman J. Ornstein and Barbara Sinclair, "Senate Styles and Senate Decision-Making, 1955-1980," *Journal of Politics* 46 (1986): 877-908. Related arguments are made in Hugh Heclo, "Issue Networks and the Executive Establishment," in *The New American Political System*, ed. Anthony King (Washington, D.C.: American Enterprise Institute, 1978); Anthony King, "The American Polity in the Late 1970s: Building Coalitions in the Sand," in *The New American Political System*, ed. Anthony King (Washington, D.C.: American Enterprise Institute, 1978); and Thomas L. Gais, Mark A. Peterson, and Jack L. Walker, "Interest Groups, Iron Triangles and Representative Institutions in American National Government," *British Journal of Political Science* 14 (1984): 161-185.

22. Timothy Cook, "House Members as Newsmakers: The Effects of Televising Congress," *Legislative Studies Quarterly* 11 (1986): 203-226; Stephen Hess, *The Ultimate Insiders: U.S. Senators in the National Media* (Washington, D.C.: Brookings Institution, 1986).

23. Barbara Sinclair, *The Transformation of the U.S. Senate* (Baltimore: Johns Hopkins University Press, 1989).

24. Ibid. See also Burdett Loomis, *The New American Politician* (New York: Basic Books, 1988).

25. Jack L. Walker, "The Origin and Maintenance of Interest Groups in America," *American Political Science Review* 77 (1983): 390-406; Kay Lehman Scholzman and John T. Tierney, *Organized Interests and American Democracy* (New York: Harper and Row, 1986).

26. Cooper, "Congress in Organizational Perspective"; Cooper and Brady, "Institutional Context and Leadership Style"; Roger Davidson, "The Legislative Work of Congress" (Paper presented at the annual meeting of the American Political Science Association, Washington, D.C., 1986).

27. Mary Parker Follett, *The Speaker of the House of Representatives* (New York: Bert Franklin Reprints, 1974), 25-26. Originally published in 1896.

28. Ibid., 69.

29. Ibid., 71-72.

30. Ibid., 96.

31. See Randall B. Ripley, *Party Leaders in the House of Representatives* (Washington, D.C.: Brookings Institution, 1967), 16-17.

32. See Stanley Bach, "Suspension of the Rules in the House of Representatives," Report No. 86-103, Congressional Research Service, 1986, and "Arranging the Legislative Agenda of the House of Representatives: The Impact of Legislative Rules and Practices," Report No. 86-110, Congressional Research Service, 1986; Bruce I. Oppenheimer et al., *A History of the Committee on Rules* (Washington, D.C.: U.S. Government Printing Office, 1983); and Follett, *The Speaker of the House.*

33. Cooper and Brady, "Institutional Context and Leadership Style."

34. Ripley, *Party Leaders in the House*, 24-25; and George B. Galloway, *History of the House of Representatives* (New York: Thomas Y. Crowell, 1961).

35. Ripley, *Party Leaders in the House*, 28.

36. Ibid., 33

37. Ibid., 32-34; Ripley, *Majority Party Leadership in Congress*, 3.

38. Lawrence C. Dodd, "The Expanded Roles of the House Democratic Whip System: The 93rd and 94th Congresses," *Congressional Studies* 7 (1979): 27-56; Sinclair, *Majority Leadership in the U.S. House.* Also see the membership list published by Congressional Quarterly in its special report on committee memberships for each Congress.
39. Randall B. Ripley, *Power in the Senate* (New York: St. Martin's, 1969), 24 passim.
40. Ibid.; Robert L. Peabody, *Leadership in Congress: Stability, Succession and Change* (Boston: Little, Brown, 1976); and David Rothman, *Politics and Power: The U.S. Senate 1869-1901* (Cambridge: Harvard University Press, 1966).
41. Floyd M. Riddick, *Majority and Minority Leaders of the U.S. Senate: History and Development of the Offices of Floor Leaders*, S. Doc. 97-12, 97th Cong., 1st sess. (Washington, D.C.: U.S. Government Printing Office, 1981), 4-6.
42. Ibid., 14.
43. Cooper and Brady, "Institutional Context and Leadership Style"; and Sinclair, "Party Leadership and Policy Change."
44. Ripley, *Majority Party Leadership in Congress*, 4.
45. For some examples, see Follett, *The Speaker of the House*; and William A. Robinson, *Thomas B. Reed, Parliamentarian* (New York: Dodd, Mead, 1930).
46. Cooper and Brady, "Institutional Context and Leadership Style," 27.
47. Ibid.; Sinclair, "Party Leadership and Policy Change."
48. C. R. Atkinson, *The Committee on Rules and the Overthrow of Speaker Cannon* (New York: Columbia University Press, 1911); Kenneth W. Hechler, *Insurgency* (New York: Columbia University Press, 1940); and L. White Busby, *Uncle Joe Cannon* (New York: Henry Holt, 1927). See also the fine analysis by Charles O. Jones, "Joseph G. Cannon and Howard W. Smith: An Essay on the Limits of Leadership in the House of Representatives," *Journal of Politics* 30 (1968): 617-646.
49. Nelson W. Polsby, "The Institutionalization of the U.S. House of Representatives," *American Political Science Review* 62 (1968): 144-168.
50. H. Douglas Price, "Congress and the Evolution of Legislative Professionalism," in *Congress in Change: Evolution and Reform*, ed. Norman J. Ornstein (New York: Praeger, 1975).
51. Cooper and Brady, "Institutional Context and Leadership Style"; and Sinclair, "Party Leadership and Policy Change."
52. Sinclair, "Party Leadership and Policy Change," 31.
53. Ibid., 34.
54. Ripley, *Party Leaders in the House*, 6. See also Richard F. Fenno, "The Internal Distribution of Influence: The House," in *The Congress and America's Future*, ed. David B. Truman (Englewood Cliffs, N.J.: Prentice-Hall, 1965).
55. John F. Manley, "Wilbur D. Mills: A Study of Congressional Leadership," *American Political Science Review* 63 (1969): 442-464.
56. Cooper and Brady," Institutional Context and Leadership Style"; and Richard Bolling, *House Out of Order* (New York: Dutton, 1965).

57. Sinclair, *Congressional Realignment*.

58. See Richard F. Fenno, *The Power of the Purse* (Boston: Little, Brown, 1966) and *Congressmen in Committees*.

59. Milton C. Cummings and Robert L. Peabody, "The Decision to Enlarge the Committee on Rules: An Analysis of the 1961 Vote," in *New Perspectives on the House of Representatives*, ed. Robert L. Peabody and Nelson W. Polsby, 2d ed. (Chicago: Rand McNally, 1969); Roger H. Davidson, "Congressional Leaders as Agents of Change," in *Understanding Congressional Leadership*, ed. Frank H. Mackaman (Washington, D.C.: CQ Press, 1981); David W. Rohde, "Committee Reform in the House of Representatives and the Subcommittee Bill of Rights," *Annals of the American Academy of Political and Social Science* 411 (1974): 39-47; Lawrence C. Dodd and Bruce I. Oppenheimer, *Congress Reconsidered* (New York: Praeger, 1977), 2d ed. (Washington, D.C.: CQ Press, 1981); Norman J. Ornstein, *Congress in Change* (New York: Praeger, 1975); Leroy N. Rieselbach, *Congressional Reform in the Seventies* (Morristown, N.J.: General Learning Press, 1977); and Thomas E. Mann and Norman J. Ornstein, eds., *The New Congress* (Washington, D.C.: American Enterprise Institute, 1981).

60. Bolling, *House Out of Order*.

61. Bruce I. Oppenheimer, "The Rules Committee: New Arm of Leadership in a Decentralized House," in *Congress Reconsidered*, ed. Lawrence C. Dodd and Bruce I. Oppenheimer (New York: Praeger, 1977) and "The Changing Relationship Between House Leadership and the Committee on Rules," in *Understanding Congressional Leadership*, ed. Frank H. Mackaman (Washington, D.C.: CQ Press, 1981); Sinclair, *Majority Leadership in the U.S. House;* Janet Hook, "GOP Chafes Under Restrictive House Rules," *Congressional Quarterly Weekly Report*, October 10, 1987, 2450-2453; and Stanley Bach and Steven S. Smith, *Managing Uncertainty in the House of Representatives* (Washington, D.C.: Brookings Institution, 1988).

62. John W. Ellwood and James A. Thurber, "The Politics of the Congressional Budget Process Re-examined," in *Congress Reconsidered*, ed. Lawrence C. Dodd and Bruce I. Oppenheimer, 2d ed. (Washington, D.C.: CQ Press, 1981).

63. Harrison Fox and Susan Webb Hammond, *Congressional Staffs* (New York: The Free Press, 1977); Michael Malbin, *Unelected Representatives* (New York: Basic Books, 1980); and Norman J. Ornstein et al., *Vital Statistics on Congress 1984-85* (Washington, D.C.: American Enterprise Institute, 1984).

64. David R. Mayhew, "Congressional Elections: The Case of the Vanishing Marginals," *Polity* 6 (1974): 295-317 and *Congress: The Electoral Connection* (New Haven, Conn.: Yale University Press, 1974); Morris P. Fiorina, *Congress: Keystone of the Washington Establishment* (New Haven, Conn.: Yale University Press, 1977). See also Richard F. Fenno, *Home Style* (Boston: Little, Brown, 1978).

65. Herbert B. Asher, "The Learning of Legislative Norms," *American Political Science Review* 67 (1973): 449-513; Burdett A. Loomis, "The 'Me' Decade and the Changing Context of House Leadership," in *Understanding Congressional Leadership*, ed. Frank H. Mackaman, (Washington, D.C.:

CQ Press, 1981); and Sinclair, *Majority Leadership in the U.S. House.*

66. Cooper and Brady, "Institutional Context and Leadership Style," 45; Bruce I. Oppenheimer, "Congress and the New Obstructionism: Developing an Energy Program," in *Congress Reconsidered,* ed. Lawrence C. Dodd and Bruce I. Oppenheimer, 2d ed. (Washington, D.C.: CQ Press, 1981); Sidney Waldman, "Majority Leadership in the House of Representatives," *Political Science Quarterly* 95 (1980): 373-393; Christopher Deering and Steven Smith, "Majority Party Leadership and the New House Subcommittee System," in *Understanding Congressional Leadership,* ed. Frank H. Mackaman (Washington, D.C.: CQ Press, 1981); David W. Rohde and Kenneth A. Shepsle, "Leaders and Followers in the House of Representatives: Reflections on Woodrow Wilson's *Congressional Government,*" *Congress and the Presidency* 14 (1987): 111-133.

67. Sinclair, *Majority Leadership in the U.S. House.* The increase in activity is based upon comparisons with Ripley, *Party Leaders in the House.*

68. Barbara Sinclair, "House Majority Party Leadership in the Late 1980s," in *Congress Reconsidered,* ed. Lawrence C. Dodd and Bruce I. Oppenheimer, 4th ed. (Washington, D.C.: CQ Press, 1989) and "The Changing Role of Party and Party Leadership in the U.S. House" (Paper delivered at the annual meeting of the American Political Science Association, 1989); Steven Smith and Forrest Maltzman, "Declining Committee Power in the House of Representatives" (Paper delivered at the annual meeting of the American Political Science Association, 1989); Roger Davidson, "The New Centralization on Capitol Hill," *Review of Politics* (Summer 1988): 345-364; Kenneth A. Shepsle, "The Changing Textbook Congress," in *Can the Government Govern?* ed. John E. Chubb and Paul E. Peterson (Washington, D.C.: Brookings Institution, 1989), 238-266; and Steven S. Smith, *Call to Order: Floor Politics in the House and Senate* (Washington, D.C.: Brookings Institution, 1989).

69. See Sinclair, "The Changing Role of Party and Party Leadership"; Janet Hook, "Speaker Jim Wright Takes Charge in the House," *Congressional Quarterly Weekly Report,* July 11, 1987, 1483-1488; and Richard E. Cohen, "Quick-Starting Speaker," *National Journal,* May 30, 1987, 1409-1413.

70. See Walter J. Oleszek, Roger Davidson, and Thomas Kephart, "The Incidence and Impact of Multiple Referrals in the House of Representatives," Congressional Research Service, 1986; and Melissa P. Collie and Joseph Cooper, "Multiple Referral and the 'New' Committee System in the House of Representatives," in *Congress Reconsidered,* ed. Lawrence C. Dodd and Bruce I. Oppenheimer, 4th ed. (Washington D.C.: CQ Press, 1989).

71. Alan Ehrenhalt, "Changing South Perils Conservative Coalition," *Congressional Quarterly Weekly Report,* August 1, 1987, 1699-1705; David Rohde, "Variations in Partisanship in the House of Representatives: Southern Democrats, Realignment and Agenda Change" (Paper presented at the annual meeting of the American Political Science Association, Washington, D.C., 1988).

72. Ripley, *Power in the Senate,* 27. See also Rothman, *Politics and Power.*

73. Ripley, *Power in the Senate*, 7.
74. Ibid., 16.
75. See especially Donald E. Matthews, *U.S. Senators and Their World* (New York: Vintage Books, 1960); also see Ralph K. Huitt, "The Internal Distribution of Influence: The Senate," in *The Congress and America's Future*, ed. David Truman, (Englewood Cliffs, N.J.: Prentice-Hall, 1965); Joseph S. Clark, *The Senate Establishment* (New York: Hill and Wang, 1963); William White, *Citadel: and The Story of the United States Senate* (New York: Harper and Brothers, 1956); and Ralph K. Huitt, "The Outsider in the Senate: An Alternative Role," *American Political Science Review* 55 (1961): 566-575.
76. Sinclair, "Senate Styles and Senate Decision-Making."
77. Ripley, *Power in the Senate;* Norman Ornstein, Robert L. Peabody, and David W. Rohde, "The Changing Senate: From the 1950s to the 1970s," in *Congress Reconsidered*, ed. Lawrence C. Dodd and Bruce I. Oppenheimer (New York: Praeger, 1977) and "The Senate Through the 1980s: Cycles of Change," in *Congress Reconsidered*, ed. Lawrence C. Dodd and Bruce I. Oppenheimer, 3d ed. (Washington, D.C.: CQ Press, 1985); Robert Peabody, Norman J. Ornstein, and David W. Rohde, "The United States Senate as a Presidential Incubator: Many Are Called but Few Are Chosen," *Political Science Quarterly* 91 (1976): 237-258; David W. Rohde, Norman J. Ornstein, and Robert Peabody, "Political Change and Legislative Norms in the U.S. Senate, 1957-1974," in *Studies of Congress*, ed. Glenn Parker (Washington, D.C.: CQ Press, 1985); Sinclair, *Transformation of the U.S. Senate;* and Michael Foley, *The New Senate* (New Haven, Conn.: Yale University Press, 1980).
78. Peabody, *Leadership in Congress;* Lynne P. Brown and Robert L. Peabody, "Patterns of Succession in House Democratic Leadership: The Choices of Wright, Foley, Coelho, 1986" (Paper presented at the annual meeting of the American Political Science Association, Chicago, Ill., 1987); see also Garrison Nelson, "Partisan Patterns of House Leadership Change, 1789-1977," *American Political Science Review* 71 (1977): 918-939.
79. Peabody, *Leadership in Congress*, 466.
80. Ibid.; Brown and Peabody, "Patterns of Succession," 2-3.
81. Brown and Peabody, "Patterns of Succession," 3. Figures have been adjusted to incorporate the 1989 leadership change.
82. Ibid.
83. Ibid.; Robert L. Peabody, "Senate Party Leadership: From the 1950s to the 1980s," in *Understanding Congressional Leadership*, ed. Frank H. Mackaman (Washington, D.C.: CQ Press, 1981).
84. Ibid., 60-61.
85. Peabody, *Leadership in Congress*, 17.
86. Ibid., 49. See also Nelson W. Polsby, "Two Strategies of Influence. Choosing a Majority Leader, 1962," in *New Perspectives on the House of Representatives*, ed. Robert L. Peabody and Nelson W. Polsby, 2d ed. (Chicago: Rand McNally, 1969).
87. Ibid., 17.
88. Brown and Peabody, "Patterns of Succession," 59.

89. Peabody, "Senate Party Leadership; Cooper and Brady, "Institutional Context and Leadership Style"; and Charles O. Jones, "House Leadership in an Age of Reform," in *Understanding Congressional Leadership*, ed. Frank H. Mackaman (Washington, D.C.: CQ Press, 1981).

90. Quoted in Jones, 119.

91. See Brown and Peabody, "Patterns of Succession," Table 1.

92. David B. Truman, *The Congressional Party* (New York: Wiley, 1959).

93. Barbara Hinckley, "Congressional Leadership Selection and Support: A Comparative Analysis," *Journal of Politics* 32 (1970): 268-287.

94. William E. Sullivan, "Criteria for Selecting Party Leadership in Congress," *American Politics Quarterly* 3 (1975): 30.

95. Ibid., 2.

96. Ibid., 35.

97. Brown and Peabody, "Patterns of Leadership Succession," 54.

98. Sinclair, *Majority Leadership in the U.S. House;* and Burdett Loomis, "Congressional Careers and Party Leadership in the Contemporary House of Representatives" *American Journal of Political Science* 28 (1984): 180-202.

99. Ripley, *Party Leaders in the House.*

100. Sinclair, *Majority Leadership in the U.S. House.*

101. Nicholas Masters, "Committee Assignments in the House of Representatives," in *New Perspectives on the House of Representatives*, eds. Robert L. Peabody and Nelson W. Polsby (Chicago: Rand McNally, 1963); and Kenneth A. Shepsle, *The Giant Jigsaw Puzzle: Democratic Committee Assignments in the Modern House* (Chicago: University of Chicago Press, 1978).

102. Randall B. Ripley, "The Party Whip Organization in the United States House of Representatives," *American Political Science Review* 58 (1964): 561-576; Lawrence C. Dodd, "The Expanded Roles of the House Democratic Whip System: The 93rd and 94th Congresses," *Congressional Studies* 7 (1979): 27-56; and Sinclair, *Majority Leadership in the U.S. House* and "House Majority Party Leadership in the Late 1980s."

103. Don Wolfensberger, "The Role of Party Caucuses in the U.S. House of Representatives: An Historical Perspective" (Paper presented at the annual meeting of the American Political Science Association, Washington, D.C., 1988); and Diane Granat, "Democratic Caucus Renewed as Forum for Policy Questions," *Congressional Quarterly Weekly Report*, October 15, 1983, 2115-2119.

104. Jones, *The Minority Party in Congress;* and Ripley, *Party Leaders in the House.*

105. Charles O. Jones, *Party and Policy-Making: The House Republican Policy Committee* (New Brunswick, N.J.: Rutgers University Press, 1964) and *The Minority Party in Congress.*

106. Peabody, *Leadership in Congress.*

107. John Pitney, "The War on the Floor: Partisan Conflict in the U.S. House of Representatives" (Paper presented at the annual meeting of the American Political Science Association, 1988); and William Connelly, "The House Republican Policy Committee: Then and Now" (Paper presented at the

annual meeting of the American Political Science Association, 1988).

108. Rohde, Ornstein, and Peabody, "Political Change and Legislative Norms."

109. Charles S. Bullock, "U.S. Senate Committee Assignments: Preferences, Motivations, and Successes," *American Journal of Political Science* 29 (1985): 789-808.

110. Walter J. Oleszek, *Majority and Minority Whips of the Senate*, S. Doc. 92-86, 92nd Cong., 1st sess. (Washington, D.C.: U.S. Government Printing Office, 1972).

111. Peabody, *Leadership in Congress* and "Senate Party Leadership"; Ralph K. Huitt, "Democratic Party Leadership in the Senate," *American Political Science Review* 55 (1961): 333-344; and Roger Davidson, "Senate Leaders: Janitors for an Untidy Chamber?" in *Congress Reconsidered*, ed. Lawrence C. Dodd and Bruce I. Oppenheimer, 3d ed. (Washington, D.C.: CQ Press, 1985).

112. Hugh A. Bone, "An Introduction to the Senate Policy Committees," *American Political Science Review* 50 (1956): 339-359; Malcolm E. Jewell, "The Senate Republican Policy Committee and Foreign Policy," *Western Political Quarterly* 12 (1959): 966-980. See also Neil MacNeil, *Dirksen: Portrait of a Public Man* (New York: World Publishing, 1970).

113. Paul S. Herrnson, *Party Campaigning in the 1980s* (Cambridge, Mass.: Harvard University Press, 1988).

114. Xandra Kayden and Eddie Mahe, Jr., *The Party Goes On* (New York: Basic Books, 1985).

115. Cooper and Brady, "Institutional Context and Leadership Style"; and Sinclair, "Party Leadership and Policy Change."

116. Polsby, "Institutionalization of the U.S. House." See also Polsby, Miriam Gallagher, and Barry Rundquist, "The Growth of the Seniority System in the House of Representatives," *American Political Science Review* 63 (1969): 787-807.

117. Sinclair, *Majority Leadership in the U.S. House*; Loomis, "The 'Me' Decade"; Hook, "Speaker Jim Wright Takes Charge in the House"; and Cohen, "Quick-Starting Speaker."

118. Jones, *Minority Party in Congress.*

119. Ibid., 22-24.

120. Ripley, *Power in the Senate*, 97; and Davidson, "Senate Leaders."

121. Ripley, *Party Leaders in the House* and *Power in the Senate.*

122. Loomis, "The 'Me' Decade."

123. Ripley, *Party Leaders in the House*, 6.

124. Sinclair, "Changing Role of Party and Party Leadership."

125. Matthews, *U.S. Senators and Their World*; and Rohde, Ornstein, and Peabody, "Political Change and Legislative Norms."

126. See Norman J. Ornstein, Robert L. Peabody, and David W. Rohde, "Party Leadership and the Institutional Context: The Senate from Baker to Dole" (Paper presented at the annual meeting of the American Political Science Association, Washington, D.C., 1986).

127. Davidson, "Senate Leaders"; and Peabody, "Senate Party Leadership."

128. Jones, *Minority Party in Congress.*

129. Sinclair, *Majority Leadership in the U.S. House.*

130. Peabody, "Senate Party Leadership."
131. Sinclair, *Majority Leadership in the U.S. House.*
132. See Cooper and Brady, "Institutional Context and Leadership Style"; Sinclair, "Party Leadership and Policy Change"; and the historical literature cited in these articles.
133. See especially Cooper and Brady.
134. For a discussion of the leadership of Rayburn's successor, see Ripley, *Party Leaders in the House.*
135. See Sinclair, *Majority Leadership in the U.S. House* and "Changing Role of Party and Party Leadership"; David J. Volger, "The Rise of the Ad Hoc Committee in the House of Representatives" (Paper presented at the annual meeting of the American Political Science Association, New York, 1978); and Waldman, "Majority Leadership in the House."
136. See Lawrence C. Dodd and Terry Sullivan, "Majority Party Leadership and Partisan Vote Gathering: The House Democratic Whip System," in *Understanding Congressional Leadership*, ed. Frank H. Mackaman (Washington, D.C.: CQ Press, 1981).
137. Sinclair, *Majority Leadership in the U.S. House.*
138. Jones, *Minority Party in Congress.*
139. For a useful early effort, to be discussed later, see Ripley, *Majority Party Leadership in Congress.*
140. Sinclair, "House Majority Party Leadership in the Late 1980s."
141. Jones, *Minority Party in Congress*; Ripley, *Party Leaders in the House*; and Peabody, *Leadership in Congress.*
142. Jones, *Minority Party in Congress*, 55-57, 82, 98-100.
143. Ibid., 190.
144. Ibid., 192.
145. Ibid., 22-24.
146. Ibid.; Peabody, *Leadership in Congress.*
147. Huitt, "Democratic Party Leadership in the Senate"; Rowland Evans and Robert Novak, *Lyndon B. Johnson: The Exercise of Power* (New York: New American Library, 1966); John G. Stewart, "Two Strategies of Leadership: Johnson and Mansfield," in *Congressional Behavior*, ed. Nelson W. Polsby (New York: Random House, 1971); George E. Reedy, *The U.S. Senate* (New York: Crown, 1986); Peabody, "Senate Party Leadership"; and Davidson, "Senate Leaders."
148. Huitt, "Democratic Party Leadership in the Senate," 344.
149. See especially Stewart, "Two Strategies of Leadership."
150. See Rohde, Ornstein, and Peabody, "Political Change and Legislative Norms"; Foley, *The New Senate*; and Clark, *The Senate Establishment.*
151. See Peabody, "Senate Leaders," 59.
152. Peabody, "Senate Leaders"; and Ornstein, Peabody, and Rohde, "Party Leadership and Institutional Context."
153. Sinclair, *Majority Leadership in the House.*
154. Davidson, "Senate Leaders"; and Patterson, "Problems of Senate Party Leadership."
155. Sinclair, *Transformation of the U.S. Senate.*
156. Jones, *Minority Leadership in Congress*, 198.

157. Ibid., 39.
158. Ripley, *Majority Party Leadership in Congress*; and Sinclair, "Determinants of Aggregate Party Cohesion."
159. Roger Davidson and Walter J. Oleszek, "Changing the Guard in the U.S. Senate," *Legislative Studies Quarterly* 9 (1984): 635-663.
160. See especially Fenno, *Congressmen in Committees*; David E. Price, *Who Makes the Laws? Creativity and Power in Senate Committee* (Cambridge: Schenkman, 1972) and "Congressional Committees in the Policy Process," in *Congress Reconsidered*, 3d ed., ed. Lawrence C. Dodd and Bruce I. Oppenheimer (Washington, D.C.: CQ Press, 1985); and Steven Smith and Christopher J. Deering, *Committees in Congress* (Washington D.C.: CQ Press, 1984).
161. Eric Uslaner, "Policy Entrepreneurs and Amateur Democrats in the House of Representatives: Toward a More Party-Oriented Congress?" in *Legislative Reform*, ed. Leroy Rieselbach (Lexington, Mass.: Lexington, 1978).
162. Loomis, *The New American Politician*.
163. Sinclair, *The Transformation of the U.S. Senate*.
164. Arthur G. Stevens, Jr., Daniel P. Mulhollan, and Paul S. Rundquist, "U.S. Congressional Structure and Representation: The Role of Informed Groups," *Legislative Studies Quarterly* 6 (1981): 415-438; and Susan Webb Hammond, Arthur G. Stevens, and Daniel P. Mulhollan, "Congressional Caucuses: Legislators as Lobbyists," in *Interest Group Politics*, ed. Allan Cigler and Burdett Loomis (Washington, D.C.: CQ Press, 1983).
165. Sinclair, *Majority Leadership in the U.S. House*.
166. See, for example, Mayhew, *Congress: The Electoral Connection*.
167. Ripley, *Majority Party Leadership in Congress*, 17-18.
168. Ibid., 182-183.
169. Jones, *Minority Party in Congress*; and Edwards, *Presidential Influence in Congress*.
170. Ripley, *Majority Party Leadership in Congress*, 187.
171. Brady, Cooper, and Hurley, "Legislative Potential for Policy Changes"; Sinclair, *Congressional Realignment*; Clausen, *How Congressmen Decide*; and Lewis Froman and Randall B. Ripley, "Conditions for Party Leadership: The Case of the House Democrats," *American Political Science Review* 59 (1965): 52-63.
172. Sinclair, *Majority Leadership in the U.S. House*.
173. See Clausen, *How Congressmen Decide*; and Sinclair, *Congressional Realignment*.
174. Paul Light, *The President's Agenda* (Baltimore: Johns Hopkins University Press, 1983).
175. For two radically different perspectives, see Mayhew, *Congress: The Electoral Connection*; and Cooper, "Congress In Organizational Perspective."

APPENDIX

The following individuals participated in the Congressional Leadership Research Project, which was organized by the Dirksen Center and led to this book.

Members of Congress: Rep. Jack Buechner, R-Mo.; Rep. William F. Clinger, R-Pa.; Rep. Martin Frost, D-Texas; Rep. Willis D. Gradison, Jr., R-Ohio; Rep. Bill Green, R-N.Y.; Rep. Henry Hyde, R-Ill.; Rep. Donald E. Lukens, R-Ohio; Rep. Matthew F. McHugh, D-N.Y.; Rep. Robert H. Michel, R-Ill.; Rep. Constance A. Morella, R-Md.; Rep. Leon E. Panetta, D-Calif.; Rep. Marge Roukema, R-N.J.; Rep. Charles E. Schumer, D-N.Y.; Rep. John M. Spratt, Jr., D-S.C.; Rep. Thomas J. Tauke, R-Iowa; Rep. Ron Wyden, D-Ore.; Sen. Alan Cranston, D-Calif.; Sen. Richard G. Lugar, R-Ind.; Sen. George J. Mitchell, D-Maine; Sen. Strom Thurmond, R-S.C.

Former Members of Congress: The Honorable and Mrs. Richard Bolling, D-Mo.; The Honorable Howard W. Cannon, D-Nev.; The Honorable J. W. Fulbright, D-Ark.; The Honorable Fred R. Harris, D-Okla.; The Honorable James Lloyd, D-Calif.

Congressional Staff: Richard Arenberg, leadership staff of Sen. George Mitchell; Janet Breslin, deputy staff director, Committee on Agriculture, Nutrition and Forestry; Richard P. Conlon, executive director, Democratic Study Group; Bill Conway, senior counsel, Water and Power Subcommittee; Dan Craig, executive assistant, Sen. Daniel Inouye; Helen Darling, legislative assistant for health policy, Office of Sen. David Durenberger; Michael Davidson, Senate legal counsel; Sharon Donaldson, deputy director, House Democratic Caucus; Andrew A. Feinstein, staff director/chief counsel, Civil Service Subcommittee; Boyd Hollingsworth, chief counsel, Office of the Assistant Republican Leader; Michael Johnson, chief of staff, Office of the House Republican Leader; Diane Liesman, administrative assistant, Rep. Edward R. Madigan; Marshall Lynam, chief of staff, Office of the Speaker of the House; David Magleby, Senate Democratic Policy Committee; Robert McArthur, staff director, Office of the Senate Republican Conference Secretary; Candice Nelson, Office of Sen. Alan Cranston; Robert Okun, executive director, House Republican Research Committee; Linda Peek, communications director, Senate Democratic Policy Committee; David Podoff, Joint Economic Committee; Peter Robinson, deputy director, Democratic Steering and Policy Committee; Thomas Sliter, director, domestic policy, Senate Democratic Policy Committee; Raymond W. Smock, historian, House of Representatives; Forest Thigpen, assistant staff director, Office of the Senate Republican Conference Secretary; Don Wolfensberger, minority counsel, Rules Committee.

Former Congressional Staff: Patrick Griffin, Gary Hymel, Christopher Matthews, Kirk O'Donnell.

Scholars: Richard Baker, historian of the Senate; Ross K. Baker, Department of Political Science, Rutgers University; Ira Chalef, Congressional Management Foundation; Christopher Deering, Department of Political Science, George Washington University; Paul Hoff, general counsel, Center for Responsive Politics; David Kozak, National War College; Peter Lindstrom, Center for Responsive Politics; Burdett A. Loomis, Department of Political Science, University of Kansas; Ellen S. Miller, Center for Responsive Politics; Garrison Nelson, Department of Political Science, University of Vermont; Samuel C. Patterson, Department of Political Science, Ohio State University; Robert L. Peabody, Department of Political Science, Johns Hopkins University; Howard Shuman, National War College; Barbara Sinclair, Department of Political Science, University of California at Riverside; Steven S. Smith, Department of Political Science, University of Minnesota.

Congressional Leadership Research Project Steering Committee: Richard E. Cohen, National Journal; Roger Davidson, Department of Political Science, University of Maryland; Alan Ehrenhalt, Congressional Quarterly; Merle H. Glick, chairman, board of directors and acting executive director, Dirksen Congressional Center; Susan Webb Hammond, Department of Political Science, American University; Charles Jones, Department of Political Science, University of Wisconsin; Frank Mackaman, director, Gerald R. Ford Presidential Library; Thomas E. Mann, Brookings Institution; Norman J. Ornstein, resident scholar, American Enterprise Institute; Frederick H. Pauls, senior specialist and chief, Government Division, Congressional Research Service; Richard C. Sachs, analyst, Government Division, CRS, and Washington project officer, Congressional Leadership Research Project; Barbara Sinclair, Office of the Speaker of the House.

Dirksen Congressional Center: Merle Glick, board of directors; Frank Mackaman, executive director.

Congressional Research Service: Stanley I. Bach, specialist, Government Division; Nancy Davenport, assistant director for special programs; Daniel P. Mulhollan, assistant chief, Government Division; Walter J. Oleszek, specialist, Government Division; Frederick H. Pauls, chief, Government Division; William Robinson, deputy director, CRS; Joseph E. Ross, director, CRS; Paul S. Rundquist, specialist, Government Division; Judy Schneider, specialist, Government Division.

Ford Foundation: Alice O'Connor, assistant project director, government and public policy.

Media: Michael Barone, *Washington Post*; Jeffrey H. Birnbaum, *Wall Street*

Journal; Jackie Calmes, *Congressional Quarterly*; Richard E. Cohen, *National Journal*; Helen Dewar, *Washington Post*; Larry Haas, *National Journal*; Janet Hook, *Congressional Quarterly*; Carol Matlack, *National Journal*; Robert Merry, *Congressional Quarterly*; Adam Pertman, *Boston Globe*; Cokie Roberts, National Public Radio; Steve Roberts, *U.S. News and World Report*; Evan Roth, States News Service; Frank Van Riper, *New York Daily News*; Tom Watson, *Congressional Quarterly*.

BIBLIOGRAPHY

Asbell, Bernard. 1978. *The Senate Nobody Knows*. Baltimore: Johns Hopkins University Press.

Asher, Herbert B. 1973. "The Learning of Legislative Norms." *American Political Science Review* 67 (June): 499-513.

Atkinson, C. R. 1911. *The Committee on Rules and the Overthrow of Speaker Cannon*. New York: Columbia University Press.

Bach, Stanley. 1986a. "Suspension of the Rules in the House of Representatives." Report No. 86-103, Congressional Research Service.

——. 1986b. "Arranging the Legislative Agenda of the House of Representatives: The Impact of Legislative Rules and Practices." Report No. 86-110, Congressional Research Service.

——, and Steven S. Smith. 1988. *Managing Uncertainty in the House of Representatives*. Washington, D.C.: Brookings Institution.

Bailey, Christopher J. 1988. *The Republican Party in the U.S. Senate, 1974-1984: Party Change and Institutional Development*. Manchester, England: Manchester University Press.

Baker, Ross K. 1980. *Friend and Foe in the U.S. Senate*. New York: Free Press.

——. 1985. "What's in It for Me: Benefits to House Members for Association with Industrial Policy." Paper presented at the annual meeting of the American Political Science Association, New Orleans, La.

——. 1987. "Fostering the Entrepreneurial Activities of Members of the House: A Realistic Approach to the Challenge of Leadership." Dirksen Congressional Center—CRS Symposium Paper, March 10.

——. 1989. *House and Senate*. New York: Norton.

Barry, John M. 1989. *The Ambition and the Power: The Fall of Jim Wright: A True Story of Washington*. New York: Viking Press.

Benenson, Bob. 1987. "Savvy 'Stars' Making Local TV a Potent Tool." *Congressional Quarterly Weekly Report*, July 18, 1551-1555.

Bolling, Richard. 1965. *House Out of Order*. New York: Dutton.

Bone, Hugh A. 1956. "An Introduction to the Senate Policy Committees." *American Political Science Review* 50 (June): 339-359.

Brady, David. 1973. *Congressional Voting in a Partisan Era*. Lawrence:

University of Kansas Press.

——, Joseph Cooper, and Pat Hurley. 1977. "Legislative Potential for Policy Changes: The House of Representatives." *Legislative Studies Quarterly* 4 (August): 385-398.

Brown, Lynne P., and Robert L. Peabody. 1987. "Patterns of Succession in House Democratic Leadership: The Choices of Wright, Foley, Coelho, 1986." Paper presented at the annual meeting of the American Political Science Association, Chicago, Ill.

Bullock, Charles S. 1985. "U.S. Senate Committee Assignments: Preferences, Motivations, and Successes." *American Journal of Political Science* 29: 789-808.

Busby, L. White. 1927. *Uncle Joe Cannon.* New York: Henry Holt.

Calmes, Jacqueline. 1987a. "Byrd Struggles to Lead Deeply Divided Senate." *Congressional Quarterly Weekly Report*, July 4, 1423.

——. 1987b. "John Murtha." *Congressional Quarterly Weekly Report*, January 3, 17.

——, and Rob Gurwitt. 1987. "Profiles in Power." *Congressional Quarterly Weekly Report*, January 3, 11-18.

Chubb, John E., and Paul E. Peterson, eds. 1989. *Can the Government Govern?* Washington, D.C.: Brookings Institution.

Clark, Joseph S. 1963. *The Senate Establishment.* New York: Hill and Wang.

Clausen, Aage. 1973. *How Congressmen Decide.* New York: St. Martin's.

——, and Clyde Wilcox. 1987. "Policy Partisanship in Legislative Leadership Recruitment and Behavior." *Legislative Studies Quarterly* 12:246.

Cohen, Richard E. 1987. "Quick-Starting Speaker." *National Journal*, May 30, 1409-1413.

——. 1989. "It Was a Transition Year in the House." *National Journal*, December 2, 2948.

——, and Burt Solomon. 1987. "Congress's Rising Stars." *National Journal*, January 24, 182.

Cohen, William S. 1981. *Roll Call: One Year in the United States Senate.* New York: Simon and Schuster.

Cohodas, Nadine. 1986. "Immigration Bill Resurrected." *Congressional Quarterly Weekly Report*, October 11, 2571-2573.

Collie, Melissa P., and Joseph Cooper. 1989. "Multiple Referral and the 'New' Committee System in the House of Representatives." In *Congress Reconsidered*, 4th ed., edited by Lawrence C. Dodd and Bruce I. Oppenheimer. Washington D.C.: CQ Press.

Connelly, William. 1988. "The House Republican Policy Committee: Then and Now." Paper presented at the annual meeting of the American Political Science Association.

Cook, Timothy. 1986. "House Members as Newsmakers: The Effects of Televising Congress." *Legislative Studies Quarterly* 11 (May): 203-226.

Cooper, Joseph. 1977. "Congress in Organizational Perspective." In *Congress Reconsidered*, edited by Lawrence C. Dodd and Bruce I. Oppenheimer. New York: Praeger.

——, and David W. Brady, 1981. "Institutional Context and Leadership Style: The House from Cannon to Rayburn." *American Political Science Review*

75 (June): 411-425.

Cummings, Milton C., and Robert L. Peabody. 1969. "The Decision to Enlarge the Committee on Rules: An Analysis of the 1961 Vote." In *New Perspectives on the House of Representatives*, 2d ed., edited by Robert L. Peabody and Nelson W. Polsby. Chicago: Rand McNally.

Davidson, Roger H. 1981. "Congressional Leaders as Agents of Change." In *Understanding Congressional Leadership*, edited by Frank H. Mackaman. Washington, D.C.: CQ Press.

_____. 1985. "Senate Leaders: Janitors for an Untidy Chamber?" In *Congress Reconsidered*, 3d ed., edited by Lawrence C. Dodd and Bruce I. Oppenheimer. Washington, D.C.: CQ Press.

_____. 1986. "The Legislative Work of Congress." Paper presented at the annual meeting of the American Political Science Association, Washington, D.C.

_____. 1988. "The New Centralization on Capitol Hill." *Review of Politics* (Summer): 345-364.

_____, and Walter J. Oleszek. 1981. *Congress and Its Members*. Washington, D.C.: CQ Press.

_____, and Walter J. Oleszek. 1984. "Changing the Guard in the U.S. Senate." *Legislative Studies Quarterly* 9 (November): 635-663.

Deering, Christopher J. "Leadership in the Slow Lane." *PS* 19:37-42.

_____, and Steven Smith. 1981. "Majority Party Leadership and the New House Subcommittee System." In *Understanding Congressional Leadership*, edited by Frank H. Mackaman. Washington, D.C.: CQ Press.

Dodd, Lawrence C. 1979. "The Expanded Roles of the House Democratic Whip System: The 93d and 94th Congresses." *Congressional Studies* 7 (Spring): 27-56.

_____, and Bruce I. Oppenheimer. 1977. *Congress Reconsidered*. New York: Praeger.

_____, and Bruce I. Oppenheimer, eds. 1981, 1985, 1989. *Congress Reconsidered*, 2d, 3d, 4th eds. Washington, D.C.: CQ Press.

_____, and Terry Sullivan. 1981. "Majority Party Leadership and Partisan Vote Gathering: The House Democratic Whip System." In *Understanding Congressional Leadership*, edited by Frank H. Mackaman, 227-260. Washington, D.C.: CQ Press.

Drew, Elizabeth. 1979. *Senator*. New York: Simon and Schuster.

Edwards, George C. 1980. *Presidential Influence in Congress*. San Francisco: W. H. Freeman.

Ehrenhalt, Alan. 1987. "Changing South Perils Conservative Coalition." *Congressional Quarterly Weekly Report*, August 1, 1699-1705.

Ellwood, John W., and James A. Thurber. 1981. "The Politics of the Congressional Budget Process Re-examined." In *Congress Reconsidered*, 2d ed., edited by Lawrence C. Dodd and Bruce I. Oppenheimer, 246-271. Washington, D.C.: CQ Press.

Evans, C. Lawrence. 1986. "Influence in Senate Committees: The Role of Formal Leadership." Paper presented at the annual meeting of the American Political Science Association, Washington, D.C.

Evans, Rowland, and Robert Novak. 1966. *Lyndon B. Johnson: The Exercise of Power*. New York: New American Library.

Fenno, Richard F. 1965. "The Internal Distribution of Influence: The House." In *The Congress and America's Future*, edited by David B. Truman, 52-76. Englewood Cliffs, N.J.: Prentice-Hall.

_____. 1966. *The Power of the Purse*. Boston: Little, Brown.

_____. 1973. *Congressmen in Committees*. Boston: Little, Brown.

_____. 1978. *Homestyle*. Boston: Little, Brown.

_____. 1982. *The United States Senate: A Bicameral Perspective*. Washington, D.C.: American Enterprise Institute.

_____. 1989. *The Makings of a Senator: Dan Quayle*. Washington, D.C.: CQ Press.

Fiorina, Morris P. 1977. *Congress: Keystone of the Washington Establishment*. New Haven, Conn.: Yale University Press.

Foley, Michael. 1980. *The New Senate*. New Haven, Conn.: Yale University Press.

Follett, Mary Parker. 1986. Reprint 1974. *The Speaker of the House of Representatives*. New York: Bert Franklin Reprints.

Fox, Harrison, and Susan Webb Hammond. 1977. *Congressional Staffs: The Invisible Force in American Lawmaking*. New York: Free Press.

Froman, Lewis, and Randall B. Ripley. 1965. "Conditions for Party Leadership: The Case of the House Democrats." *American Political Science Review* 59:52-63.

Gais, Thomas L., Mark A. Peterson, and Jack L. Walker. 1984. "Interest Groups, Iron Triangles and Representative Institutions in American National Government." *British Journal of Political Science* 14:161-185.

Galloway, George B. 1961. *History of the House of Representatives*. New York: Thomas Y. Crowell.

Gibb, Cecil A. 1969. "Leadership." In *The Handbook of Social Psychology*, IV. 2d ed., edited by Gardner Lindzey and Elliot Aronson. Reading, Mass.: Addison-Wesley.

_____. ed. 1969. *Leadership: Selected Readings*. Harmondsworth, England: Penguin.

Graber, Doris A., ed. 1984. *Media Power in Politics*. Washington, D.C.: CQ Press.

Granat, Diane. 1983. "Democratic Caucus Renewed as Forum for Policy Questions." *Congressional Quarterly Weekly Report*, October 15, 2115-2119.

Gross, Donald A. "Changing Patterns of Voting Agreement Among Senatorial Leadership, 1947-1976." *Western Political Quarterly* 37:120-142.

Gurwitt, Rob. 1987. "Henry Hyde." *Congressional Quarterly Weekly Report*, January 3, 14.

Hall, Richard L. 1987. "Participation and Purpose in Committee Decision Making." *American Political Science Review* 81:105-127.

Hammond, Susan Webb. 1987. "Committee and Informal Leaders in the U.S. House of Representatives." Dirksen Congressional Center—CRS Symposium Paper, July 14.

_____, Arthur G. Stevens, and Daniel P. Mulhollan. 1983. "Congressional Caucuses: Legislators as Lobbyists." In *Interest Group Politics*, edited by Allan Cigler and Burdett Loomis. Washington, D.C.: CQ Press.

_____, Daniel P. Mulhollan, and Arthur G. Stevens, Jr. 1985. "Informal Congressional Caucuses and Agenda Setting." *Western Political Quarterly* 38 (December): 583-605.

———, Daniel P. Mulhollan, and Arthur G. Stevens, Jr. Forthcoming. *Informal Congressional Groups in National Policymaking.* Washington, D.C.: American Enterprise Institute.

Hechler, Kenneth W. 1940. *Insurgency.* New York: Columbia University Press.

Heclo, Hugh. 1978. "Issue Networks and the Executive Establishment." In *The New American Political System,* edited by Anthony King. Washington, D.C.: American Enterprise Institute.

Herrnson, Paul. 1988. *Party Campaigning in the 1980s.* Cambridge, Mass.: Harvard University Press.

Hess, Stephen. 1986. *The Ultimate Insiders: U.S. Senators in the National Media.* Washington, D.C.: Brookings Institution.

Hinckley, Barbara. 1970. "Congressional Leadership Selection and Support: A Comparative Analysis." *Journal of Politics* 32:268-287.

———. 1980. "The American Voter in Congressional Elections." *American Political Science Review* 74 (September): 641-650.

History of the Committee on Rules, A. 1983. Washington, D.C.: U.S. Government Printing Office.

Hook, Janet. 1987a. "Speaker Jim Wright Takes Charge in the House." *Congressional Quarterly Weekly Report,* July 11, 1483-1488.

———. 1987b. "GOP Chafes Under Restrictive House Rules." *Congressional Quarterly Weekly Report,* October 10, 2450-2453.

———. 1988. "Byrd Will Give Up Senate Majority Leadership." *Congressional Quarterly Weekly Report,* April 16, 975-978.

———. 1989. "New Leaders Felt Their Way Gingerly Through the Session." *Congressional Quarterly Weekly Report,* December 2, 3284.

Huitt, Ralph K. 1961a. "Democratic Party Leadership in the Senate." *American Political Science Review* 55:333-344.

———. 1961b. "The Outsider in the Senate: An Alternative Role." *American Political Science Review* 55:566-575.

———. 1965. "The Internal Distribution of Influence: The Senate." In *The Congress and America's Future,* edited by David B. Truman. Englewood Cliffs, N.J.: Prentice-Hall.

———, and Robert L. Peabody. 1969. *Congress: Two Decades of Analysis.* New York: Harper and Row.

Jacobson, Gary C. 1987. *The Politics of Congressional Elections,* 2d ed. Boston: Little, Brown.

———, and Samuel Kernell. 1981. *Strategy and Choice in Congressional Elections.* New Haven, Conn.: Yale University Press.

Jewell, Malcolm E. 1959. "The Senate Republican Policy Committee and Foreign Policy." *Western Political Quarterly* 12 (December): 966-980.

———, and Samuel C. Patterson. 1986. *The Legislative Process in the United States.* 4th ed. New York: Random House.

Jones, Charles O. 1964. *Party and Policy-Making: The House Republican Policy Committee.* New Brunswick, N.J.: Rutgers University Press.

———. 1968. "Joseph G. Cannon and Howard W. Smith: An Essay on the Limits of Leadership in the House of Representatives." *Journal of Politics* 30:617-646.

_____. 1970. *The Minority Party in Congress.* Boston: Little, Brown.

_____. 1981. "House Leadership in an Age of Reform." In *Understanding Congressional Leadership,* edited by Frank H. Mackaman, 117-134. Washington, D.C.: CQ Press.

_____. 1982. *The United States Congress: People, Place and Policy.* Homewood, Ill: Dorsey Press.

Kayden, Xandra, and Eddie Mahe, Jr. 1985. *The Party Goes On.* New York: Basic Books.

King, Anthony. 1978. "The American Polity in the Late 1970s: Building Coalitions in the Sand." In *The New American Political System,* edited by Anthony King. Washington, D.C.: American Enterprise Institute.

Kingdon, John W. 1984. *Agendas, Alternatives and Public Policies.* Boston: Little, Brown.

Kramer, Gerald H. 1971. "Short-Term Fluctuations in U.S. Voting Behavior, 1896-1964." *American Political Science Review* 65 (March): 131-143.

Light, Paul. 1983. *The President's Agenda.* Baltimore: Johns Hopkins University Press.

Loomis, Burdett A. 1981. "The 'Me' Decade and the Changing Context of House Leadership." In *Understanding Congressional Leadership,* edited by Frank H. Mackaman, 157-179. Washington, D.C.: CQ Press.

_____. 1984. "Congressional Careers and Party Leadership in the Contemporary House of Representatives." *American Journal of Political Science* 28 (February): 180-202.

_____. 1988. *The New American Politician.* New York: Basic Books.

Mackaman, Frank H. 1981. "Introduction." In *Understanding Congressional Leadership,* edited by Frank H. Mackaman. Washington, D.C.: CQ Press.

MacNeil, Neil. 1970. *Dirksen: Portrait of a Public Man.* New York: World Publishing.

Malbin, Michael. 1980. *Unelected Representatives.* New York: Basic Books.

Manley, John F. 1969. "Wilbur D. Mills: A Study of Congressional Leadership." *American Political Science Review* 63:442-464.

Mann, Thomas E., and Norman J. Ornstein, eds. 1981. *The New Congress.* Washington, D.C.: American Enterprise Institute.

Masters, Nicholas. 1963. "Committee Assignments in the House of Representatives." In *New Perspectives on the House of Representatives,* edited by Robert L. Peabody and Nelson W. Polsby. Chicago: Rand McNally.

Matthews, Donald E. 1960. *U.S. Senators and Their World.* New York: Vintage Books.

Mayhew, David R. 1974a. "Congressional Elections: The Case of the Vanishing Marginals." *Polity* 6:295-317.

_____. 1974b. *Congress: The Electoral Connection.* New Haven, Conn: Yale University Press.

Miller, James A. 1986. *Running in Place: Inside the Senate.* New York: Simon and Schuster.

Neimi, Richard G., and Herbert F. Weisberg, eds. 1984. *Controversies in Voting Behavior,* 2d ed. Washington, D.C.: CQ Press.

Nelson, Garrison. 1977. "Partisan Patterns of House Leadership Change, 1789-1977." *American Political Science Review* 71 (September): 918.

_____. 1985. "Leadership Selection in the U.S. Senate, 1899-1985: Changing Patterns of Recruitment and Institutional Interaction." Typescript, 1985.

Oleszek, Walter J. 1972. *Majority and Minority Whips of the Senate*. S. Doc. 92-86, 92d Cong., 1st sess. Washington, D.C.: U.S. Government Printing Office.

_____. "Party Whips in the United States Senate." *Journal of Politics* 33:955-979.

_____, Roger Davidson, and Thomas Kephart. 1986. "The Incidence and Impact of Multiple Referrals in the House of Representatives." Congressional Research Service.

Oppenheimer, Bruce I. 1977. "The Rules Committee: New Arm of Leadership in a Decentralized House." In *Congress Reconsidered*, edited by Lawrence C. Dodd and Bruce I. Oppenheimer, 96-116. New York: Praeger.

_____. 1981a. "The Changing Relationship Between House Leadership and the Committee on Rules." In *Understanding Congressional Leadership*, edited by Frank H. Mackaman, 207-226. Washington, D.C.: CQ Press.

_____. 1981b. "Congress and the New Obstructionism: Developing an Energy Program. In *Congress Reconsidered*, 2d ed., edited by Lawrence C. Dodd and Bruce I. Oppenheimer, 275-295. Washington, D.C.: CQ Press.

_____. 1985. "Changing Time Constraints on Congress: Historical Perspectives on the Use of Cloture." In *Congress Reconsidered*. 3d ed., edited by Lawrence C. Dodd and Bruce I. Oppenheimer. Washington, D.C.: CQ Press.

Ornstein, Norman J., ed. 1975. *Congress in Change*. New York: Praeger.

_____. 1987. "Can Congress Be Led?" Dirksen Congressional Center—CRS Symposium Paper, February 24.

_____, Thomas E. Mann, and Michael J. Malbin. 1989. *Vital Statistics on Congress, 1989-90*. Washington, D.C.: CQ Press.

_____, Thomas E. Mann, Michael J. Malbin, Allen Schick, and John F. Bibby. 1984. *Vital Statistics on Congress 1984-85*. Washington, D.C.: American Enterprise Institute.

_____, Robert L. Peabody, and David W. Rohde. 1977. "The Changing Senate: From the 1950s to the 1970s." In *Congress Reconsidered*, edited by Lawrence C. Dodd and Bruce I. Oppenheimer. New York: Praeger.

_____, Robert L. Peabody, and David W. Rohde. 1985. "The Senate Through the 1980s: Cycles of Change." In *Congress Reconsidered*, 3d ed., edited by Lawrence C. Dodd and Bruce I. Oppenheimer. Washington, D.C.: CQ Press.

_____, Robert L. Peabody, and David W. Rohde. 1986. "Party Leadership and the Institutional Context: The Senate from Baker to Dole." Paper presented at the annual meeting of the American Political Science Association, Washington, D.C.

Parker, Glenn R. 1985. "Stylistic Change in the U.S. Senate: 1959-1980." *Journal of Politics* 47:1190.

Patterson, Samuel C. 1970. "The Professional Staffs of Congressional Committees." *Administrative Science Quarterly* 15 (March): 22-37.

_____. "Legislative Leadership and Political Ideology." *Public Opinion Quarterly* 27:399-410.

_____. 1987. "Problems of Senate Party Leadership." Dirksen Congressional Center—CRS Symposium Paper, June 2.

_____, and Gregory A. Caldeira. "Party Voting in the United States Congress." *British Journal of Political Science* 18:111-131.

Peabody, Robert L. 1976. *Leadership in Congress: Stability, Succession and Change*. Boston: Little, Brown.

_____. 1981. "Senate Party Leadership: From the 1950s to the 1980s." In *Understanding Congressional Leadership*, edited by Frank H. Mackaman. Washington, D.C.: CQ Press.

_____. 1984. "Leadership in Legislatures: Evolution, Selection, Functions." *Legislative Studies Quarterly* 9 (August): 441-473.

_____. 1985a. "House Party Leadership: Stability and Change." In *Congress Reconsidered*, 3d ed., edited by Lawrence C. Dodd and Bruce I. Oppenheimer. Washington, D.C.: CQ Press.

_____. 1985b. "Leadership in Legislatures: Evolution, Selection, and Functions." In *Handbook of Legislative Research*, edited by Gerhard Loewenberg, Samuel C. Patterson, and Malcolm E. Jewell. Cambridge, Mass.: Harvard University Press.

_____, Norman J. Ornstein, and David W. Rohde. 1976. "The United States Senate as a Presidential Incubator: Many Are Called But Few Are Chosen." *Political Science Quarterly* 91:237-258.

Pitney, John. 1988. "The War on the Floor: Partisan Conflict in the U.S. House of Representatives." Paper presented at the annual meeting of the American Political Science Association.

Polsby, Nelson W. 1968. "The Institutionalization of the U.S. House of Representatives." *American Political Science Review* 62:144-168.

_____. 1969a. "Two Strategies of Influence: Choosing a Majority Leader 1962." In *New Perspectives on the House of Representatives*, 2d ed., edited by Robert L. Peabody and Nelson W. Polsby. Chicago: Rand McNally.

_____. 1969b. "Policy Analysis and Congress." *Public Policy* 18 (September): 61-74.

_____. 1970. "Strengthening Congress in National Policy-Making." *Yale Review* 59 (June): 481-497.

_____, Miriam Gallagher, and Barry Rundquist. 1969. "The Growth of the Seniority System in the House of Representatives." *American Political Science Review* 63:787-807.

Price, David E. 1971. "Professional 'Entrepreneurs': Staff Orientations and Policymaking on Three Senate Committees." *Journal of Politics* 33 (May): 316-336.

_____. 1972. *Who Makes the Laws? Creativity and Power in Senate Committee*. Cambridge: Schenkman.

_____. 1985. "Congressional Committees in the Policy Process." In *Congress Reconsidered*, 3d ed., edited by Lawrence C. Dodd and Bruce I. Oppenheimer. Washington, D.C.: CQ Press.

Price, H. Douglas. 1975. "Congress and the Evolution of Legislative Professionalism." In *Congress in Change: Evolution and Reform*, edited by Norman J. Ornstein, 2-23. New York: Praeger.

Ranney, Austin. 1983. *Channels of Power*. New York: Basic Books.

Reedy, George E. 1986. *The U.S. Senate*. New York: Crown Publishers.

Riddick, Floyd M. 1981. *Majority and Minority Leaders of the U.S. Senate: History and Development of the Offices of Floor Leaders*. S. Doc. 97-12, 97th Cong., 1st sess. Washington, D.C.: U.S. Government Printing Office.

Rieselbach, Leroy N. 1977. *Congressional Reform in the Seventies*. Morristown, N.J.: General Learning Press.

Ripley, Randall B. 1964. "The Party Whip Organization in the United States House of Representatives." *American Political Science Review* 58:561-576.

———. 1967. *Party Leaders in the House of Representatives*. Washington, D.C.: Brookings Institution.

———. 1969a. *Majority Party Leadership in Congress*. Boston: Little, Brown.

———. 1969b. *Power in the Senate*. New York: St. Martin's.

———. 1988. *Congress: Process and Policy*. 4th ed. New York: Norton.

Roberts, Cokie. 1987. "Leadership and the Media in the 100th Congress." Dirksen Congressional Center—CRS Symposium Paper, October 27.

Robinson, Michael J. 1981. "Three Faces of Congressional Media." In *The New Congress*, edited by Thomas Mann and Norman J. Ornstein. Washington, D.C.: American Enterprise Institute.

Robinson, William A. 1930. *Thomas B. Reed, Parliamentarian*. New York: Dodd, Mead.

Rogers, Lindsay. 1962. *The American Senate*. New York: Knopf.

Rohde, David W. 1974. "Committee Reform in the House of Representatives and the Subcommittee Bill of Rights." *Annals of the American Academy of Political and Social Science*. 411:39-47.

———. 1988. "Variations in Partisanship in the House of Representatives: Southern Democrats, Realignment and Agenda Change." Paper presented at the annual meeting of the American Political Science Association, Washington, D.C.

———, Norman J. Ornstein, and Robert L. Peabody. 1985. "Political Change and Legislative Norms in the U.S. Senate, 1957-1974." In *Studies of Congress*, edited by Glenn Parker. Washington, D.C.: CQ Press.

———, and Kenneth A. Shepsle. 1987. "Leaders and Followers in the House of Representatives: Reflections on Woodrow Wilson's 'Congressional Government.'" *Congress and the Presidency* 14:111-133.

Rothman, David J. 1966. *Politics and Power: The U.S. Senate 1869-1901*. Cambridge, Mass.: Harvard University Press.

Rubin, Richard L. 1981. *Press, Party and Presidency*. New York: Norton.

Salisbury, Robert H., and Kenneth A. Shepsle. 1981. "Congressman as Enterprise." *Legislative Studies Quarterly* (November): 566.

Scholzman, Kay Lehman, and John T. Tierney. 1986. *Organized Interests and American Democracy*. New York: Harper and Row.

Shepsle, Kenneth A. 1978. *The Giant Jigsaw Puzzle: Democratic Committee Assignments in the Modern House*. Chicago: University of Chicago Press.

———. 1989. "The Changing Textbook Congress." In *Can the Government Govern?*, edited by John E. Chubb and Paul Peterson. Washington, D.C.: Brookings Institution.

Shuman, Howard. Forthcoming. "Lyndon Baines Johnson." In *Profiles in Senate Leadership*, edited by Richard A. Baker and Roger H. Davidson. Washington, D.C.: CQ Press.

Sinclair, Barbara. 1977. "Determinants of Aggregate Party Cohesion in the U.S. House of Representatives, 1901-1956." *Legislative Studies Quarterly* 2 (May): 155-175.

————. 1981. "Majority Party Leadership Strategies for Coping with the New House." *Legislative Studies Quarterly* (August): 391-414.

————. 1982. *Congressional Realignment.* Austin: University of Texas Press.

————. 1983. *Majority Leadership in the U.S. House.* Baltimore: Johns Hopkins University Press.

————. 1985. "Agenda Control and Policy Success: The Case of Ronald Reagan and the 97th House." *Legislative Studies Quarterly* 20 (August): 291-314.

————. 1986a. "Party Leadership and Policy Change." In *Congress and Policy Change,* edited by Gerald Wright, Leroy N. Rieselbach, and Lawrence J. Dodd. New York: Agathon Press.

————. 1986b. "Senate Styles and Senate Decision-Making, 1955-80." *Journal of Politics* 46 (November): 877-908.

————. 1986c. "Senate Norms, Senate Styles and Senate Influence." Paper presented at the annual meeting of the American Political Science Association, Washington, D.C.

————. 1989a. *The Transformation of the U.S. Senate.* Baltimore: Johns Hopkins University Press.

————. 1989b. "House Majority Party Leadership in the Late 1980s." In *Congress Reconsidered,* 4th ed., edited by Lawrence C. Dodd and Bruce I. Oppenheimer. Washington, D.C.: CQ Press.

————. 1989c. "The Changing Role of Party and Party Leadership in the U.S. House." Paper presented at the annual meeting of the American Political Science Association.

Smith, Steven S. 1987. "Informal Leadership in the Senate: Opportunities, Resources and Motivations." Dirksen Congressional Center—CRS Symposium Paper, September 30.

————. 1989. *Call to Order: Floor Politics in the House and Senate.* Washington, D.C.: Brookings Institution.

————, and Christopher J. Deering. 1984. *Committees in Congress.* Washington, D.C.: CQ Press.

————, and Forrest Maltzman. 1989. "Declining Committee Power in the House of Representatives." Paper presented at the annual meeting of the American Political Science Association.

Stevens, Arthur G., Jr., Daniel P. Mulhollan, and Paul S. Rundquist. 1981. U.S. Congressional Structure and Representation: The Role of Informed Groups." *Legislative Studies Quarterly* 6 (August): 415-438.

Stewart, John G. 1971. "Two Strategies of Leadership: Johnson and Mansfield." In *Congressional Behavior,* edited by Nelson W. Polsby, 61-92. New York: Random House.

Sullivan, William E. 1975. "Criteria for Selecting Party Leadership in Congress." *American Politics Quarterly* 3 (January): 25-44.

Torcom, Jean E. 1973. "Leadership: The Role and Style of Senator Everett Dirksen." In *To Be a Congressman: The Promise and the Power.* Edited by Sven Groennings and Jonathan P. Hawley. Washington, D.C.: Acropolis Books.

Truman, David B. 1959. *The Congressional Party: A Case Study.* New York: Wiley.

United States. House of Representatives. Commission on Administrative Review.

1977. "Administrative Reorganization and Legislative Management." *Final Report*. H. Doc. 95-232, 95th Cong., 1st sess.

Uslaner, Eric. 1978. "Policy Entrepreneurs and Amateur Democrats in the House of Representatives: Toward a More Party-oriented Congress?" In *Legislative Reform*, edited by Leroy N. Rieselbach, 105-116. Lexington, Mass.: Lexington.

———, and Margaret Conway. 1985. "The Responsible Electorate: Watergate, the Economy and Voter Choice in 1974." *American Political Science Review* 79: 788-803.

Verba, Sidney. 1961. *Small Groups and Political Behavior: A Study of Leadership*. Princeton, N.J.: Princeton University Press.

Volger, David J. 1978. "The Rise of the Ad Hoc Committees in the House of Representatives." Paper presented at the annual meeting of the American Political Science Association, New York.

Waldman, Sidney. 1980. "Majority Leadership in the House of Representatives." *Political Science Quarterly* 95 (Fall): 373-393.

Walker, Jack L. 1983. "The Origin and Maintenance of Interest Groups in America." *American Political Science Review* 77:390-406.

West, Darrell. 1987. *Congress and Economic Policymaking*. Pittsburgh: University of Pittsburgh Press.

White, William. 1956. *Citadel: The Story of the United States Senate*. New York: Harper and Brothers.

Wilson, Woodrow. 1885. *Congressional Government*. New York: Meridian Books.

Wolfensberger, Don. 1988. "The Role of Party Caucuses in the U.S. House of Representatives." Paper presented at the annual meeting of the American Political Science Association.

CONTRIBUTORS

Ross K. Baker is a professor of political science at Rutgers University and the author of *House and Senate* (1989) and *Friend and Foe in the U.S. Senate* (1980). He served as a special assistant to Sens. Walter F. Mondale, D-Minn., and Birch Bayh, D-Ind., and as a speechwriter for Sen. Frank Church, D-Idaho. In 1982-1983, he was a consultant to the Democratic caucus, U.S. House of Representatives. He writes a regular column on national politics for the *Los Angeles Times*.

Susan Webb Hammond, professor of political science and director of the University Honors Program at American University, received her Ph.D. from Johns Hopkins University. She has written on congressional organization and reform and is coauthor of *Congressional Staff: The Invisible Force in American Lawmaking*. She is currently working on a study of informal caucuses in the U.S. Congress.

John J. Kornacki is the executive director of the Everett McKinley Dirksen Congressional Leadership Research Center. He also teaches political science and government at Bradley University and at Sangamon State University. He has written about public policy formation and is currently managing a four-year research project on congressional leadership.

Norman J. Ornstein is a resident scholar at the American Enterprise Institute for Public Policy Research, codirector of *The People, Press and Politics*, and cofounder of the National Commission on the Public Service. His articles and reviews have appeared in the *Washington Post, New York Times, Wall Street Journal, U.S. News and World Report*, and *Newsweek*. He has made frequent appearances on National Public Radio's *All Things Considered*, ABC's *Nightline*, and CBS's *Face the Nation*. He is the author of *The People, Press and Politics; The American Elections of 1982; The New Congress; Interest Groups, Lobbying and Policymaking;* and *Vital Statistics on Congress, 1989-1990*.

Samuel C. Patterson is a professor of political science at Ohio State University and managing editor of the *American Political Science Review*. His Guggenheim Fellowship (1984-1985) to initiate a study of congressional parties and leadership was supported by grants from the Brookings Institution and the Dirksen Congressional Center. He is coauthor of *The Legislative Process in the United States* (1986), *Comparing Legislatures* (1979), and *Representatives and Represented* (1975), coeditor of the *Handbook of Legislative Research* (1985), and recipient of the 1986 Fenno Prize of the American Political Science Association.

Cokie Roberts is a congressional correspondent for National Public Radio and ABC News. Prior to joining NPR in 1978, she covered the Greece-Turkey-Cyprus beat and, after returning to the United States, produced public affairs and children's programs in Washington, D.C., and Los Angeles. She was the cohost of a weekly program on Congress, *The Lawmakers* (1981-1984), for PBS. She is the recipient of numerous awards, including the 1986 Everett McKinley Dirksen Award for Distinguished Reporting on Congress.

Barbara Sinclair is a professor of political science at the University of California, Riverside. She received her Ph.D. from the University of Rochester. Her publications on the U.S. Congress include *Congressional Realignment* (1982), *Majority Leadership in the U.S. House* (1983), and *The Transformation of the U.S. Senate* (1989). She is currently studying the evolution of majority party leadership in the modern House of Representatives.

Steven S. Smith is an associate professor of political science at the University of Minnesota. He has taught at George Washington and Northwestern universities and was a senior fellow in governmental studies at the Brookings Institution. He has authored or coauthored four books on Congress: *Committees in Congress* (two editions), *Managing Uncertainty in the House of Representatives*, and *Call to Order: Floor Politics in the House and Senate*. He is currently working on a book on policy leadership in Congress.

INDEX

Advisers, 63, 67
Agenda setting, 98-99
Albert, Carl, 16, 122
Aldrich, Nelson, 110, 118
Allison, William, 36, 110, 118
Amendments, 43, 80-81
Arms Control Caucus, 61
Aspin, Les, 95

Baker, Bobby, 50
Baker, Howard, 3, 16, 50, 92, 122
    as majority leader, 4, 47-48
    leadership style of, 20-22, 37, 38,
        142
    on legislative scheduling, 44
Baker, Ross K., 3, 4, 27, 145
Barkley, Alben, 49
Barnes, Michael, 90
Bauman, Robert, 141
Bennett, Charles E., 95
Boggs, Thomas, 122
Boll Weevils, 61
Bolling, Richard, 63
Bone, Hugh, 128
Bonior, David E., 125
Bork, Robert, 92
Brademus, John, 122
Bradley, Bill, 6
Brady, David W., 102, 111-113, 130
Breaux, John B., 48
Broder, David, 105
Brokers, 63-64, 67

Brown, Lynne P., 122, 123, 125
Bullock, Charles, 127
Byrd, Robert, 3, 16, 20, 48, 122
    on amending activity rules, 81
    leadership style of, 23, 37, 51, 95,
        142
    on partisan obligations, 45-46
    relationship with press, 87
    on Senate leadership, 42-44, 49-50
    on television coverage, 93
    as whip, 47

Cable television, 2, 92-93, 106. See
    also Media; Television
Calmes, Jacqueline, 63
Campaign activity, 103, 106-107
Campaign committees, 128-129
Campaign finance, 82
Cannon, Joe, 102, 112, 138
Caucuses, 60-62, 125, 145
Chaffee, John H., 48
Cheney, Richard, 23, 86, 95, 122
Clark, Joseph, 21
Clay, Henry, 108, 124
Coalition building, 63-64, 103-104,
    136
Coelho, Tony, 23, 86, 123, 125
Cohen, William S., 38, 92
Committee leaders
    House, 6, 58-60, 67, 68
    party leaders' relationship with,
        132-134

Senate, 73-74, 78-80, 82, 120
Committee on Party Effectiveness (House Democratic Caucus), 3, 29-32
Committees
  assignment to House, 126
  assignment to Senate, 73, 74
  campaign, 128-129
Committees in Congress (Smith and Deering), 59
Conference, 125
Congress
  development of party leadership offices, 108-110
  expansion of staff, 14
  external variables impacting, 101-107
  functions, 97-101
  institutional environment, 107-108
  leadership changes' impact on, 13-16
  organization, 9-10
Congressional caucuses, 125, 145
Congressional leadership. *See also* House leadership; Party leadership; Senate leadership
  challenges to, 23-24
  characteristics, 10-11, 124-125
  congressional functions, 97-101
  Congress members' needs and expectations of, 123, 149
  external variables impacting, 101-107
  impact of changes in Congress, 13-16
  impact of environmental changes on, 1-3
  impact of television on decision making, 94-95
  informal. *See* Informal House leadership; Informal Senate leadership
  interactions and interrelationships, 129-136
  legislative success, 146-148
  need to study, 11-12
  proposed research agenda, 148-152
  selection, 121-124
  styles and strategies, 136-146

Conservative Opportunity Society (COS), 61, 140
Conway, Margaret, 104
Cooper, Joseph, 102, 111-113, 130
Courter, Jim, 61
Cranston, Alan, 46, 48
C-SPAN broadcasts, 2, 92-93. *See also* Media; Television

Danforth, John C., 38, 91-92
Daschle, Thomas A., 48
Davidson, Roger, 127, 131, 143-144
Deering, Christopher, 59
Democratic Congressional Campaign Committee, 127, 129
Democratic Policy Committee, Senate, 47
Democratic Study Group, 60
Democrats
  party structure in House, 125-127
  party structure in Senate, 127-128
  party unity among Senate leaders, 39-40
  Senate succession, 47-49
Dirksen, Everett M., 37-38, 47, 122
Discussion group leaders, 6, 62
Dixon, Alan J., 48
Dodd, Lawrence, 127
Dole, Robert, 3, 5, 16, 48, 122
  leadership style of, 20-22, 37, 142
  on legislative scheduling, 44
  media strengths, 8, 22, 51, 87, 89, 95
  as minority leader, 50, 144
  partisan performance, 46
Domenici, Pete V., 48
Douglas, Paul, 21
Downey, Thomas J., 6, 62

Eisenhower, Dwight D., 49, 139
Elections
  party role in, 102-104
  primary, 112
  short-term forces, 104-105
Electronic press releases, 94
Entrepreneurship, House, 27-32
Environment, external, 2-3, 51
Ervin, Sam, 92

Index 183

Evans, Rowland, 18

Fenno, Richard, 28
Filibusters
change in rules, 21-22, 81
frequency, 45
Floor Activity
control, 116
increase in Senate, 43
televised debates, 93
Foley, Michael, 119
Foley, Thomas S., 10, 23, 31, 122, 125
leadership style, 24, 66
media availability, 86
Follett, Mary, 108
Followers, 65
Foote, Joe S., 87, 90
Ford, Gerald R., 140
Ford, Wendell H., 48
Frank, Barney, 90
Free, Diedra Sullivan, 136

Gephardt, Richard A., 23, 29, 95,
123-124
Germaneness rule, 73, 74, 81
Gingrich, Newt, 23, 122
media use, 8, 93
Gore, Al, 92
Gorman, Arthur, 36
Gramm, Phil, 7
media use, 85, 91
Gray, William H., III, 23
Griffin, Robert, 47

Halleck, Charles, 140
Hammond, Susan Webb, 5, 6, 57, 145
Hearings, televised, 91-93
Helmke, Mark, 87, 89
Helms, Jesse, 21, 22, 89
Herrnson, Paul, 128
Hess, Stephen, 75, 106
Hinckley, Barbara, 124
House leadership. See also Congres-
sional leadership; Party leadership
entrepreneurship and, 27-29
House structure and, 65-66
informal, 5-6, 144-145
coalition builders, 63-64

committee, 58-60
discussion group, 62
within caucuses, 60-62
identifying, 57-58
issue, 62-63
questions regarding, 67-68
staff as, 64
structure of House and, 65-66
timing, 66
institutional environment, 9
relationship with Senate leadership, 135
strategies and style of majority,
136-139
strategies and style of minority,
140-141
techniques available to, 29-32
House members
campaign activities, 103
media coverage, 106-107
House of Representatives
characteristics, 57
differences between Senate, 120-
121
leader identification, 57-58
policy-making techniques, 29-32
regimes, 110-111
1890—1910, 111-112
1920—1970, 112-114
postreform House circa 1975,
114-118
television coverage, 2, 15, 88-89
Huitt, Ralph K., 127
Hyde, Henry J., 63, 90

Incumbent party leaders, 49
Individualism, 17-23
Informal House leadership. See also
House leadership
coalition builders, 63-64
comittee, 58-60
discussion group, 62
within caucuses, 60-62
identifying, 57-58
issue, 62-63
questions regarding, 67-68
research on, 144-145
staff, 64

structure of House and, 65-66
timing, 66
Informal Senate leadership
    conditions, 79-83
    context of, 72-77
    motivations, 77-79
    policy, 80-81, 144-145
Inouye, Daniel, 23, 48
Institutional maintenance, 99
Interest groups, 15, 105, 116
Issue leaders
    House, 59, 62-64
    Senate, 77

Jacobson, Gary, 104
Jewell, Malcolm, 128
Johnson, Lyndon Baines, 1, 122,
    leadership style of, 17-19, 21, 37,
    42-43, 49, 120, 141-142, 147
Johnston, J. Bennett, 23, 38, 48, 95
Joint Economic Committee, 30
Jones, Charles O., 36, 127, 130, 140

Kayden, Xandra, 129
Kefauver, Estes, 92
Kennedy, Edward, 47, 89
Kennedy, John F., 49
Kernell, Samuel, 104
Knowland, William, 38, 122

Lawmaking function, 97-98, 144,
    146-148
Leaders with portfolio, 57, 58, 145
Leaders without portfolio, 57, 58, 63,
    145
Leadership. *See also* Congressional
    leadership; House leadership; Senate
    leadership
    characteristics, 10, 124-125
    components of individualism in,
        16-17, 24-25
    followers and, 65
    personalized, 37-39
Leahy, Patrick, J., 48
Legislative success, 146-148. *See also*
    Lawmaking function
Legislative work, 43-44
Long, Gillis, 3, 29-32

Loomis, Burdett A., 28, 131, 145
Lott, Trent, 86, 122
Lugar, Richard G., 48, 89
*Lyndon B. Johnson: The Exercise of
    Power* (Evans and Novak), 18

McCain, John S., 48
McCarthy, Joseph, 92
McClure, James A., 48
McCormack, John W., 16, 122, 147
McFall, John, 122
MacKay, Buddy, 61
Mahe, Eddie, 129
Majority leader, House
    origin of, 109
    relationship with minority leader,
        135
    strategies and style, 140-141
Majority leader, Senate
    media exposure of, 95
    vs. minority leader, 70
    powers of, 73-74, 110, 119-120
    relationship with minority leader,
        135
    rules, 71
    strategies and style of, 141-143
Mansfield, Mike, 2, 16, 47, 147
    leadership style of, 19, 37, 49-50,
        142
    working relationship with presi-
        dents, 49
Mansfield Principle, 41
Markey, Edward J., 90
Martin, Joe, 140
Masters, Nicholas, 127
Matthews, Donald, 75
Mazzoli, Romano L., 59
Media
    access, 51, 75-76, 85-89
    achieving recognition through, 89-
        90, 116
    changing role, 105-106
    coverage of hearings, 91-93
    impact of political parties, 9
    influence of, 7-8
    leaders use, 85-89
    local coverage, 93-94
    policy making by use of, 4, 31-32

print, 86
talents and skills appealing to, 90-91, 123
television. *See* Television
use of press secretaries, 87
Mediating leadership, 41-42
Metzenbaum, Howard M., 22
Michel, Robert H., 8, 16, 122
media use, 86, 91
Mills, Wilbur, 113
Minority leader, House
media exposure, 86
origin, 109
relationship with majority leader, 135
strategy and styles of, 140-141
Minority leader, Senate
vs. majority leader, 135
strategies and style, 143-144
Mitchell, George J., 5, 8, 23, 24, 48, 92, 127
Morse, Wayne, 21
Moynihan, Daniel Patrick, 89
Mulhollan, Daniel, 145
Murkowski, Frank H., 48
Murtha, John, 63
Muskie, Edmund S., 41

Natcher, William H., 91
Newspaper exposure, 106. *See also* Media
Nickles, Don, 48
Norms change, 14
Northeast-Midwest Congressional Coalition, 61
Novak, Robert, 18
Nunn, Sam, 74, 79

Obey, David R., 3
Oleszek, Walter J., 127, 143-144
O'Neill, Thomas P. "Tip," 16, 66, 122
on camera panning of chamber, 92-93
use of media, 88-89
Orators, 63-64, 67
Ornstein, Norman, 2-3, 13, 88, 116, 119, 142

Partisanship, 39-40, 45-47
Party cohesion, 147
Party leadership. *See also* Congressional leadership; House leadership; Senate leadership
development of offices, 108-110
group access to, 136
incumbent, 49
influence on informal leaders, 59-60, 66
relationship with committee leaders, 132-134
relationship between House and Senate, 135
relationship between majority and minority, 135
relationship with members, 100-101, 130-132
relationship with president, 134-135
strategies and style, 136-144
Party maintenance, 99
Party structure, 125-129
Party system
character, 101-104
short-term forces, 104-105
Patterson, Samuel C., 4, 5, 35, 127
Payne, Sereno, 109
Peabody, Robert L., 37, 39, 110, 119, 121, 123, 125, 142
Peek, Linda, 87
Personalized leadership style, 37-39
Peters, Ronald, 109
Photographic opportunities, 87-88
Policy action, 3, 29-30
Policy Committee, Senate, 128
Policy leadership, Senate, 71-72
conditions for, 79-83
context of informal, 72-77
motivations, 77-79
Policy magnetism, 3, 29
Political climate, 42-43
Political cover, 3-4, 30-31
Political parties, 9. *See also* Party system
Polsby, Nelson W., 102, 112
Potentially centralizing rules, 114-115
Potentially decentralizing rules, 114-

115
President
    interactions with congressional
    leaders, 10-11
    leaders' strategies regarding, 138-
    139
    relationship with party leaders, 49,
    134-135
Presidential ambition, 78-79
Presidential election, 104-105
Presidential speeches, 88
Press releases, electronic, 94
Press secretaries, 87
Price, Douglas, 112
Price, Melvin, 95
Primary elections, 112
Print media, 86. *See also* Media
Proxmire, William, 21, 46
Pryor, David, 48

Rayburn, Sam, 13, 15, 63, 115, 137-
    139, 147
Reagan, Ronald, 88, 105, 117, 129,
    146
Recess press, 92
Reed, Thomas B., 109, 138
Republican Policy Committee, Sen-
    ate, 46
Republicans, Senate
    committee activities, 46-47
    leadership succession, 47-49
    party structure, 128
    party unity, 39-40
Research environment, 8-11
Resource expanding rules, 115
Rhodes, John, 16
Riddick, Floyd, 110
Ripley, Randall, 104, 109-111, 113,
    118, 119, 126-127, 131, 146
Roberts, Cokie, 7, 8, 85
Robinson, Tommy A., 90
Rogers, Lindsay, 35, 51
Rohde, David, 119, 142
Roll-call voting, 39, 44, 45
Rothman, David, 110
Rules
    House vs. Senate, 120-121
    impact of changes on leaders, 14,

21-22
Rundquist, Paul S., 145
Russell, Richard, 21

Satellite transmission, 93
Schumer, Charles, 62
Scott, Hugh, 47, 122
Senate
    changing of guard, 52
    characteristics, 17
    differences from House, 120-121
    party unity, 39-40
    power distribution, 118-120
Senate leadership
    changes, 35-36
    collegial nature, 40-41
    differences between majority and
        minority, 50
    informal, 6-7, 71-72, 145
        conditions for, 79-83
        context, 72-77
        motivations, 77-79
        policy, 80-81
    in institutional context, 17-23
    mediating nature, 41-42
    partisan, 39-40
    peculiarities, 4-5
    personalized, 37-39
    relationship with House leadership,
        135
    relationship with media, 51, 75-76,
        87-96
    selection, 121-124
Senate party leadership problems, 42
    context, 42-43
    external relations, 51
    leaders' role, 49-51
    management, 43-45
    party, 45-47
    succession, 47-49
Senators
    campaign activities, 103
    media coverage, 106-107
    resources available, 74-76
    time in home states, 44-45
Shepsle, Kenneth A., 127
Simon, Paul, 89
Simpson, Alan K., 45, 48, 59

Sinclair, Barbara, 8-9, 28, 37, 97, 102, 104, 111, 112, 116, 119, 127, 130, 138, 142, 145.
Smith, Steven, 6, 7, 59, 63, 71, 145, 146
Socioemotional leadership, 37
Solarz, Stephen J., 90
Soundbite, 90-91
Speaker of the House
  access to media, 86
  between 1890—1910, 111-112
  origin of, 108-109
  selection, 121, 122
  styles, 136-139
Special orders, 92-93
Staff, 64, 87
Stakeout, 88
Stevens, Arthur, 145
Stevens, Ted, 46, 48, 50
Stewart, John G., 50
Structure, 65-66
Subcommittee assignments, 73
Subcommittee chairs, 58-59, 115
Succession, 47-49
Sullivan, William, 124-125
Sunshine reform, 114

Taft, Robert A., 38, 122
Task specialist, 37
Television. *See also* Media
  cable, 2, 92-93, 106
  effects of use on decision making, 94-95
  impact, 2, 15, 19, 87-96, 105-106

  leaders use of, 51, 75-76, 87-96, 106-107
  local coverage, 93-94
  new technology, 93-94, 106
Timing, 66
Traficant, James A., 90
Truman, David B., 39, 41, 124

Uslaner, Eric, 104, 143

Voting, roll-call, 39, 44, 45

Walker, Robert S., 93
Ways and Means Committee, House, 109
Webster, Daniel, 40
Weicker, Lowell, 21
Wherry, Kenneth, 47
Whip, House
  origin, 109-110
  role, 126
  selection, 122, 123
Whip, Senate
  origin, 110
  selection, 122
  use, 47
Whitten, Jamie L., 90
Wilson, Woodrow, 36, 42
Wirth, Tim, 29
Wolfensberger, Don, 127
Wright, Jim, 16, 31, 122, 125
  leadership style of, 23, 24, 66, 117, 139
  media relations, 86, 90